NAVAJO TEXTS
BY
PLINY EARLE GODDARD

Originally published by
THE AMERICAN MUSEUM OF NATURAL HISTORY
PUBLICATIONS IN ANTHROPOLOGY, 1933

ISBN 9798670079433
*Cover Design by Bernhard Michaelis*

Hastiin Tł'ohtsahii (Mister Buffalo Grass) agreed in 1923, to tell some stories to the linguist Pliny Goddard. It was the first ever accurately recorded texts. The collaboration lasted less than a year, and the results remained unpublished for a decade, because Goddard passed away in1928 while he was preparing this myth for publication, and Hastiin Tł'ohtsahii also died shortly after.

It fell to Gladys A. Reichard, who had a work and most likely also romantic relationship with Goddard, to finish this project. She had accompanied Goddard on a field trip to the Navajo reservation during 1923, and she returned with him again in 1924 and 1925. She had enjoyed her fieldwork with him, and continued his work, particularly in terms of editing the manuscript of the Shooting Chant, after his death.

PLINY EARL GODDARD
*In Memoriam*

CONTENTS

# INTRODUCTION

Posthumous works are always unfair, unfair to author and unfair to editor. When writing the author always makes mental reservations about the finished product which no editor can supply. The editor realizes his deficiencies and the best he can do is to choose between two interpretations. He fears that the one he selects may not have been the author's final choice, but has no alternative. He can rarely fill in gaps left by queries. This is particularly true of the work presented in the following pages. The Navajo texts were collected in 1923 and 1924 by Doctor Pliny Earle Goddard who died July 12, 1928. Doctor Goddard had recorded the texts at the dictation of Sandoval, a Navajo, learned in his lore, but not a medicineman. Since the untimely death of Doctor Goddard, Sandoval has also died. There is therefore no immediate means of checking over the text as it is written. It had been typed, carefully translated, and worked over several times. But, as is always the case in matters of this kind, queries were noted with the hope that on a subsequent trip the author would be able to get more accurate translations or explanations.

Doctor Goddard had devoted practically a lifetime to the study of the Athapascan languages. He therefore omitted much in his notes which cannot now be filled in, for he kept common words and phrases in his head. Fortunately in this paper the full text had been transcribed. It is here presented with a keen appreciation of the editor's shortcomings. I realize thoroughly its deficiencies due to lack of detailed knowledge of the Navajo language and of Doctor Goddard's specific intentions.

It seems expedient to print these texts which are practically the first to be published in standardized orthography. We have some texts of Matthews which, however, do not give a true picture of the language, as his purpose was to describe the chants and not primarily to study the language. There is at the present time a movement afoot, led by Doctor Edward Sapir of Yale University, to collect a large body of text and grammatical material of the Navajo. This material will differ from Doctor Goddard's when published, in that special care is being taken to record pitch accent and length.

From the literary standpoint it is almost impossible to have too much Navajo material. The texts here presented illustrate well the beauty of Navajo narrative. "He made his mind forked," that is, "He made him think two ways so he could not concentrate on what he was doing," is only one example of the unusual type of Navajo thought.

The texts are also abundantly illustrative of the Navajo use of direction, color, natural beauty, abstract and all-inclusive beauty, four-fold repetition, etc.  It is deeply to be regretted that we may not have Doctor Goddard's own interpretation of Navajo literary style of which he was unusually appreciative and with which he had closely identified himself.

Besides being the first accurately recorded texts, this body of myth has also the distinction of not belonging to a definite chant.  Sandoval, who lived at Shiprock, New Mexico, laid no claim to being a chanter. His power (for good) was however recognized by all in his own neighborhood and elsewhere.  "No, he knows no chants, but his story is the best for it accounts for the Navajo much farther down[1] than any of the others."  These were remarks frequently made of the origin tale (pp. 9–57, 127–147).  Sandoval learned the stories from his maternal grandfather *ba'iłinkojε*[2].

Besides, this version contains much that was heretofore not known of the Navajo as, for example, the orderly account of the months, the constellations which usher them in, the "soft feathers" belonging to them, and the activities which go on in those months.  There are, of course, many incidents which are recorded by Matthews[3] and the Franciscan Fathers,[4] but the text not only gives an entirely different impression of the thought and style, but furnishes details, the omission of which by Matthews was very annoying, especially since his references indicate that he knew details of the girls' puberty rite, for example, and other ceremonies which are of great importance to the Navajo student, even though tedious to record.

All of these texts were recorded in summer, at a time when the rattlesnakes were out.  It is not "good" to tell them at this time and the fact accounts for the omissions.  In one case, Sandoval would not tell a portion of the story which was highly significant, but the next day he announced that he had "made medicine" to make himself immune from any evil effects which might ensue, and proceeded to fill in the gaps in the narrative.  In other cases it was necessary to wait for the winter months when the ground was frozen.  Certain songs (p. 168 *e.g.*) were too sacred and precious ever to be given up.

There are a few pages (158–160) for which there were literal translations, but for which I can find no free translation.  I was consequently forced to make it myself and I apologize for any misinterpretations and

---

[1]That is, in lower worlds.
[2]Reichard, Gladys A., Social Life of the Navajo Indians (*Columbia University Contributions to Anthropology*, vol. 7, New York, 1928), Gen. I D, 557 who was highly respected for his knowledge.
[3]Navaho Legends (*Memoirs, American Folk-Lore Society*, vol. 5, New York, 1897).
[4]*An Ethnologic Dictionary of the Navaho Language.* St. Michaels, Arizona, 1910.

inadequacies, assuming at the same time full responsibility for them. The two stories included in pages 76–85, 158–160 are stories of witchcraft and, as such, of extreme potency. The notebook records a remark of Sandoval's, "If people knew I knew this story they would call me a wizard."

Nothing could be more unfortunate for an individual.[1] He is suspected, avoided, feared, but respected. The respect accorded him is not the same as that enjoyed by the learned Navajo, but rather honor induced by coercion based on fear and suspicion, respect of form for one's own defense rather than of admiration for intellect and personal success (*hojoni*). Sandoval was always honored in the "good" way. He never practised witchcraft, but he stated that even his knowledge of one who had practised it would lay him open to suspicion were it known.

The apparently innocent pages which record the stories of witchcraft are an excellent example of things which to us are trivial, but which to the native, are most highly significant.

"The Creation of the Horse" is a tiny bit illustrative of Navajo literary charm in a nutshell. It is comparable with a similar tale of the Mescalero Apache,[2] but has a very different twist, particularly at the end.

The last tale describes the origin and scattering of the people and sheds additional light on the possession of pets by the Navajo. Such possession has been interpreted as totemism by Matthews[3] and Kroeber.[4] The interpretation has been refuted by the Franciscan Fathers[5] and by myself.[6] This tale seems to me to corroborate our interpretation. The pets, bear, panther, and snake, were protectors and saviors but were attached to indefinite groups before the scattering of the clans and there is no evidence of a specific kinship as of descent or of vision experience for them. They are more distinctly Navajo protectors than clan totems.

I hope some day to extract the enormous mass of ethnological material contained in these texts as well as in mythological material already published in English. Before that time I expect to have the opportunity of becoming acquainted with that ethnology as it is still being lived. Until that has been done (by myself or some one else) I must be content to point out the vast possibilities for additional knowledge contained in these texts of Doctor Goddard.

[1]Cp. Reichard, *loc. cit.*, 148.
[2]Notes of P. E. Goddard.
[3]The Gentile System of the Navajo Indians (*Journal of American Folk-Lore*, vol. 3, pp. 89–110, 1890), 106.
[4]This series, vol. 18, 148.
[5]*Ethnologic Dictionary*, 424.
[6]*Social Life*, 33.

The alphabet employed in the text is that published in Smithsonian Miscellaneous Collections, vol. 66, no. 6.   It should be noted however that b, d, and g are intermediates in sonancy while g is fully sonant. The velar intermediate is represented by $\gamma$.

GLADYS A. REICHARD.

# TEXTS AND LITERAL TRANSLATIONS

## THE EMERGENCE

naxodo'ołɛ xolgela djɪn, ni'xodɪłxɪł xolge'la djɪn.   ni'dixodɪłxɪł
Water was everywhere it was called they say.   Earth black it was called they say.   Earth was black

xolgela djɪn.   sa'łai xolgela djɪn.   tsɪndasakat xolgela djɪn.   yołɣai
was called they say.   Word one it was called they say.   Trees standing it was called they say.   White
shell.

dana'ɛł xolgela djɪn.   doł'iji dana'ɛł xolgela djɪn.   yołɣai ndi'aʻ
waves move it was called they say.   Turquoise waves moved it was called they say.   White shell stands
vertical

xolgela djɪn.   doł'ijɛ ndi'aʻ xolgela djɪn.   kodji (east) xa'adolɛłdji'-
it is called they say.   Turquoise stands vertical it is called they say.   Here where it will be east

la djɪn.   dɪłxɪł dandildoila djɪn.   łaɣaigo dandildocla djɪn.   dɪłxɪł
it was they say.   Black rose up they say.   White rose up they say.   Black

łaɣai bɪł exedildogi akwi atsɛhastin xazlį djɪn.   yołɣai nadą́lgai
white together rise with each other, there First Man became they say.   White shell white corn

didjol doxonot'innɛ yɪł xazlį djɪnnɛ.   ko doł'ijgo daandildola djɪnnɛ.
round end invisible (?) with he became they say.   Here blue rose up they say.

łɪttso dandildola djɪnnɛ.   ɛxɛdildo'la djɪnnɛ.   akwi' atsɛɛstsan xazlįla
Yellow rose up they say.   They rose up together they say.   There first woman became

djɪnnɛ.   ditciłɛ nadą́łtsoi nadadɪtdjol dohwonot'innɛ yɛł xaslį djɪnnɛ.
they say.   Abalone yellow corn end round invisible with it she became they say.

dɪnnɛhɛ nihidiyala djɪnnɛ.   adɛ nt'c dɪłxɪłgo danadildondɛ kǫ'
The man started to walk they say.   Then it was black rose up fire

dzɪttsą djɪnnɛ.   łagaigo danadildo'go kǫ dzɪłtsąnegoʻ tc'ɛ najnta djɪn.
he discovered they say.   White when it rose up fire where he saw in vain he looked they say.

tadɛ tc'ɛ naznɛztą' djɪn.   akoʻ inda' sizɪnnɛdo sizį' djɪnnɛ.   tsin
Three times in vain he looked they say.   There now where he stood he stands they say.   Stick

nazdɪtą djɪn.   ɛdzitsi djɪn.   ado bik'ɛsdɛs'į djɪn dɪłxɪłɛldo djɪn.
he took up they say.   He stuck in the ground they say.   Then on it he looked they say.   Black went
they say.

łagai xaldo djɪn.   akǫdji niya djɪn.   kodɛ łɪt djɪn.   da'iskɪt binna
White came up they say.   There he came they say.   Here smoke they say.   Around hill

djoɣał djɪn.   xat'ilą' kǫ xoɣanli'tc'ɛ nacda'.   nixal li' kǫn djɛɣałɛ,
he walked they say.   What here house is in vain I came.   You the one walking.   Here you walk?

xat'ilagodo  ca  djɛɣadala?  nǫcini'.  tsɛɣadn'dɪnnɛ  ɛkǫ'la  djɪn.
Why nobody comes to me? I think. Rock crystal the fire was they say.

andzodza djɪn.  akoci'  andzodza djɪnnɛ.  dɪɫxɪɫgo danadildo' djɪn.
He went back they say. There he went back they say. Black came up they say.

ndɛ kǫ nadzɪltsą djɪn.  ɫakgai dannadildo'go akogo nadzitdza'
Then here fire he saw again they say. White when it came up again then he went again

djɪn.  ndɛ' t'ado bik'izniyada djɪn.  nadzitdza djɪn.  anadzittsi ado
they say. Then she did not find where she came back again they say. Then

tsɪn nazdɪtą djɪn.  anadzitsi djɪn.  bik'ɛtsidɛz'į djɪn.  kǫ' djo'innɛgo
she stuck up stick she took up again they say. She stuck it up again they say. The one she saw
say. The one she saw

bik'idjigo akoandɛ daisk'itla djɪn.  adɛ lɪt djɪn.  doɫ'iji kǫla djɪn.
on the side there hill was they say. Then smoke they say. Turquoise fire was they say.

kǫxoganle' doc'įdalla djɪnnɛ,  niɣą'leɣi?  akǫ' nannaɫɛ?  xastį
Here someone living I did not see she said, Are you walking? Here did you come? Old man

adjɪnnɛ djɪn.  xat'ilxanna?  tsɛɣadndinɛ nikǫla ce doɫ'ijɛ cɛkǫla.
said it they say. Why is that you? Rock crystal your fire, mine turquoise my fire is.

xat'ila binigɛ t'a'aɫa' ndji'acle?  a aihididit'ac.  xago'onɛ' caɣandɛ.
Why separate we stay? We don't want to stay far away. Let us live together. "All right, my house."

adɛ axadjit'aj djɪn.  kodi ɫa'dacdiyo djɪn.  ma'itoyiɫdjiɫela djɪn.
There they went together they say. Here somebody came they say. Water coyote it was they say.

di to dɛat'lɛla djɪn.  taɫka nailtila djɪn.  ɛic aɫtsogo bɪɫ exozinela
This water all over the water he runs they say. Everything with he knows

djɪn.  kwɛdɛgo ɫa'nazdidza djɪn.  attsɛ xackɛ ma'ila djɪn.  ma'itcitɫakgai
they say. Before we know somebody he came they say. Old Man was afraid to call *attsɛ xackɛ*[1]
Coyote it was they say. Coyote blanket

yikasdzazla djɪn.  noxok'ɛ 'aɫtsogo bɪɫ exozinla djɪn.
was girded on they say. The land all with he knows they say.

kodɛ' danadildɛ djɪn.  bidjat kodaniɫnɛz djɪn.  biji' adaɫts'isiyɛ
Here they came they say. Their legs so long they say. Their bodies were small

djɪnnɛ.  tsasnaɫsoi la djɪn.  bɛzǫz daxolǫla djɪnnɛ.  dadiccicla djɪn.
they say. Yellowjacket it was they say. His sting they have they say. They sting they say.

adɛɫ ącla djɪn.
They witch with it they say.

kodɛ' ɫa' nadilde' djɪn.  dįgo adaɫk'isisiyɛ bɛ'ɛ' dadicco'la djɪn.
Here another came they say. Four, short (?) (slender) their shirts were black they say.

na'azǫzi la djɪn.  kodɛ' ɫa' nadildɛ djɪn.  dįgo dadiɫxiɫdjinɫa
Tarantula it was they say. Here another came they say, four. They were black

---

[1] This may be a note about Sandoval, the informant.—G. A. R.

woletc'ijin la djin. bizǫz naxodlǫla djin. adiɫɣ̨acla djin. kode'
black ants were they say.     His sting he has again they say.     They witch with it they say.     Here

ła na'dikai djin. t'at'ɛ' nadadiɫxiɫ djin. bat'ɛ'adinla djin. xwoledjinla
another came they say three.     All over black they say.     He has nothing they say.

djin aɫts'isigi bat'ɛ'adin. kehwit'įle la djin. ado ts'idesdeɫ djin. ade'
small he has nothing.     They want to live there they say.     They do not want them to move they say

axedaiɫhiljic axedaiɫhilɣ̨ac nahilts'e djin. ts'ideskai djin. atsehastį
they sting each other they witch each other they kill they say.     They begin scatter around they say
                                              They not doing right, they go crazy.     First man

adjinne djin. tc'indac beɫ kexodjett'į ni djin. bets'an ni' beɣa
said it they say.     No use we live with them he said they say.     From them earth they went

dika djin. ade hake xanasa djin. ni' doɫ'ij dasakaatla la djin. ade'
through they went they say.     Then on it after them (?) they moved up they say.     Earth blue was lying
                                                                                         they say.     Then

doɫ'ij nǫxonel'ądji kexat'ila djin. nat'aggi djin. dadoɫ'ij at'exo doli
blue extend in everv direction they were living they say.     Those that fly they say.     Just blue they were
                                                                                                    blue bird.

djin. ts'an djin. ts'andistissi ts'anłan djo·ɣe. t'ǫxodjiyu djin. ni'
they say.     Jay they say.     Jay small, chapparal jay, bluejay.     It was crowded they say.     World

xwoɫts'isi djin. ado ade akwoxot'ego axanadikai djin. bets'an ni'
was small they say.     Then they did the same way.     They witched each other they say.     From them
                                                                                                      earth

be(ɣ)a nailde djin. ni' ła dasakat djin. xana'akli djin. atsehastį
they went through they went again they say.     World another lay on they say.     They moved up they
                                                                                         say.     First man

djin. atseesdzan djin. ma'itoi yildjiɫe djin, ma'i djin. e xanasde
hey say.     First woman they say.     Water coyote they say.     Coyote they say.     Those came up

djin. ni' łittso dasakatdji' ado ni' doɫ'iji dasakage' kexat'ineni'
they say.     World yellow to where it lies there earth blue from where it lies those living

ąɫtso xaik'e xanassa djin. ako nahwot'ela djin. kodji xa'adji dziɫ
all after them came up they say.     There they found it was like this they say.     Here east mountain

sa'ąni. sisnadjinne holgela djin. cada'ą bitc'iddji sa'ąni tsodziɫ
stood, Blackbelt (Pelado Peak) was called they say.     South toward one stood Mt. Taylor

holgela djin. e'ądji dok'o'osłit holgego sa'ąla djin. kodji nahokǫsdji
is called they say.     West San Francisco is called stands they say.     Here north

debentsa' holgego sa'ą la djin. ałni'gi' dziɫną'odiɫe xolgego sa'ą lá
La Plata (Sheep large) being called stands they say.     Middle *dziɫną'odiɫe* being called stands

djin. hat'a bitc'iddje' dabilage' dziɫtc'ol'į· holgego sa'ą la djin.
they say.     Beside it on east side just beyond from its top *tc'o'łį'* called stands they say.

akwi hwolajinε bitsi'daltcigε kεxotc'itt'įla djin. doxodjigε (t'oxodjijni) kεxotcitt'įlε djin. hwillatc'iłts'oi dinnε kεxotc'itt'inla djin. hwolεtci dinnε kεxotcitt'inla djin. hwollεtci sisnadjinnε sa'ani ha'a dolełdji'tci bitc'iddji' dol'iji ɑcki adji xodjitlǫla djin. dinnε nakadzad nakai bikąi yił kεxat'į la djin. łok'atso bikąi bεxolǫ la djin. xaxonigε' biką dinnε yił kεxat'į la djin. k'at ɑnnat'alεdji' yołgai ba'adε xwillonla djin. εsdzan nligo xolon la djin εsdzan nakadzaa nakai ba'adi yił xwillon la djin. łok'atso ba'adε yił xwillonla djin. xahwonεst'in ba'adε yił xwillonla djin. kodjigo dził łibai holgεlε djin. adji t'adji nadanłbai bεxowillon la djin. k'at toxodjila' ła djin. atsεhastin ɑnnε djin. k'at axadaxic dolka ł'istso nat'ani ahwodilya djin. cac nat'ani ahwodilya djin ma'itso nat'ani ahwoilya djin. nɑsdǫitso nat'ani ahwodilya djin. adε t'abastin nat'ani ahwodilya djin. ela djiłt'εgo ɑcdlą' nat'ąni adε ahoot'ila djin.


nat'ani adalyani' yandastin' djin. dik'at ałk'ε dadodlεł dikε nahalyaigε' xaditda' axaso'gεgo digisdołεł inda ado'tc'ą e ba xadzitda dzitsa adjitia djin. ną' k'at. nihila' axiłyadanot'εhi axanda'ogε'. natdli xwillǫ la djin. εsdzan ił' innε e xwillǫ la djin. ąłts'a tc'uini'ilεdolεł εsdzan į̄ł'įnε bεxonnissan la djin. dinnε iłjnε ałdo bεxonissinla djin. ako k'at axot'εgo tc'oni tc'anjni' į̄lε xolągo nadlε la djin. atsεhastin ni djin. atsεhastin nadanłgai e lastsi silį djin. atsεesdzan nadanłtsoi e k'idolya djin. dol'iji ɑckiyεn e dol'ij nadą k'idolya djin. k'at dził łibaidji kεxodjitt'inε ni xi k'at tcǫ'ini'į dindε adjoljinεn dadadada ni djin. dindi ałna holdjij djin. akwεilago nadanłbai nałdazdzaεn łago nakǫdji' danεsk'ɑn na'o la djin. na'ołεisł'innε dįgo nałdaz djin. t'o axayuigo nda nεst'ą djin. nadąa alya djin. aladj nat'ani djilinnεnni' xadolyala djin. atsεhastįn xaxonigε dinnε ajdila la djin t'ado yadjiłti diłxiłgo dandildo' djin. dįndi diłxiłgo daɑndildo la djin. do'its'aida djinnε. akεdε nat'ani daddjillεngi tc'ε dats'ists'ą djinnε. aikεgo diłxiłgo danadildo djin. akεdε nat'ani djililnεnnε yadjiłti' djinnε. do'its'aida djinnε. akεdε dadjillεnεn yanadjiłti djinnε. do'its'ąida djin. akεdε yanadjiłti la djin. doits'ąida djin. akεdε yanadjiłti la djini. tabastin-

There black ant its head red lived there they say. Many people | they
did the same thing they say. Yellow ant people lived there they say.
Red ant | people lived there they say. Ant Pelado Peak which stands
east where will be | toward it turquoise boy there he lives they say.
People twelve walking around | males with him lived they say. Large
reeds male they have they say. Mirage | male people with they live
they say. Now where sunset will be white shell female | were they say.
Women there were they say. Women twelve walking | female with they
live they say. Large reeds female with they live they say. | Mirage (heat
upon) female with they live they say. Here (East) mountain gray
named | they say. There turkey gray corn with he lived they say. Now
will be many | they say. First man spoke they say. Now they live
as married. Large snake chief | they made they say. Bear chief they
made they say. Wolf chief they made | they say. Panther chief they
made they say. Then Otter chief they made | they say. Five they were
chiefs then (?) they say.

Chiefs those they made council they say. After this one on another
clans will be. From your own if you marry (?) | you will go crazy then
go in the fire because of that in the future they are afraid | they say.
Now go ahead. Those who like each other let them marry. | Hermaph-
rodite will live they say. Woman work that he lives they say. Both
sides | he will know woman work he knows they say. Man work too |
he knows they say. Then "Now like this you will know after this |
hermaphrodite was," they say. First Man said they say. First Man
white corn that seeds became | they say. First Woman yellow corn
that she planted they say. Turquoise Boy that one blue | corn
he planted they say. Now mountain gray there who live "You now
your turn" | four when he danced "dadadada" said they say. Four
times back and forth he danced they say. Doing that way | there next
gray corn he dropped. Next these cantaloupe beans | they say spotted
(pinto bean), four times he dropped they say. Much then got raised |
they say. Corn they made they say. First chief who was she committed
adultery with they say. | First Man, Mirage Man he went to (?) they
say. He did not talk. Then they talked while black | arose they say.
Four times black arose they say. They didn't hear anything they say. |
Second chief who was in vain they listened for they say. After that black
| came up they say. Second chief who was talked they say. They
didn't hear | they say. Next who was talked again they say.
They didn't hear they say. Next | he talked again they say. They
didn't hear they say. Next he talked they say. That otter |

nɛn yanadjiltilɛ xalct'iɛgo doits'ạida? djɛnɛ djin. di kɛxoit'ini
haila ninni yil'a· djinɛ djin. haila bik'aant'ɛ bɛkɛnti' nihiltc'inna'ạ
lạ'ạ nɛ djin. atsɛhastin nladɛ nadlɛ xago bidonni· ni djin. adɛ
niya djin. haila 'asạ na yila ni djin. t'acic'ị ni djin. ledzạ· haila
na'ila ni djin. t'acicla ni djin. adɛ'ecạ' haila na'ịnla? t'aci k'idila
at'ɛ ni djin. haicạ' tcacdjɛ' na'ịlla? t'aciicla ni djin. bɛ'ɛjoca hai
na'ila? adistsin cạ hai nala t'aci'icla? ni djin. tosdjɛ cạ' hai naila
t'aci'icla?

t'adolaiyan dị yiska· at'ɛli· djin. t'adọadlạ do' djin. nla dɛnnɛ
adɛcdlinl adotc'iyan ca'anlɛ. adɛcinl aldo'. ɛsdzannɛ ayoi a'cidinnit. ado cadilala e bik'ɛ anct'ɛ ni djin. atsɛhastin nockọl holge
xact'ɛdalɛ'. t'adats'inanni xwodji hwɛ'ina ai k'at xacte dazdilya.
cikɛbiyajjigɛ' ạniltso dinnɛ dannolinnɛgɛ' ạnltso ts'ɛna ndika·.
dako nickọl anltso xast'ɛdalya. anltso bɛ ts'ɛnạ· ni'ildɛ'. kojigo
dinnɛ kɛxat'i. kojigo ɛsdzan kɛxat'i silị'. bitago ayu'it'ɛ' to nilị'
silị'. k'idolya djin. dinnɛ djin da'ak'ɛ anaxolya djin. esdzanyɛdjɛ'
adilni' danadil djin. k'idadɛlɛ' djin. t'abɛxoniltɛl nt'ɛ k'ɛdolya djin.
ako nadạa dalya djin. kojigo ɛsdzan do' nadạadalya djin. dinnɛdji
k'ɛdadeslago billago kinna'dolya· djin. ɛsdzandji bo'ogo kinaldalya'
isila xani' dabitcigo k'ɛdolya djin. akogo nakidi djin. dinnɛdji
nabillago ɛsdzandji t'anabitc'igo k'innaesla da'dɛsdla djin.

akogo tadɛ djinni'. dinnɛdji nabilladi djin. ɛsdzandji ɛtdin silị djin.
dinnɛdji dịdi k'ɛdolya djin. ɛsdzandji dịdilɛxɛñkɛ ɛtdin djin. ako ditcin
biniɣạ djin. atsị' axibitdịn xwonina djin. xa'ọl axan. doits'aida·
dinnɛ la xattc'ị. xatdji tahilɣot djinnɛ. i'ɛl djin. la tananalɣot
djin. nana'ɛl djini. naki i'ɛl djin. la' tananalɣot djin. nana'ɛl
djinni. dị djin. akogo dakɛgo nat'ani dzillinɛ nọckọl bɛ tsɛt'na
nijniya djin. nda salla djin. xwotc'oba'· naxas'ạla djin. tsɛ'na
nats'itdza djin. xale itɛdolɛl xat'icbɛ' nasọxwontilɛ dolɛl, ɛsdzanni-
yɛnnɛ atc'oba· naxasạla. nakɛgo nat'ani djilɛnɛ xanadzodzi
djin. docbaxatc'obaida djinnɛ djin. ak'ɛgo nat'an djilɛni xanadzodzi

talked "What is the matter we do not hear?" he said they say. "Those who live here | who your mind changed," he said they say. "What makes you that way? You don't talk. Tell us." | "Very well," he said they say. First Man, "Yonder hermaphrodite to come here tell," he said they say. Then | he arrived they say. "Who pot made for you?" he said they say. "I made for myself," he said they say. "Plate who | made for you?" he said they say. "I made it for myself," he said they say. "Little cup who made for you?" "I planted it | it is," he said they say. "Who metate made for you?" "Just I made it," he said they say. "Hair brush who | made for you?" "Stirring sticks who made for you?" "I made them," he said they say. "Little water basket who made for you?" | "I made it." |

He hadn't eaten four days (?) they say. He had not drunk too they say. "Go on for me | I want to drink. Something to eat prepare for me. I want to eat too. The woman scolded me badly. | Then she was false to me because of that I am thus," he said they say. First Man, "Boat called | you get ready. They will find out who (?) is stronger. That now they begin to get ready. | Boys small all men that class all across we go." | So large boat all they made ready. All with it across they arrived. Here | men lived. Here men lived it became. Between large water flowed | became. They planted they say. Men farms they made again they say. Women | they make loud song they say. They planted they say. Full width (?) all they planted they say. | Then they raised corn they say. Here women too raised corn they say. Men | when they planted beyond age they planted they say. Women didn't plant all over they planted they say. | Then twice they say. Men again more women quarter they planted they say. |

Then three times they say. Men more again they say. Women was all gone they say. | Men fourth time they planted they say. Women would have been four times nothing they say. Then famine | killed them they say. Meat they were dying for they say. "Bring boat," they said. They didn't hear | men one spoke. She ran in the water they say. She drowned. Another ran in water | they say. Drowned again one they say. Two drowned they say. Another ran in the water they say. Again another drowned | they say. Four they say. Then second chief who became boat with across | he arrived they say. They were thin they say. Starving he found they were they say. Across | he came back they say. "What will we do? What with no increase will be? Those women | poor are living." Next chief again spoke | they say. "They are hungry for meat," he said they say. Next chief was spoke again |

djɩnnɛ. akɛdi nat'ani djilɛnɛnɛ xanadzodzi djɩn. k'atdji ba'' ako daznizi dazdillɛ bɛ' xwaddɛnɛst'ɛ? la'ą tc'obanihini adat'ɛla ni djɩn. atsɛxastɩn hwol'ago t'akanɛ' at'idalinilɛ. iladį ąnłtso tsɛtnan'. nano'nił ąłts'o tsɛtnan' na'nil djɩn. k'at aidɛ t'anołtso tadaditdogis. akogo nadanłgai bɛ ndadadołtsi·. akɛdi taditdį· atdąodadołnił. asdzani aidɛ do' ałts'o tadadidogis ai nadanłtsoi yɛ ndadadołtsa. bikɛdi taditdin atdą atdadolnił da dalnił· k'at t'ado axandat'ɛni dį yidołkał. ado'inda ałt'andoka.

akogoci atsɛɛsdzan nadaozdɛs'ą la djɩn. t'aąltsoni bik'ɛti'-hwioɛnni''. ditcɩn adat'e bikɛ't'uisinni' atc'ą adat'e. bik'ɛt'uisɩnni''· ɩnda cidjekɛt a·daxazɛ·l djɩnni djɩn. t'ani nɛɩnla caxastin ya la biniɣɛ xanaxat'a nazdiłgizlɛl djɩnni. xaxastin naniz'ą djɩnnɛ. t'aci aik'ɛdɛcdlɛl djini djɩn. nlɛ ni' xwodiłxɩldɛ ma'tc'it yɛ' ɩdiya xa'a ba·natzɩs'ąla djɩn. nadzilit badjinlala djɩn. to iłną isdlįgi tɛxołtsodi biyaji naki danaɛłkǫani baadjiłdɛlgo bɛ· ts'ittsadzisla djɩn. akogo koji łagaigo koji dandildo djɩn. koji do' desk'az xaslį djɩn. kodɛ łakgaigo dadadit'a djɩn. kodigo doł'ijgo yit'a djɩn. kodigo łɩttsogo yit'a djɩn. kodɛ diłxɩłgo yit'a djɩn. dodat'innɛ nikɛ (?) nixɛxot'indjɛ e xɛt'a djɩn. kojigo gɩnts'o diłxɩł axwodol'ą djɩn. kojigo gɩnłbai axwodol'ą djɩn.

kodɛ yɛnɛ' ndjilgot djɩn. to at'ela djɩnnı djɩn. t'annıa djinigo ndjilwot' djɩn. ɛ'adji daihitihi xwodol'ą djɩn. t'anila to at'ela djɩnigo ndjilɣot djɩn. kojigo to bɛnoxolnihi axwodolnit' djɩn. todji'ndiɣai djɩn. t'anni to la djinat djɩn. tatłatka naseya' djini djɩn. ndjilgot' djɩn. k'acą xa it'elɛ djini djɩn. atsehastin ca'ałtcinnɛ djɩnad djɩn. sɩsnadjɩnnɛ bilatadji daditdi'ika djɩnni djɩn. 'ądji daxadildɛ' djɩn. t'akɛ xwodjitt'indɛ' xadɛyɛ at'i·n la djinnɛ djɩn. xadeyat'iynit'ąnɛ ąnłtso 'adɛ'·dał dził xwo'ą'i atsehastin sɩsnadjɩnne łɛjyɛnnɛ· nazdidja djɩn. tsodził łɛyɛnnɛ· nazdidja djɩn. dok'ooslid łɛj nozdidja djɩn. dɛbɛntsa łɛjyɛnnɛ nazdidja djɩn. dziłna'odiłi łɛyɛ' nazdidja djɩn. tc'ol'į łɛji nazdidja djɩn. ąłtso xanaza akɛdɛdadildɛ djɩn. doł'iji ackiyį ałtin diłxɩł lok'atso bikąi yiłgo daididja djɩn. bikɛdɛ dinnɛ nakadzada nakai dadildɛ' djɩn. bikąi bikɛdɛ xaxonigɛ dɩnnɛ bikąi danadildɛ' djɩn. kodɛ adɛgo sɩsnadjɩnnɛ. sa'ąnɛ ha'ądolɛłdɛ'go yołgai at'ɛd lokatso ba'adɛ ałtį· tsɛlkanɛ tał'axalɛ djik'ɛ akwiya dadicɣɛt yił da·nɛdidja djɩnnɛ. bikɛdi

They say. Next chief was spoke again they say. "Now (?) | then they have found out adultery. Are they punished enough?" "Yes, poor they are," he said | they say. First Man, "After this as long as you live do not hurt them. Tell them all across you take them." | All across they took them they say. "Now these all of you bathe." | Then white corn with dry yourselves. After that pollen from top to bottom sprinkle. | Women those too all wash. Those yellow corn with you dry. | After that pollen from top to bottom sprinkle. Then not have intercourse | four days. Then you may come together.

Now First Woman she was in command they say. All under her | they were unfortunate, famine they had. Unfortunate they were hungry for meat. Unfortunate | my girls drowned he said they say. "True you make the living my husband. | What because of it they teach you should I twist it," she said. Her husband she gave charge of matters. "Just I | will do as he wants," she said they say. Here earth was black coyote blanket with he came. | She gave him instructions they say. Rainbow she gave him they say. Water across where it flows *texoltsodi* | its young two were swimming. Lassoing them with it he drew them out they say. Then here | white here it loomed up they say. Here too cold it became they say. Here white | they were flying they say. Here blue they fly they say. Here yellow they fly they say. | Here black they fly they say. Unknown ones on the earth living those flew they say. | Here hawks black he sent they say. Here gray hawk he sent they say.

Here they came back they say. "Water it is," he said they say. "It is true," saying | he came back they say. South humming bird he sent they say. "It is true water it is," saying | he came back they say. Here is Water he is boss of he sent they say. Egret they say. | Truly water is he said they say. On water I walked he said they say. He returned they say. | "What we do about it?" he said they say. First Man "My children," he said they say. "Pelado Peak | on its top we will go," he said they say. There they moved they say. "All those living on the world | come (?)," he said they say. (?) all (?)|First Man Pelado Peak soil took up they say. Mt. Taylor | soil he took up they say. San Francisco Peaks soil he took up they say. La Plata Mountain soil | he took up they say. *dzilna'odili* soil he took up they say. *tc'ol'ị* soil he took up they say. | They all went up. After him they came they say. Turquoise boy bow wood black large reed male | with he came they say. After him men twelve living came they say |males. After them mirage people male came they say. Here | west Pelado Peak which it stands White Shell Girl reed large female bow | mulberry from the bottom of water (his name). Back in I go. Mountain mahogany with they came they say. Afterward |

dinnɛˈ nakadzada nakai ba'adi ɛsdzan nlini danadildɛ djin. bikɛdɛ
xaxonɛstin danadilka djin. xat'ɛgota? docino'łni'dala dziłłabaidɛ taji
danazdidza djin. sisnadjinnɛ. sa'annɛnnɛ ałnigo tobinnɛs'ą djin.
dilaahaiyula sizzɛɛnnɛ. bai'sɛnnala ɛsdzan ni djin. atsɛhastin t'egicą
hini'nadolel xadic xininadolɛłˈ djikɛ akwiya dadicγɛt' nɛ djin. doda· ci
nabikandɛcdat ni djin.

taﬂ'axalɛ dinnigo dɛgo adjolγot djin. adɛya yago nɛzdilgot djin.
taﬂ'ago yɑ'adjolwat djin. adɛ azeˈɛnnɛ bił xadzizwot' djin. e bidjalyɛ' e
bidzozgɛ djin. t'aﬂ'axalɛ' sisnadjinnɛ bilatadji to nɛsąt djin. lok'atso ɛtsi
djin. dego bidɛyol djinnɛ ya bɛnisa djin. biyigo ayingo xazlį djin. bida'nakai
djin. taji yehwɛnonɛl'ą xatsɛ'ɛn tahidjil djin. bɛtallɛwoc bigizigai
yabɛnissa djin. kwɛdɛ' to nol'ąnł taji djini djin. doxaxozt'idɑllɛ xala
'indza hastin xwodjinnɛ djin. tsinłkałɛ xatsi' ndizγis djin. ałtą'įla'
djin. biyaildɛ djin. lok'atso agonɛ' xantsa djin. yatɑt'a xasde''
djin. kodę' ayuɛ xaxast'ą djinnɛ. tɛxołtsodɛ bidɛ' k'isdɛł'ijgo.
xat'ilaba xat'i. cɛcik'tɛ kodɛ ma'iyɛnnɛ ma'itc'it' yiłakatszaz. dici
bąaxat'i ni djin. ądo ditcili ts'ą djin. nł'iz bixadɛłbį djin.
tobidɛstcit ła djin. taditdin doł'ij taditdin djin. t'ɛłxaditdin djin.
taditdin djin. bidɛgi'jgɛ' daihiską djin. ma'i ni djin. doda dała' na-
nandɛctɛł dɛlda didɛ ni'łakkai dasakadji adɛ bi'ildɛ bɛ niłtsąbaką bɛc'įlɛ
niłtsa ba'ad bɛc'įlˈ do'. k'osdiłxił bɛc'įlɛ do'. tc'ilati hojon bɛc'įł do'.
nɑnsɛ' bɛc'įl do'. bɛni'xodɛlɛ'lɛ do' bɛxincnalɛ do'. akola axwodjinniłɛ
ni djini. t'ałai ba'adɛ ba nazn-iłti djin. tcuwocyicts'ądza djin. to iniłxaj
djin. woni'tc'idintso· xotc'a adjila djin. atsɛ beost'an xat'agi ałna' datsiznil
djin. atsɛk'izditsoi xatsiyadɛ ałna' datsiznil djin. ni'dasikadji djinne
baγajninnil djin. to la djin. xacł'ic łałk·a xadzizł'in djin. kodjigo
tc'inctaihiłgai hwolge danałk'ǫn djin. didjitt'ɛ gooxinɛgɛ' at'ɛgo atsɛbɛst'an bitagɛ axidɛlna atsɛbest'an axidɛlna da siz la la djin. adɛ' tałkadɛ
tuiyiłdlatgo to hannɛdɛłdla djin.

---

ˈOr, xat'ɛgic xinenadolel.

persons twelve living female women were came they say. Afterward |
mirage they came they say. "Why didn't you tell me?" Mountain
brown turkey | one came they say. Pelado Peak which stands half-
way water reached they say. | "Where my medicine I forgot," he told
his wife they say. First man "Somewhere I have to die. | Back I will go,"
he said they say. "No, I | for you after it I will go," he said they say. |
Blue heron up he went they say. Down hard he started they say. |
Bottom of water he came down they say. Then that medicine with | he
came out they say. That his legs he is named they say Bottom-of-water
(?) Pelado Peak its top water came they say. Large reed he stuck | up
they say. Up he blew it they say. Sky it reached growing they say. In
it nodes it became they say. They started up | they say. Turkey was at
the end his tail stuck in the water they say. It was washed it became
white. | Sky it reached, they say. "Here water let it stop," (turkey) said
they say. They couldn't get through. | "? old man," he said they say.
Woodpecker his head (?) they say. It became thin | they say. He got
through they say. Large reed it grew up in they went up | they say. Sky
hole they moved up they say. Here he followed them up they say.
tɛxoltsodɛ his horn end blue. | (They were scared because he came). "Why
did he come up my boys. Here coyote coyote blanket was tied. "That |
he came for," he said they say. Then abalone basket they say. Jewels
it was filled with they say. | Water ores too they say. Pollen turquoise
pollen they say. Cattail pollen they say. | Pollen they say. Between his
horns they put it they say. Coyote said they say. "No, I won't give you
all. | One this white fabric then with it rain male I will make | rain female
I make with it too. Black cloud I make with it too. Flowers I make with
it too. | Vegetation I make with it too. Ground wet too I will live with
it (World white lies they come afterward.)" "That way as you say," | he
said they say. One female he gave him they say. Water falling they
heard. Water went down | they say. Cicada his headband he made they
say. Tail fastened (to arrow) his forehead crossing each other he put on |
they say. Tail yellow back of his head crossing each other he put they
say. Earth where it lies through | he drilled they say. Water was they say
(?). Mud on he took up they say. Water was there foot deep and built
up with mud. East | Grebe named came wading on the water they
say. He looks like him this way | feathered arrow on his forehead across
each other tail fastened on across each other were lying they say. Then
spreading out the water | as he came opened out around him they say.

atsɛbɛst'an   naidinil   djɪn.   bizɛgonɛ' yiiłgɛ  djɪn.   bidjɪltcidɛ
ła'iyit  gɛt  djɪn.  ałna'  xaiyizǫz  djɪn.  xago'nɛ'  cc'idlɛ  xałni  djɪn
ako dini' hɛyalɛxałni djɪn.  xat'icbɛ ɛdolnił.  t'aałdi't  ałna  naxaxots'anɛgɛ'
ni' atsɛbɛst'an  naidinil  djɪn.  wonnɛstc'idi  at'i  djɪn.  bitdjɛgonɛ'ałna'
haiyizǫnz djini.  xagonɛ'  k'at ce'idlɛ  akogo  t'c  nɛheya'łlɛ.  t'ado xadzi'da
djɪn.  to  ɛyiłdlạt  djɪn.  bikɛgo  toina'  djɪn.  kwɛdɛ'go  tc'ictạilgai  doł'ij
ɣatc'i  nadilgwot'  djɪn.  t'adojnilk'ołɛ  djinił'ị  djɪn.  tohanc  xananai
dɛłdlạt  djɪn. atsɛk'izditsoi bitagɛ dasɪnnillɛnɛ naidinil djɪn. xago ce'itdlɛ
bizɛdɛ yiłgɛt djɪn.  bidjɪltcidɛła'i yiłgɛt djɪn.  ałna  haiyizonz djɪn.  akodɛ
kwɛɛ nɛheya lɛ ha'icbɛadołnił t'ạłdint ałna'.  hahots'angɛ' atsɛk'isditsoiyɛ
najdinil djinnɛ.  xat'icbɛadolnic xagonɛ'  ni'go ce'idlɛ djɪnni.  ni  hadje
gonɛ'  ałna'  xadzizǫz  djɪn.  doxadzi'da  djɪn.  cada'adjɛgo tohanɛ' anai'
iłdlat djɪn.  taxanni' bikɛ dananɛztị djɪn. 'alɛdɛgo tcịct'axiłgai łɪttsogo
xatc'in nadilgo' djɪn.  to xanaidɛłdlạt djɪn.  adɛ t'adonilk'ołɛ hwon ł'i
djɪn.  k'oxanni nihwoka.  dɛnnɛ donaɣada.  atsɛbɛst'an bɛtaɣɛ' ałna'
dasɪnnillɛ'ni' naidinil djɪn.  koɣannɛ nihwoka dɪnnɛ donaɣada xałni
djɪn.  bizɛ gonɛ' yiłgɛt djɪn.  bidjɪltcidɛ yiłge djɪn.  ałna' hayizǫz djɪn.  ako
ce'idlɛ ni djɪn.  tcịct'aiłgai łɪttso anne djɪn.  akohot'e' nɛheyalɛ xałni
djɪn.  e'cyabe adolnił ạłdịt.  ałna haho ts'ạgɛ ako xani. 'atsɛbɛtsan nazdinil
djɪn.  haɣonnɛgo ce'idlɛ djɪnni djɪn.  wonɛstc'idists'o' cịctahiłgai łɪttso
doxadzi'da djɪn.  toxanɛ anaiyiłdlin djɪn.  e'ạlɛdjɛgo bikɛgo to dananɛstin.


nahokosdɛgo tcịctaihiłgai diłxiłgo bɛtc'in xatc'ị' nnạdilgwot' djɪn.
toxananaidɛłda djɪn.  xagocci xwonił'ị djɪn.  t'ado nik'ołi hwodo
djannɛ t'adojnilk'ołi djɪn.  nił'i djɪn.  koxanni nohwoka dɪnnɛ,
donaɣada bɛtaɣɛ atsek'izditsoi bizɛ ganɛ' niłgɛt djɪn.  bitciłdjidɛ ałna'
hanaiyizǫnz djɪn.  ako ce'idlɛ akodɛ nɛhcyallɛ ni djɪn.  tc'inct'aihiłgai
diłxiłgo aicayadɛ bɛɛdołnił djini djɪn.  t'a'aiłdint ałna' xaxwotsan-
nɛɣɛ' xagonnɛ'nigo ce'idlɛ atsɛk'itsoi xadje gonɛ' ałna' xadzonz
djɪn.  doxatdzi'da djɪn.  tcinct'aihiłgai diłxił tohanɛ' nahok'ǫsdjigo

Feathered arrows he took off they say. In his mouth he put them they say. In his mouth | he stuck in they say. His anus the other he put in they say. He drew them out passing each other they say. That way "What I did," he told him they say. | "Then here you may live," he told him they say. "Nothing to do with it," | he said. Already hole through. Passing each other a hole is | you. Feathered arrow he took off they say. Cicada did it they say. In his heart passing each other | he drew out they say. All right now way I do then you may live. Not he spoke | they say. Water he plowed they say. After him water went they say. From here bird blue | came to him they say. Staring he looked at him they say. | He splashed water around him they say. Yellow feathered arrows his forehead which were placed he took they say. "This way I do." | His mouth he put in they say. His anus one he put in they say. Passing each other he drew them out they say. "Here | you may live." Gosh. It is already hole. Yellowtail arrows | he took off they say. "Gosh," saying. "All right," saying, "you like I do," he said his heart | in passing each other he drew out they say. He didn't speak they say. Toward the south | he plowed water they say. Water opened out after him flowed they say. From the west grebe yellow | to him came they say. Water he threw out they say (water came around his breast). Then staring he look at him | they say. Around here "Earth people do not live," they say. Feathered arrows his forehead across each other | which lay he took they say. "Around here Earth people don't live," he said to him. | His mouth in he put they say. His anus he put in they say. He drew them out they say. "Now | like I do," he said they say. Yellow said it they say. "Then here you will live," he told him | they say. "Gosh already done." Hole already it has been drawn through. Feathered arrows he took | they say. "All right," saying, "As I do it," he said they say. Cicada grebe yellow | didn't speak they say. Water he plowed they say. Toward the west after him water flowed.

From the north grebe black to him came they say. | He plowed water they say. Hard he looked at him they say. He too he stared | they say. Hard he looked they say. "Here person | does not live. His forehead yellow feathered arrow his mouth he put in they say. His anus passing each other | he drew them out they say." "Now as I do here you may live," he said they say. Grebe | black "Gosh, easy way," he said he said they say. Already done passing each other they have been drawn. | "All right, as I do," Yellow feathered arrow his heart in crossing each other he drew | they say. He didn't speak they say. Grebe black water north |

anaiyiłdlą djın. tohane ananiłxaj djın. tohane ałtso 'ina' djın. da siγε'εnnε' adįgo' 'ałtso ina' djın.  tontεl εxε xınyınnigε silį djın. dobisoxodǫn'įł-
dalla t'anacidol'įt djini djın. todassiγįla djini djın. dįgo tcınct'aihiłgai
dasεt'ila. toxanε' εcdit ałtso ina' xacł'ic t'εya. kodεgo hannε' najna'a djın.
dołijila yołgaila ditciłila tcεłtciila bacinila dεstciila tadıtdindoł'ijila tadıt-
dinla tsınbitadıtdinla nihikεdidjın. yadits'ą holgε djın. ni'hodissǫns holgε
djın. akǫ biyε'l alya djınnε. nł'izεn acłago tadıtidinnε do' dεstci acdla na
nahodołtstigo. nıłtc'ibiyajε xannε' nziz'ą djın. 'e bε adzozkan silį' djın.
bε dεna nahodolts'ı'. adε' dį djin niyol dį ł'ε niyol djınnε. k'addatsi'ı·
naholtsai na hwodo'nni't djın. candınbiyaji kadjiya djın. nahactc'it
bidadzodza djın. kodo xacł'ıj bε xidεnxεlgo bidadzodza djın. t'ihįg'annε'
nahwotts'ailad djın. djini djın. djoxołtsaila sołtį' hwodon'ni't' djın.
t'axalo· ni djın. atsεhastin ma'its'o djın. nacdoitso djın. ma'itso atsabitse
bε xadilya djın. nacdoitso xanε nadąizai bε xadilya djın. ado mai'ito-
yitdjıłε e atse' xadjiya djın. akεdi atsεhastin xadjiya djın. bikεdi atsεεs-
dzan xaiya djın. akεdi atsεhack'ε (xaiya djın). bikεdi adε xanaza djın.
ni' łakgai dasakadji' xasdε adε. s'ın dists'ą' djın. 'adε nacdoitsoyεnnε
mai'itso yıł nixε'na djın. akogo nacdoitso xadadodzıns xwodoni djın.
ndadjildloc nohozlidji 'ado nt'εhwołıłnadεl djın. djo· mai'itso xadadzıs-
dzįz djınnε. di nixxε dadjini djın. nacdoitso xanε' anasazε dabikınninεgε
xadzεzdzįz djın. eba kis'anε bikin daholǫ naxwonnlįdji' nadą binizin djın.

ni'hodiłxiłyeñgε'
ni'hodoł'ijεyeñgε
ni'xaltsoyeñgε
ni'xalgaiyeñgε'.
la'dajdiłxiłyeñgε'
ła'dajdoł'ijyeñgε
ła'dajıltsoyeñgε'
ła'dadjilgaiyeñgε'

eba· dįgo ał'anat'ε djınnε.

he plowed they say. Went away they say. Water all goes through they say. | Log like that which lay there four ways all was gone they say. All around ocean gathered together became they say. "Hard they fought with me | I made it none (?)" he said they say. "Water had been on top," he said they say. "Four grebes | lived on it. Water all gone all disappeared mud sticks up." Now word he brought back they say. | Turquoise, white shell abalone red shell jet powdered iron ore, blue of flowers, | pollen, tree pollen. Those above us living sky rattles are called they say. | Spotted spring called they say. Over there their pay was made they say. Jewels five, pollen too ores five | make it dry. Small wind message took they say. These he begged for them (pay for making medicine) it became they say. | With it they pay they make it dry. Then four days it blew, four nights it blew they say. Now maybe | it is dry he said they say. Son-of-sunshine (small badger) went above (?) they say. Badger | he came down they say. So far mud with he was black they say. He came down they say. "A little | it is dried up," he said they say. "It is dry, this day let us go," he told them they say. | "Wait," he said they say, First Man. Wolf they say. Panther they say. Wolf eagle-tails | with they decorated they say. Panther he mixed corn wasted not good corn (that is with broken kernels) with they decorated they say. Then water coyote | plays tricks to get water that one first came up they say. Next First Man came up they say. After him First Woman | came up they say. Next first warrior came up they say. After him then they moved up they say. | Earth white where it lay. Then they moved up. Song he heard they say. Then that panther | wolf with overtook him they say. "Then panther you pull out," he told them they say. | They trotted there you who have them they were mixed up well they missed him they say wolf they pulled up | they say. "This ours," they said they say. Panther himself Pueblo ancient Pueblo people those having houses | pulled up they say. Pueblo their houses they have like us corn they like they say. | Song:—

> From the earth black,
> From the earth blue,
> From the earth yellow
> From the earth white.
> One from where they were black,
> One from where they were blue,
> One from where they were yellow,
> One from where they were white.

Because of that four colors were they say.

ts'addɛk'at ałtso xazna xoɣan dolɛł xodǫ'nit' atsɛhastin. anni
xa'alɛdɛgo lok'atso biką'ɛnnɛ ɛ'ąlɛ dɛgo lok'atso ba'adɛ ałtc'i' dɛstsi'
cada'ądɛ' ałtindiłxił binitsi nahokǫsdɛ ałtįtsɛłkanɛ binitsi bɛ xoɣan alya
djın. nadąnłgai nik'ago t'adįdɛ bɛ'ɛcdlicdo˙ xodonnit' djın. kodɛyɛ hojǫgo
caɣą są'ali sa'ąnaɣai hoɣan są'alɛ bik'ɛhojon nligo sa'alɛ xodǫni djın.
nadjigo kisannɛ anasazi dadjilinɛ daiidą xasł'ic bɛ kin adadjila djın.
xoɣan didjol alyąagi' tc'ɛ dɛkai ca'ałtcinnɛ xadatdilyi 'atsɛhastin atcinni
djın. tatcɛ 'adilliłnɛ' xwodjinni djın. tca'' datsɛla' xacindja xodjınni
djın. xacitdjala djinni djın. ta tsǫtsɛ' 'e xadjisdjalad djın. njonigo tatcɛ
adjilalad djin. nammazgo xasł'ic bɛ dzizłɛ''lad djın. dɛzdiłdjɛlad
djın. tsɛhɛnnɛ dįgo tsitdza'djinilad djın. djinıłgailad djın. kojigo
ts'oxodza adjila djɛn. nohokǫs bitc'idjigo nijongo xaldzizgo adjila djın.
akwiya tsɛhɛnnɛ dįgo nɛjnnillad djın. mai' tc'itłakgai dajdınniłballa
djın. nabikaɣɛ tc'itłagai xolge dajdɛnniłballad djın. nabakaɣɛ
diłxił naską˙ xolge danajnıłballad djın. bakaɣɛ k'ɛɛstcin xolge dannaj-
dannıłbal djın. akogo dį dajdɛnnıłbal djın. oo o hwu tatcɛ xo˙dje'i˙.
nisnildɛ djın. niisdɛ djın. bidjidje djın. nihwonɛti˙ djinni djın. 'atsɛhastį
tca'' adjanni djın. phu phu phu phu ni djın. tatcɛ axodɛzso djın.


ła'ya hanadjidjɛ' djın. we xastį xodjinni djın. tca'' xadjinai bidaɣɛ
nina'ą djinni djın. tsin asdza yɛ nina'ą djınni djın. tatsotsɛ'' diłxiłɛ yɛ
nina'ą. noahosdzan yɛ ninɛ'ą saannaɣai bɛ noxoɛdziłgo yɛ nina'ą.
k'addɛ tc'ɛsdeskaiyɛ xatto' ałtso xaxa dahaztɛł djın. akwi ado xata
adaxastsalgo tc'ɛna'ildɛ djın. kisannɛ dadjıllɛnnɛgɛ' xakin daxollonnɛgɛ
e doda c do tatcɛ adjidjɛ'da. atsɛhastin daxadjo'icdji xoɣan ditdjol
alyanɛ 'adjɛt'ɛ tatcɛdjidjɛ'. xoɣan alyą binololdɛ djın. atsɛhastin djın.
atsɛɛsdzan djın. atsɛackį djın. 'atsɛat'ɛd djın. akodɛgo atsɛhastin
kwot'ɛgo nɛztį djın. atsɛɛsdzą nadɛgo nɛztį djın. bɛtaɣɛ bɛɛzɛ' siłtsozgo
idjį' tcosładɛ dɛstɛjgo kodo ayannıłti djın. xact'ɛgo yałti djın. kwɛdɛgo
atsɛasdzą' yałti djın. xact'ɛgo nla tcitɛjnnɛ tc'ɛadzists'ą djın. daat'ɛgo
azdits'igo xos'į djın. t'ado iłxajɛ yiską djın. djıñgo dakt'ɛgo sad nabakągo
dɛdɛsdzinł. dzinɛdziñgo bitc'in nadjitdago ndiłxił djın. nahwonadjitdago

Now all moved up. "House will be," he told them, First Man said
it. | At the east reed large male, at the west large reed female toward each
other he stuck up. | South oak he leaned against it, north mulberry he
leaned against it. With it hogan was made | they say. White cornmeal
just four places I will rub on he said they say. Over there | Pueblos ancient
Pueblos their clans already mud with house they had built they say. |
"Hogan round made we are tired we walk. My children, we will rest,"
First Man said | they say. "Sweathouse you make," he told him they say,
beaver. "Stone one some you bring up," he told him | they say. He has
brought them up," he said they say. Stones those he had brought up.
Good sweathouse | he had made they say. Being round clay with he plas-
tered they say. He had made a fire | they say. Those stones four he had
put in they say. They had become white hot they say. Good | door he
made they say. North its side hole for the rock he made they say. | In
there stones four he had put they say. Coyote blanket white he had
hung | they say. On that white blanket called he had hung they say.
On that | black fabric called he had hung they say. On that calico
figured (?) called he hung | they say. Then four he hung they say,
"Ooohwu sweathouse go in." | They started they say. They came they
say. They went inside they say. "We are crowded," he said they say,
First Man. | Beaver he said it to they say. "Phu phu phu phu," he said
they say. Sweathouse became larger. |

Others came in they say. "Wey, old man," he said to him they say.
Beaver "Those who came up on top | they built it," he said they say.
"Stick woman with he built it," he said they say. Stones black with | he
built it. Earth with he built it. Old age living with in safety (?) with he
built it. | Now those were tired traveling their water all came to the
surface they say. Then | all over being rested they went out they say.
Pueblo their clans their houses | they have, those not sweathouse they
make. First man those he led, hogan round | those who made they
go in sweathouse. Hogan which was made they went in they say. First
Man they say. | First Woman they say. First Boy they say. First Girl
they say. Then First Man | this way he lay they say. First Woman in
front (?) lay they say. Between them his medicine lying | toward it
arms under head they two lying thus began to talk they say. Softly they
spoke they say. Here (in front) | First Woman spoke they say. Softly
that side those two lying in vain listened they say. Nearly hearing | it
became light they say. Not sleep it was day they say. During the day the
same way words more they talk again | they listened for. Listening toward
them when he goes they stop (talking) they say. When they go away |

ai yananiłti djɪnnɛ. ł'ɛnaxasdlį djɪn. nanɛztɛj ɑnda xot'ɛgo naxosį djɪn. dasabą̄γą̄go naxos'į djɪn. djɪ̃ngo sabananiγa djɪn. daxact'ɛgo naxiłidjį dakɑtt'ɛgo nanɛctɛj djɪn. xact'ɛgo sabananiγa djɪn. naxosį djɪn. t'ado nazdizts'a djɪn. nacidjictɛji a yananiłti djɪn. djɪ̃ngo t'o ladɛ nadjitdadjɪn 'atsɛacki.

ł'ɛ naxasdlį djɪn.   dakwot'ɛgo 'ałdijgo nanɛjdjol djɪn. ł'ɛ biγa yałtįgo nanɛską djɪn. atsɛacki adjinni djɪn. xadzodzi djɪn. t'ado 'alxoci dį yiską djɪn. djɪngo dį tsɛbi nasdlį djɪn. atsɛ'ckį xadzodzi djɪn. xat'įla do'hɑnnał bahwɪnt'ici? bainoxt'i daidilwocxe'la, bił nits'adazkį kwc xawodzi kwi sa sɪllį djɪn. atsɛhastin xadzi' doboxots'ɑn dobainit'ila? atsɛacki ɑnni djɪn. akwot'ɛgola e xozɑn xwoł'ago· są'aγą̄go bitc'in hwont'igo kɛhwit'ilɛgo sąγą̄ bɛtc'i' hwɑnt'ilɛgo bɛnit'į djoxona'ai yai·nt'įla djɪn. dził xodollɛłgɛ yaint'įla djɪn. nixididzi xodollɛłgɛ' yaint'įla djɪn. tsɪn' xodollɛcłgɛ' yaint'ila djɪn. k'ɑt di ni' bika' axot'ɛlɛgɛ yaint'ila djɪn.

ni'nil djɪn. ałai'go akᵊjnda'go axwo'dilya djɪn. tsaddik'ɑt bandildɛgo e axɛjnda'a t'ado xadazdɛs'į xołyaalgo djɪn. xat'ilobandał ni? djɪn. bits'anndɛs'į djɪn. bik'i ilka djɪn. dobandent'ɪnda djɪnni djɪn. atsɛhastin anadza djɪn. nakɪskɑnnɛ nakɛgo ɑłła axɛznda djɪn. tsiddałnigo xadɛłyago akɛjndaxa· t'ado łanadadɛs'į' kodɛ danadilgo djɪn. bik'i ilka djɪn. xat'ila baxwɪnt'i ni djɪn. do bawɪnt'ɪnda bitcɪnni djɪn. 'aigɛ dobaxwɪnt'ɪndala 'ɑnnanadza djɪn. nanɛ́ską djɪn. tago 'ɑłła axɛjnt'i sɛzlį djɪn. k'addɛ 'ą̄łtso xadilnɛgo· t'ado xanadazdɛs'į kodɛ danadilgo djɪn. bɛts'ɑn bik'i nailka djɪn. xat'ila bandaxat'i ciłna'acgo ni? djɪn. dobandɛt'ɪnda ts'ɪtdɛ t'adobandɛt'ɪnda. ɑnnanadza djɪn. dįgo nanɛska djɪn. dįgo 'ɑłła axɛjnt'i sɛzlį djɪn. tsɛtdadi do' hastį bɛnołni· xatc'ɛdjinnɛ bokǫ' e bɛkǫ' bɛdjuxona'ai bɛ dinnoldo xodo'ni djɪn. bokǫ' e bɛ' djuxona'ai nilγai djɪn. oldjɛ́nɛ tsɛłγa'dndinnɛ oldjɛ bɛ nildzil djɪn. ɛbą̄ oldjɛ dobɛxozdoda.

the others talk again they say.  Night came again they say.  They two lie down again the same way it is light again | they say.  They talking it is light again they say.  During the day they talk they say.  Softly | evening again the same way they two lie down they say.  Softly talk continues they say.  It is light again | they say.  Then they couldn't hear they say.  Those lying other side they talked again they say.  Daytime | over there he stood First Boy.

Night became again they say.  This way toward each other they lay huddled up they say.  Night through | talking it became day again they say.  First Boy addressed them they say.  He spoke they say.  Not | sleeping four nights they say.  Days four; eight became they say.  First Boy spoke | they say.  "Why | not before us you talk?  What you talk about we can't sleep.  Sleep | bothered us," this he spoke then language became they say.  First Man spoke, | "What we are going to do we talk about?" | First Boy said it they say.  "That way we would like to know."  After that Old Age toward living (?).  We living here Old Age toward | how we shall do we talk about.  Sun they talked about they say.  Mountains which will | be they talked about they say.  Months will be they talked about they say.  Trees which will be | they talked about they say.  Now this earth on it how it will be they talked about they say.

He put down they say.  One place those guarding he placed they say.  Now he working | those guarding not they see him he stepped in they say.  "What are you doing?"  he said they say. | From him he hid it they say.  On it he spread they say.  "We are not talking about anything," he said they say.  First Man | went back they say.  Next day two place they sat as guards one beyond the other they say.  Half when they had made | the guards not saw him here he came they say.  On it he spread they say. | "What you talk about?"  he said they say.  "We talk about nothing," he told him they say.  "So, | you talk about nothing," he went back they say.  It was day again they say.  Three places one beyond the other lines became | they say.  Now all as he finished not they saw him again here he came they say. | From him on it he spread they say.  "What you talk about, my cousin?"  he said they say. | "Now we talk about nothing."  He went back they say.  Fourth time it was day | they say.  Four places one beyond the other circles became they say.  "Rock pollen old man you invite Black God | his fire that his fire with sun with make hot," he said they say.  His fire that with sun | red hot they say.  The moon rock crystal moon with was a little warm they say.  Because of that moon | does not make heat.

at'ihigo bɛxolinlɛ xodon'ni djın. bɛnɛnałac xolgɛlɛ xodon'ni djın. nałac xolge di binị' xidɛkallɛ bɛits'oslɛ xodonni djın. binị' naγaci ałtai hidjallɛ xodon'ni djın. nɛstịn bidje ɑlya djın. di' (2nd) niłtc'its'osi xolgɛlɛ xodon'ni djın. hastịsɑkk'ai bɛits'os ɑlya djın. bɛni' djadi ałtai hidjɛ'lɛ xodon'ni djın. xadots'osi xolge bidje ɑlya djın. niłtc'itso xolgɛlɛ xodon'ni djın. ɑttsɛ'ɛtso bɛits'oslɛ xodonni djın. xak'ɑz bidje ɑlya djın. bị' ałta hidjallɛ xodonni djın. zasniłt'ɛs xolgɛlɛ xodonni djın. tin bıtdje djın. ik'aisdai bɛits'oslɛ xodonni djın. atsabiyaj xolgɛlɛ' atsabɛt'o delxinłlɛ. gaxat'ɛ bɛits'os ɑlya djın. nlo' ditdjollɛ bidje ɑlya djın. bigi' γa' ałta' idjalɛ. ga daxott'ịnlɛ djın. xoztcịnt xolgɛlɛ xodon'ni djın. dibɛni bɛits'ozlɛ xodon'ni djın. tcilditł'idɛ bıtdje ɑlya djın. ts'iddɛ ndɛzi'gonɛ' naγaci dałtcilɛ xodonni djın. k'ɑt xadjiłtso djın. cịdji'ye hit'atcil olgɛlɛ xodonni djın. deł bɛits'os ɑlya djın. e bini ndɛkalle djın. tc'il bitci' bidje ɑlya djın. at'ạtso xolgɛlɛ xodonni djın. niłts'ạ bɛits'os ɑlya djın. niyol bidje ɑlya djın. binị djadi dadoltcił xadonni djın. ya'icdjactcillɛ xolgɛlɛ xodonni djın. djadɛyac bɛits'os ɑlya djın. t'ixigo tc'ıl binnạ'dɑntalɛ xodon'ni djın. xadots'osi bidjela djın. ya'icdjatso xolgɛlɛ xodon'ni djın. ndjijoc bɛits'os ɑlya djın. xado' bidje' ɑlya djın.

binɛ' bị xadołtcil xodon'ni djın. nladɛ' dilγɛ binị naidodji' xadonni djın. bịyaj bɛts'ɛkiγɛ dacitdjallɛ xodonni djın. binị nạts'osi holgele xodonni djın. niłtsạ' bikại bɛits'oslɛ xodonni djın. nd'ạ ts'osi bidje ɑlya djın. binị nt'atso xolgɛlɛ xodonni djın. tc'il dɑnt'ạna xwonel'a djın. bidje ɑlya djın. dikodɛ niłts'a ba'at bɛits'os ɑlya djın. k'ɑtdɛ ạltsodje xastan ninil djın. kɑddla hai hiyidji' dadadoγał. doł'ijɛ ackiyₑ xadola'ai ɑnt'inɛ xodjınni? djın. sisnadjinɛ sa'anɛ xa'ata bitcitdjɛ aict'i djini djın.

"Little it will give light," he said they say. | "Month Spider will be named," he said they say. "Spider called this month; animals traveling its soft feather," he said they say. "Month mountain sheep | with each other they will go," he said they say. Heat shimmering its heart was made they say. "This Slender Wind | will be called," he said they say. *hastinsakk'ai* its soft feather was made they say. "Month antelope | with each other will go," he said they say. "Heat slender called its heart was made they say. "Big Wind will be called," | he said they say. "First big its soft will be feather," he said they say. Cold its heart was made | they say. "Deer with each other will go," he said they say. "Snow-cooked it will be called," he said they say. | Ice its heart they say. "Morning star (Milky Way) its soft feather, will be," he said they say. Young Eagle it will be called. | Eagle its nest will be warm Rabbit track its feather was made they say. Hail round its heart was made | they say. In it rabbits with each other will go. Rabbits will breed they say. "Horns-lost it will be called," he said | they say. "This month Say's phoebe its soft feathers, will be," he said they say. Clouds with small hail its heart was made," they say. "Now | end of month mountain sheep will give birth," he said they say. Now winter is passed they say. Summer begins. | "Little Vegetation it will be called," he said they say. Crane its soft feather was made they say. That month cranes will migrate they say. | Vegetation its heart was made they say. "Leaves-large it will be called," he said they say. Rain its soft feathers | are made they say. Wind its heart is made they say. "Month antelope have young," he said they say. | "Seeds-about-to-ripen it will be called," he said they say. Young antelope its soft feather is made they say. "Little | vegetation will get ripe he said they say. Slim warm (planting time) its heart was they say. "Seeds-large | it will be called," he said they say. Rain little strings its soft feathers was made they say. Heat its heart was made they say.

"Month deer have young," he said they say. "Then Pleiades month comes up," he said | they say. "Young deer on their backs they will lie," he said they say. "Month Slender-ripe will be called," | he said they say. "Rain male it soft feathers," he said they say. Ripe slender its heart was made | they say. "Month Ripe-large will be called," he said they say. Vegetation all ripe it ends they say. Its heart | was made they say. This rain female its soft feather was made they say. Now all six | he placed they say. "Who inside will step. Turquoise Boy "Wherefrom | are you?" he said they say. "Pelado Peak which stands by it east side I am," he said they say. |

doł'iji ackį ɑnnє. biɣidji' dadadinnał xodjinni djın. dєlnє'' łok'atso nakits'adago na baɣa dєdlitgo nt'a satądo xaniɣєdinє. yєnє' bił dadadika. e bє donєyєtįgo nditdalє xodjinni djın. lą'ą djınni djın. dacєt'є dodozє bitdį dєcała ebi dana ndicdalє. t'acdo' nxidєeyala. e tsiddєdanołtє naxokєnałdєhc djini djın. nєznatdįdoba'ą. nakigo cєtįnlє djınni djın. akogo ndinnєlє. yołgai ackį yєnє' xadzodzi djın. xadola ɑnt'innє? sısnadjınnє sa'ąnє є'a bitc'itdji' yołgai ɑckį niclınє aicict'i djıni djın. oldje'' biɣidjє' daditdinnał xodjini djın. k'ɑt ba xadidabąhigє ahwodonil go 'ałta ndilniłc xodjinni djın. dįgo adlac nt'i t'ado nadatsiltsɑnnє anidє.' kodє mą'i hiɣał djın. bits'an bik'i ninasti djın. kodє atsєhastįnє xwolxwonє' djın. niłtc'ibiyajє bigołnє.   tsidic ɑddatdonił xodjınni djın. nladє xactcєcdjınnє bokǫ' bєkєdє yailgolɑd djın. xat'єgo donixilnida yiłni? djın. nladє djuxona'ai banaldє akє yictci djın. xat'iciiłi djın. xacdjєcdjınnє yainiłts'oz djın. baxatdji djın xadjicdjınni. gaaa ni djın. abinizǫnz djın. daihitє djın. ai nda yinɑłdzitla djın. tcinnɑlgotla djın. xoniłtsogo kodo gittsєgai. dєgo gittsєgai yago gittsittso doł'ijє yє ndєzzǫlɑd djın. ditcıłє yє ndєzǫ'lɑn djın. bacinє yє ndєzzǫlɑd djın. yołgai yєndєzzǫla djın. tsєɣadndinnє yє ndєzzǫlɑd djın. acdlago ndєzǫlɑd djın.

bєt'a sєtąlɑd djın.   nadє t'ado biłxwєdjilnє. xat'єgo ca sıtts'an ndannołin. di yєnє' dju bidayє xwonaxolnє' djın. dojdonida dacidonila ni djın.   daąłtso dzitdiłgє'j dacidonєla ni djın. mą'i dala'ni akott'єndi t'ado cinik'є astsagida ni djın. atsєєsdzą̨n nni' bikєgoiti't ni djın. nianє bik'єgo. asdza 'ąłtsoi bik'єtuxwisi'ni' aciak'indєcdłeł cidinnit'. nnє bik'єgo toxołtsodi biyaji ts'it tasasilla ndi'ayat'єgє yistsą ni djın. adolni djın. xat'icidi nigo naididzitєnnє' itagє nintą djın. kodє niłtc'ibiyajє akє xastin xołnaxonnє'. e dotc'єjntago dodołniłda nzin xwodjınni djın. di doł'ijgo yєndєzǫgє tcił doł'ij gє'ıł'į xodjınni djın. ł'ıtsogo yєndadzǫgє ditcıłє 'ıł'į tcil dadınnot'inł nzego ɑtt'į, bacinє yєndєzǫ' tcil bit'ą ałtsǫ' dinnot'ą nzingo ɑtt'į. dzıł dijigona'alє nzigo ɑtt'i xodjınni djın. ai łigaigo yєndєzǫgє yołgai yıł'į dzıłlata dadodzɑs nzįgo ɑt'i xodjınni djın.

Turquoise Boy said it. "Inside you step," he told him they say. Horn large reed | twelve holes having, your shirt put it under. Mirage People those with you travel. | That with not seeing you will you pass by," he said they say. "All right," he said they say. "Well, person's | death I pass that with you will pay me. Just not your people. These wherever on the earth | they move," he said they say. "One hundred and two my roads will be," he said they say. | "This place so many (?) persons will die." White Shell Boy that one he spoke to they say. "Where are you from?" | "Pelado Peak which stands west side White Shell Boy I belong I am," he said they say. | "Moon inside you step," he told him they say. "Now after this doing something if it will happen | each other you will change," he said they say. Four places they watch not in line | they saw him he came. Here coyote walked they say. From him on it he put they say. Here First Man | he instructed him they say. Small wind told him. "Something bad he is going to tell him," he said | they say. There Black God his fire his place he had gone they say. "Why didn't they tell us?" | he said to him they say. Over there sun they made, picture he made they say. Don't know what kind they say. | Black God he handed it to they say. He got angry they say. Black God. "Gaaa," he said they say. | He tore it up they say. He ran off they say. That one only he was afraid of they say. He ran off they say. | So long so much white. Above white below yellow blue with | he had drawn lines across they say. Abalone with he had drawn lines they say. Jet with he had drawn lines they say. | White shell with he had drawn lines they say. Rock crystal with he had drawn lines they say. Five | he had drawn lines they say.

His blanket fold in it lay they say. ? not he told him. "Why from me | you hid it? This is first," he told him they say. "You are not going to tell me," | he said they say. "All I make crooked you tell me," he said they say. Coyote, "Sure I did that | not my leadership I did it," he said they say. "First Woman you were leader," he said they say. | "You being leader I did it. All her leadership was unfortunate 'I want to win' you told me. You | being leader *toxoṭtsodi* its young I took out (?) little better I did," he said they say. He said it | they say. What saying drawing in center he put down (a stick) they say. Here wind young | First Man he told. "That if it is not taken on it will not happen he thinks," he told him they say. | "This blue he drew with grass green he represented," he told him they say. "Yellow with he drew | abalone vegetation getting ripe he means it is. Jet he drew with vegetation its leaves all | fallen he means it is. Mountains black across he means it is," he told him they say. This | white with drawn white shell made with mountain tops snow lies on he means it is," he said to him they say.

dide tseɣadndɩnnε yendεdzǫgε' to ąłtsǫ dadotɩnłgo nzɩgo ati
xodjɩnni djɩn. ako atsεhastin di doł'ɩjgo bεndɩndzola tcil doł'ɩjgε' inlala
bidjɩnni djɩn. ditcɩłe bεdεnzogε' tcil 'ąłtso dinnotɩnł nzingo nt'i bidjɩnni
djɩn. bacinε bεndinzogε' at'a·n ąłtso ndinnotago dzɩł t'ałijigo na'allε
nzɩgo ɑnt'ɩ bidjini djɩn. yołgai bεndnzǫgε dzɩłłata dadodzas nzingo
nt'i bidjini djɩn. tseɣadndεnε bεdnzogε to ałtso dadotɩnł nzɩgo ɑnt'ɩ
bidjini djɩn. ładji xastan nǫnilla. ładji do' xastan nǫnilla. xacai'it'εlε.
ade' djilta dolgεł. xaic bε nasxwont'ilε. di bε nnatntallε. k'ɑt nila banakai
banadza djɩn do xaida djuxona'ai yεnε konε ninil djɩn. djuxona'ai
xodollełgi kwɑtt'εgo adεdεst'a djɩn. bini doł'ij go xodolεł. xodon'ni
djɩn. binik'ε xactcɩgo bizεk'ε xactcɩgo biyada' na ettsogo bidε doł'ɩjgo
bidε' bɩłεbaanigε (bɩłdanogεł) yεgo daiista djɩn. ya daxayε xodon'nigo
bąda'ist'a·. adzilł'ijtso xolge. atsεxastin yi'al dindε yε'yoł at'ε yεnε-
nεsɑl djɩn. hidεzna djɩn. yaxanεya· hiya djɩn. akodidjε' nacdalε.
haiya' dzaxadzis xolge'djε t'adjin nacdalε. akwi nacdɩlε. doł'iji łɩ bεn-
dicdąhi akwi nadɩlε ni djɩn. kodo kodji' t'obεlya. axilɣałε dobitts'ilgo
ni djɩn. deya djɩn. k'asą' dadjistc'ilgo i'i'ą djɩn. doa'bεsoxodonł'ɩdala
xodon'ni djɩn. xondzadji denahidεsda djɩn. ako nadεsdza djɩn. nakidi
dεya djɩn. t'a konanada djɩn. dobεsoxodobεjda xonεzɣa djɩn.
tadi dεya djɩn.


t'a konanada djɩn. dobεts'odobεjda xonnεzɣa djɩn. dakondzadjɩ
dεnaxεdεsda djɩn. dɩdi dεdεsda djɩn. k'a dɩnda yat'ε xodonni djɩn. k'ɑt
noxosdzan kwɑtt'εgo niɩłso djɩn. noxasdzan xolge djɩn. sɩsnadjɩnnε
la djɩn. yołgai bε xadildiya djɩn. tsodzɩł nit'a djɩn. doł'ijε bεxadilya
djɩn. doɣoslɩd ditcɩłi bε xadilya djɩn. dεbεntsa bacinε bε xadilya djɩn.
dzɩłnaxodɩłε xa'anεɣε bε xadilya djɩn. nɩ' bidje ɑlya djɩn. djoli nł'ij
bizε bε xadilya djɩn. ni bidje disdjol ɑlya djɩn. yoditdzil xolgelε xodon'ni
djɩn. nɩłtsą dzil xolgelε xodon'ni djɩn. dzɩł dεst'i djɩn. kodjεgo nεs'ą
go ɑlya djɩn. dzɩł noxozɩłi bitsits'in ɑlya djɩn. bεc bε xaditt'εgo ɑlya

This rock crystal with drawn water all frozen he means it is," | he told him they say. Then First Man "This blue you drew with vegetation green you made," | he said to him they say. Abalone you drew with vegetation all fallen off you meant you did," he told him | they say. "Jet with you drew leaves all fallen off mountains just black across | you meant you did," he told him they say. White shell with you drew mountain tops snow lies you meant | you did," he said to him they say. "Rock crystal with you drew water all turned to ice you meant you did,"| he said to him they say. One side six you put down. Other side too six you put down. What will it be. | Don't do any more it will be named. What with will you make beyond. This with we get mixed. Now you | do it." From him he went home they say. Sun in here he put they say. Sun | they are going to make. This way they began to sing they say. "Its face blue will be," he said | they say. "His eye mark making black his mouth mark making black. His cheek horizontal yellow, his horn blue | with mirage (?) he placed they say. Sky on saying | he put it up. *adzall'itso* (a medicine) called. First Man he chewed it four places he blew it was with he sprinkled it | they say (?). It began to move they say. On the sky he went they say. "Here middle I will go. | Here reservoir *dzaxadzis* where it is called just there I will go. There I will eat dinner. Blue horse the one I ride | there he will eat," he said they say. So much from there for fun he made. "Somebody goes down not strongly," | he said they say. He went they say. Nearly when they were roasting it set they say. "You nearly burned them (?)," | he said to him they say Farther up he went up again they say. Then he went again they say. Twice | he went they say, it was hot they say. It was frightfully hot they say. | Three times he went they say. |

Just it was hot they say. It was warm they say. Farther up | he raised it again they say. Four times he raised it they say. "Now | it is right," he said they say. Then map this way they made they say. Map called was named they say. Pelado Peak | was they say. White shell with it was decorated they say. Mount Taylor stood up they say. Turquoise with it was decorated | they say. San Francisco Peaks abalone with it was decorated they say. La Plata Mountains jet with was decorated they say.| *dziłnaxodiłε* mirage with was decorated they say. Earth its heart was made they say. *djoli* hard jewels | with was decorated they say. Earth its heart round was made they say. "Bead Mountain it will be called," he said | they say. "Rain Mountain it will be called," he said they say. Mountain he placed they say. This way (south) lying he made it | they say. *noxoziłi* skull was made they say. Lava with covered it was made |

djɪn. binago bɛsist'oɣɛ adastsi' djɪn. bɛ bits'ą xwoniɣɛ'lɛgo. adastsi djɪn. aidɛ tsɛsdjin adaz'agɛ silį djɪn. yuwotcogo ɛ'adjɛgo nacdjɪjgo ɑlya djɪn. bɛtɛldzi to xadazlįgo ɑlya djɪn. dį xɑlgaigo xɑlgaidɛn nlado xolgelɛ xodon'ni djɪn. kodɛ to djɪnlido tsɛlakan atcajdjic do' xodon'ni djɪn. k'ɑt nli bił'adi to ałnasdlį xolgelɛ adɛ. ako xadą'ąnɛ sɪsnadjinnɛ baxolonɛnnɛ kidɛdołɛ xodon'ni djɪn. dlodzɪłgai ndictci' gɛjdila djɪn. dlojicinɛ tc'o· gijdila djɪn. tsɑnłannɛ dɛstsin gijdilla djɪn. xaze gɑt gijdilla djɪn. adonda adjilandɛ tc'il bina' daxatc'inyangɛ' at'ɛ gidadɛzla djɪn. edik'ɑt nokaxolɑd djɪn. adɛinda atsɛxastin sɪsnadjinnɛ nɑzdidja. tsodzɪł disdja. doɣosłił nɑzdidja. dɛbɛntsa nazdidja. dzɪł ł'ij bik'i dasisdilni djɪn. t'adįgo dzɪłnaodɪłeyɛn xanigɛ djik'aj bik'i dzinil djɪn. djol'i'yɛ nł'ij bize bik'i dzinil djɪn. xaiyɛ tsɛ xaiz'ą xodonni djɪn. tsɛnaltc'ocɛ cilą djɪnni djɪn. tsɛhɛnnɛ djik'ajɛ djɪnnɛ t'obɪłda'dɛsni djɪn. tsɛ xadazt'i sili djɪn. niyanɛzinni dįgo dɛzi djɪn. xadot'a djɪn. ni'ɛnnɛ ąłtsą dɛdɛstsǫ djɪn. dzɪłɛnnɛ dadanɛssą djɪn. xagocɛdanjot sili djɪn. ne'ɛ adazso djɪn. tsɛsdzɛztąn akwɛ baxanastɛ djɪn. k'addɛ izlįdji' djɪn.


dilɣɛ nidja djɪn. atsɛts'ozi nidja' djɪn. xastinsɑkk'ai ni'nil djɪn. atsɛtso kwɛ'nni' ninil djɪn. kwɛ'nnɛ' yikaisdai ɑlya djɪn. gaxat'e ɑlya djɪn. naxokǫsbikąi niltį djɪn. naxokǫs bi'adɛ niltį djɪn. kwɛ bɛkǫn ɑlya djɪn. mai'i bisǫ kodɛ nɛsdji djɪn. cidi (?) sizzonlɛ nigo bɛdaɣaan haiinij. phw ni djɪn. sǫnłitcigo daihissi djin. sǫ axaaninɛɣaz djɪnnɛ. kǫ yɪłka djɪn. phw phw phw ni djɪn. eba sǫ' t'ado exozinnɛ bɛsłin djɪn. xajo sǫ' ninıłɛ ma'i at'i djɪn. inda bɛlya nidjɪn. ako nanɑtdza djɪnni. kodjɛ' djuxona'ai xalyagɛt'ɛgo tsɛkɛ' nita djɪn. yołkɑłgo dok'ɛdodatda. ałtsisigo ła nanalya djɪn. yołkɑłgo noxok'ɛ bɛ oxozindo xani'go djɪnnɛ. nanɛska djɪn.

they say. Around it arrowheads they stuck up they say. With from it they keep them away. They stuck | them up they say. These black peaks sticking up became they say. Way on the west side lying | they were made they say. Its breast water springing up was made they say. "Four-Prairies prairies | will be called," he said they say. "Here water will flow, pericardis, diaphragm too," he said | they say. "Now stream (?) its base waters flowing across each other will be called. There their seeds Pelado Peak | those having let them plant," he said they say. Gray pine squirrel pines he planted they say. | Black squirrel spruce planted they say. Bluejays piñon planted they say. Small squirrel cedar planted | they say. Then all people vegetation its seed whatever they eat all he planted | they say. This on they are now they say. Then First Man Pelado Peak he put down. | Mt. Taylor he put down. San Francisco Peaks he put down. La Plata Mts. he put down. Soil on it | he put down they say, all four. That *dziłnaodiłe* mirage stone ground up on it he put they say. | Turquoise hard jewels on it he put they say. "Who brought up?" he asked they say. | Cañon wren, "I did," he said they say. That stone the ground up pieces they sewed back and forth they say. | Rocks stand in line became they say. Those standing under the earth four places they stand they say. They began to sing they say. The earth | from each other they began to stretch they say. Those mountains began to grow up they say. | They became very large they became they say. Earth they stretched they say. In Mesa Verde there they have them they say. Now it is completed they say.

Pleiades he placed they say. First star he placed they say. *xastinsak'ai* he placed they say. | Morningstar next he placed they say. Next Milky Way was made they say. "Rabbit tracks" was made | they say. Dipper male he placed they say. Dipper female he placed they say. Then his fire | was made they say. Coyote his star here he placed they say. "These will be my stars," saying his beard | he pulled out. "Phw," he said they say. Red stars appear they say. Stars he gathered together they say. | Up he threw them they say. "Phw phw phw phw," he said they say. Because of that stars not planned they are clustered they say. | Good stars he was going to put Coyote did it they say. "Anyway looks nice," he said they say. Then he went back they say. | Here sun made like on rock he put they say. Forever it remains. | Small another they make again they say. At dawn on earth with it knowing they tell they say. | It was day again they say.

ła dadzɩzsa djɩn. dadzɛssado dį nɩskago baiyatin djɩn. xadjila
ndjilɖla xodon'ni djɩn. xa'adji tc'ɛ ndjin'ac djɩn. cada'adji' ndjɩz'ac
djɩn. ɛ'adji ndjɩz'ą djɩn. nahokǫsdji' ndjɩz'ą djɩn. 'ąłtsogo adjitdin
xodon'ni djɩn. ałkɛ'na'aci olge bicnota djɩn. xadjɩnnaigɛ bidado
xadjijajnt'ɛ. nloyat'e xattsi djɩccogo dzɩzda djɩn. bikɛ'xaxodissi' djɩn.
eba tc'įndi diłtsɛgo xaxodissi djɩn. ndjitt'ajn nloyadɛ dzɩzda. akwiya
nadjidlela adzɩzda xodjɩnni djɩn. donnɛdɑllɛ ixodon'ni djɩn. dotcoyɩn-
ndjɩtdlɛdɑllɛ xodonni djɩn. doitci·dɑllɛ xodonni djɩn. dajnɛltɛlɛ nɛntɛlɛ
xodonni djɩn kɛłannɛ diłxiłgo xadɛlya djɩn. tosiɣi djɩn akwiya elgo djɩn.
xanɛzɛlgo do'annɛddallɛ. ma'i at'ɛ djɩn. nił'ɛ yɩł ndilwo djɩn.    di
xannazɛlgocnt'ɛ doannɛnɑllɛ ni djɩn. ma'i di annɛ. dayiłxandɛ djɩn.
tsɩnnɛni' xanazɛl djɩn.    ebaˑ xɑnni' ndaxwidlɛ djɩnnɛ. diɛnnɛ
daiiltsɩtndɛ djɩn. 'e t'a'annɛ sili djɩn.


kodɛ tsɩn yaxolɣałłɛ dadiya djɩn. tcoɣɩn silila ni djɩn. doxatsi
yiɣadɑllɛ daxatsi łijingo xodon'ni djɩn. k'ɑddɛ tcicgai dadiya djɩn.
całtcinnɛ sɩttsi' ałtsǫ' yigaila ni djɩn. dila dɩnnɛ ayudɛgo ndalnic
xodon'ni djɩn. gɛdiłdlɛ. tcij ndɛ. tsdzɑn la'i ałai. xannanic tciyandɛ
adjiłi. ɛsdjɑndɛ ndjiɣɛłɛ. dɩnnɛ bandjiɣɛłɛ xodonni djɩn. kwidɛ'
ma'i dadilgo djɩn. ciłna'acgo asigɛ ni djɩn. ebạˑ dɩnnɛ dɛntcigɛ sili djɩn.
atsɛɛsdzan tsɩnnazdɛjkɛz djɩn. ts'adi ci·cik'ɛ xodollɛł nzi batsɩnnazdɛzkɛz
la djɩn. di ɛsdzaɣi dodacida dɛcniłna. ɛsdzɑnnɛ adjil'andɛ ako dadjɩt-
t'inlɛ. nzǫ tsɩnnadɛzkɛzla djɩn. dɩnnɛ ɛsdzɑnnɛ tsɩtdɛ ba xołdaxogɛllɛ
ako ajanɛ'. dɛnɛ kwɛ xolonɛ. ɛsdzan do' bɛnaltc'ai xodollɛł nzįgo yant-
sɩzkɛ(z) la djɩn. yołgai djoc ɑlyalɛ djɩn. doł'ijɛ zɩs ɑlyalɛ djɩn. dɩnnɛ
xatdjɛgɛ xatcinɛn yiɣidɩz xack'anɛ. xatcin yɩł taila djɩn. xadastosolɛ
djɩn tcɛłtci ihiilalɛ djɩn. djoccɛ ila·yiyigonɛ' iyigɩł djɩn. ɛsdzandjɛ
xatdjɛgɛ xattcin binanadɩz djɩn.    ɛsdzɑn xatdjɛgɛ yi·dizɛnnɛ xack'an
yɩłiłta ɑnnanalya. doł'ij zɩssɛnɛ yiyigonɛ' ɑnnanalya. tołannastcin e

One died they say. He died. Four when it was days they talked about it they say. "Where | will they go," he said they say. East in vain two arrived they say. South two arrived | they say. West two arrived they say. North two arrived they say. "All places he isn't," | they said they say. The Two-one-behind-the-other-who-go put on a mask they say. Where they emerged its mouth | they two stood. Down there her hair combing she sat they say. They became nervous they say. | Because of that ghost when one sees he becomes nervous they say. They two came back, "Below she sits. Down there | one goes one sits," he said they say. "They do not die," he said they say. | "Women will not have menses," he said they say. "They will not have babies," he said they say. "Just the same people will be," | he said they say. Skin dressing stick black was painted with they say. Water stood there they say. In that he threw it they say. | If it floats up they won't die. Coyote it was they say. Ax with he threw they say. "This | if it floats up they will not die," he said they say. Coyote this he said. It sank they say. | The stick floated up they say. Because of that his mind will come to life again he said. This | one went down they say. That surely dead became they say.

Here sapsucker came they say. "Menses have become," he said they say. "Not his hair | will become gray, his hair black," he said they say. Now western robin came they say. | "My children, my head all has become gray," he said they say. "These men hard you work," | he said they say. "They plant. Wood they bring. The women they work, | what they eat she prepares. Woman may marry. Man may marry," he said they say. There | Coyote came they say. "My cousin, I am married," he said they say. That because people marry it became they say. | First woman thought about it they say. "I leader will be," she thought she studied about | they say. "These women not just I (?) commit adultery. Women as a class will do that thinking," | she studied about it they say. "Man woman hard they will separate. | Men here will have. Women too their medicine will have," thinking she studied about | they say. White shell vagina was made they say. Turquoise penis was made they say. Man | from his breast loose cuticle she rubbed off. Yucca fruit its skin with she mixed they say. Her clitoris | coral (red shell) was made they say. The vagina inside she put they say. Woman from | her breast her loose cuticle she rubbed off they say. Woman from her breast what was rubbed off yucca fruit | mixed with she made again. Turquoise that penis in she put again. All kinds of water |

bił tc'el alya djin. benets'alle biniγe djin. kodji djoc nita djin. ałtcistci sizenni nita djin ebą. benatc'a besdzoł djin. zis dała ayla djin. ebą k'at axadjitt'ajgo nisł'ad dji esdzan sida' djin. k'at ts'iddokos xodoni djin. ts'esdzestando' zisenne bentsekes ts'etna' daxezdel djin. asdzandje bets'innadezkez, k'asą' ts'etną t'ałni djin t'axaannahildel djin. bił'ane biłexone ebą. binsikes dǫnezdala djin. didolγoc xodon'ni djin. zize dilγaj djin. xaγoci daxizdel djin. asdzandji' nadilγaj djin. doxots'it dilγajla djin. axidinnodził naxodonni djin. axet'inłdil djin k'at nadadolγoc. xodo'ni djin zise. tcidilγaj djin. ndexajistc'i djin. djoce nadilγaj djin. nde' biji njongo dilγaj djin. xaji' zi(l)gela djin. dinne k'at xodonni djin. k'at xał'eγone' abedziłe. ma'i kode nilgo djin. bidaγa xaiinij djin. ya'isi djin. yik'idji' isoł djin. inda' belya ni djin. ma'i esdzan bił'egone' abedzil djin. dinne do' bił'egone' abedził djin. k'at agotsa djin.


atsesdzą sinnadezkezgo ł'istso akego nat'ani tcillinne dinne' biłni djin. iłxacla djin. cac dakego nat'ani nadjitłinne dinne' ndzidzǫnsla xodon'ni djin. ats'axwedelde djin. ł'istso nakode cace do djin. ats'axwedelde djin. nacdoitso do' adądaxast'ąda ebą ili djin. tabastine dodaadaxast'ada ebą bakaγe ili djin. yołkago ts'ede dagot'ele ats'axodi'niłle nat'ąni ndadjodlełle daxodoni djin. (Omission of winter time material). k'at nihila' nałde xodon'ni djin. ba ntsi nanakesgot'e ni djin. atsexastin dinne xodollełgi aiłnila djin. (Omission to 48 years after they come up.) tsedestąγi aibe atde'bi adadjikai xazli djin. adajnt'i. mos bendadjakai xazli djin. axidaznts'in djin. dajnni' xazli djin. t'o'axayoi dajnezna djan. dobidedladdjillene doł'ije ma'i istcin djit'enne doli istcin djit'enne ayac tcin djitenne xatsi doł'iji bedjisł'icnaxalene. doł'ije xadat'e 'astsi bą'adilni' atsełgai nakidzata binannezą' ye'anni. atsełtci' nakidzada binannesa. aidjillinne xołhaiinna, dziłnadjinne bigijge' kittsilbito' xolgedje xołbitdai'ina łą xwanaxai djinne t'akwatt'ego be'axanajdikai. t'axwatt'ego najntne djin. ałk'in nadaxodjitda. bitts'an xadjontna

that with herbs was made they say. She will be pregnant for that they say. Her vagina she placed they say. | Beside it the penis she placed they say. That is why medicine she spit on it they say. Penis both was made | they say. Because of that now when they get married left side woman sits they say. "Now you think," | she said they say. Mesa Verde the penis thought across (his) mind goes they say. | Woman thought again. Nearly across halfway back it reached | they say. Her hips in between. That is why her thinking is not long they say. "Let them shout," she said | they say. Penis shouted they say. Very loud it went they say. Woman shouted again they say. | Not hard she shouted they say. "Let them have intercourse," she said they say. They had intercourse they say. | "Now let them shout again," she said they say. Penis shouted they say. He did shout loud they say. | Vagina shouted they say. Now her voice well shouted they say. His voice he had lost they say. | Man "Now," he said they say. Now is her crotch put it in. Coyote there came | they say. His beard he pulled out they say. He stuck them in they say. On it he blew they say. "Now it looks nice," he said | they say. Coyote woman crotch in he put it they say. Man too in his crotch he put it | they say. Now they are thus they say. |

First woman when she was thinking about it great snake second chief who was people he bit they say. | He killed them they say. "Bear next chief who was people he tears up," he said | they say. They discharged them they say. Great snake and bear two they say. They discharged them they say. | Panther didn't do anything because of that he is of value they say. Otter did nothing | because of that his hide is of value they say. To this day (?) bad if they do they will discharge them. "Chiefs | will be," they said they say. (Part omitted which can be told only in winter). "Now | where you like you go," he said they say. "I am thinking about something else," he said they say, First Man. | (Omission.) "People will be," he told them they say. | Mesa Verde that with gourd dipper they travel it happened they say. They poison people. Cat they travel with | it happened they say. They bewitch people they say. They began to die it happened they say. Many of them were dying | they say. A well-behaved girl (is) turquoise coyote image, blue bird image | birds' images her hair covered with she had. Turquoise disc standing | one puts hands on. White tails twelve were around its border she had. Red tails twelve | were around its border. That tribe with her moved away. Ute Mountain its gap, *kittsil* its spring | place called with her they moved. After a year the same way they did. The same way they were dying along | they say. Each other they suspected. From them they moved |

djın. xats'abitoγi nadjıntna djın. tsınnadεsdε djın. dodaddisxisditts'ada
'ado xana'ona djın. dziłicdlai bεyadji nat'anε djillınnε xadzotsi djın.
xadjinai bił'adji kondineł djınnε djınnε. 'adziltso lą xodoni djın. t'ą'danaz-
dina djın. k'at kınteł hwidolgeł gεna djın. ado xanadildε djın. nεdaxoba
djın. diγindınnε dobidεdlattcillınnε xoydiolgεlxan'niga dεnε xattinatdja
djın.


ła'a kǫ a'ozdε' kindoł'ijε xwołxanaxona djın. t'akona xoldilidjın
xana'onαd djınnε. ła dakǫ djın adakεtcilt'εgo tsεdεze'ą' biyaγε na'inα
djın. ado tsεbiya αnni'ądji bananεstą'. aiyonxot'εkεyala nαnsε'
dobitdį'xoyεdαlla bį xolola naγacci xolola djadi. xolola dınnε' dobit-
dinxεlgεdαlla xodonni djın. nαnse yidani solti' xodontni djın. adε
ąłtso na djın. akogo djuxona'ai εsdzannε bik'i xodjilleładj djın.
naxoditdai xolge djın. asdzą' αlilleago xodjεlle' t'adoεxozınnε inilts'-
ątlαdj djın. iniltsąda nast'ai yiskago actci djın. nast'ai naididzigo
niitc'ilε ainigεi 'att'ilα djın. yictcindo acdląda yiskago nεt'axoyanε sili
djın. nαlgo djın. acdlada bεnaxago dεnnε axoyanεdolełgo ebinigε
axat'inilαdj djın. tsodził yina' nαlgo sili djın. bik'a illa djın. ga hiγa
djın łεts'o' niyiγε djın. dǫntso' baniya djın. xat'ila xana' sittsoi biłni
djın. nijε bitc'in dınna. djuxona'ai nta gont'ε biłni djın. akǫ dinyadε
xodε ła' ndjiga djın. kodji dadina xałni djın. nadzıllit at'εla djın.
tsodził bilatadji' xołdaiεsdel djın. sısnadjınnε bilatadji setat bilatadji'
xołdaiisdel djın. djuxona'ai bitc'εdadji' xołnixindeł djın. i'a'itsε'na'
xolgedji' xolginni'alαdj djın. kǫxonε noxokabinnε' donaγada xat'ila
xainiya xałni? djın. djuxona'ai kodε nıłtc'ibiyajε xolxwolnε djın.
nts'ıntdzago act'i bidinni' xałni djın. nıłtc'ibiyajε (Omission) lą'
siγε'lαnlin dani xałni djın. djuxona'ai yałnidji xwolnαtt'ajn (Omission)
dį hwiska djın. bałkεγε yałni xayatdzadzıs xolgege nijna'acgo bitt'a
dolni djın. łεdzattsoi xayi'a djın. to yixizi djın. tadıtdin ixiyitdja djın.

they say. Dolores they moved they say.   They began witching they
say.   They did not listen | then they moved, they say.   Mountains
five below chief spoke they say. | "*xadjinai* its base we will go,"
he said they say.   All of them, "All right," they said they say.
Back they came | they say.   Then Aztec where it is called they
came they say.   Then they began to fight they say.   They made war |
they say.   The holy people the fine girl they wanted to kill, spirit
people they came | they say.

Some there they stayed.  House blue with her they moved they say.
There they came to fight they say. | They moved away they say.   Some
there they say.  A few Mesa Verde below they stopped | they say.   Then
Chaco Cañon they went to look.  "Great for farms, fruit | no need to
hunt, deer they were, mountain sheep there were.  Antelope there were,
game | was plentiful," they said they say.  Fruit good.  "Let us go,"
they said they say.  Then | all they say.  Then sun woman on her (had
intercourse) they say. | Picks-up-little-things she was named they say.
Woman magically had intercourse she didn't know it.  She found she
was pregnant | they say.  When she was pregnant nine days she gave
birth they say.  Nine months | will be born it is thus because of that they
say.  Born fifteen days grown up he became | they say.  He ran (a race)
they say.  Fifteen years man will be grown that is why | it is that way
they say.  Mt. Taylor around it he ran it became they say.  His arrow
he made they say.  Rabbits he killed | they say.  Pack rats he killed they
say.  Large fly came to him they say.  "What you doing, (going ?),
my grandson," he said to him | they say.  "Your father to him you go.
The sun your father is," he told him they say.  There if you go | some-
thing stands (?) they say.  "That step on," he told him they say.  Rain-
bow it was they say. | Mt. Taylor its top it went with him they say.
Pelado Peak, its top | it went with him they say.  Sand dunes its top it
went with him they say.  Sun in front of door it landed with him they
say.  Magpie tail | where it is called it came with him they say.  "In
here with us do not go around.  What | you come for," he asked they say,
Sun.  Then small wind instructed him they say. | "'I have a hard time I
am,' you tell him," he told him they say, small wind.  "Yes, | my son
you are truly," he said they say, Sun.  Center of sky they two came.
(Omission.) | Four days they say.  Center of sky from where it is called
when they two came his pocket he put his hand in | they say.  Gold plate
he took out they say.  Water he put in it they say.  Pollen he put in
they say. |

taixinil djɪn. acdla bɛ nɪɫtsɛ xaɫni djɪn. tc'ɛ djɪɫ'ɪ̨t djɪn. nɑjnitca
djɪn. banajnaka djɪn. datdidi kwiila djɪn. yi''naxwoɫtsai djɪn. bit'a
nayi'a djɑn. nɪɫtc'ibiyajɛ bibɛnɪɫɛ' xozindo xodont'nigo xadjattagɛ
daixiszit djɑn. ebɛ nɪɫɛxozigo adinɪɫ xaɫni djɪn. xoɫninɪɫxinat'ajn.
doɫ'ijɛ ɫazɛ' xadja' badasɛnnɛlgo ebitc'ɪ̨' xajdɪnnoɫnɛlgo. ɑsdzą naxadidai
biyaj ɛyuitt'ɛci doɫ'ijɛ naidja xa'nigo. xat'ɛgila' naidinɪɫ xa'nigo tc'ɛ
bina'idɛkit. kɪn dasa'andɛ 'atdɛn cigodɛ. ɑtdɪn dajdini djini djɪn.
tc'ɛ bandatcɪɫni' djɪn. tciyan tc'ɛ dabɪttc'ɪnni djɪn. sɛst'i tc'ɛ badaba-
djɪnni djɪn. haɣonɛ' ɫa' nihinɪl tc'ɛ xaɫni djɪn. ɛsdzan nadɛctɛɫ e bɪɫ
nanaaclɛ nɛzdzalɛ xak'ɛkinsɑnnɪllɛ adjɪnni djɪn. dodɑnni' djɪn. nihinɪl
ni djɪn. xaɣo'onɛ' sɛɛst'ɛ bɪɫ ɪɫk'ɪdji'. dakats'ɑsts'ɪddɛ ebɛ' adɛdikaɫ
nigo xatci xanɛ'nɪɫ djɪn. ts'ɪttsą naxalɛgo hɛsɫ'ǫlɛ djɪn naki aɫdɛsɛs e'
xadɛsbigo sɛst'i bɪɫ ɪɫk'ɪdji' bidjɪnni djɪn. lɑn ni djɪn dakwi di dolɛɫ
aɫadɛ? ni djɪn. niilka djɪn. bɪtt'ago 'inilka djɪn. bidadolnindɛ
ts'a xaita djɪn.


daka'tsɑsts'ɪddɛ yihidja djɪn. ci itsɛ' tc'ɛ bidjɪnni djɪn. adjic
kat tc'ɛ bidjini djɪn dodani djɪn. cicɛdaka' at'ɛ acitsɛnidjɛn lą' bidjɪnni
djɪn. adzikat djɪn. bigai ninɪɫnɛ' djɪn. xaosbɑd djɑn. sɛɛst'aiyɛn
nadji'kwiilago doɫ'ijɛ t'a'i xwɑnnai'inil djɪn. ɫa kwɑɫt'ɛgo xaxwodɛnnɛsną
tciyan. oxaiyoi xaiyosbą djɪn. xwonnasdo na'ilgɛ'ɛ yidɛsba djɪn. xakɪnnɛ'
ąɫtso xayosba djɪn. di kɪn naxazɪɫbaniɣɛ' nakɫɣɛ do' tciyan do' dat'ɛ
ɛsdza ɫa' bɪɫ ɪɫk'idji' xaɫni djɪn. ɛsdzan aɫai' xayosba djɪn. ado xodɛsba
djɪn. dɪnnɛ' t'adjɪtt'ɛ aidi ano't'ɛ nixidzɪɫbanigɛ' doɫ'iɫazɛ' ano't'ɛ
bɪɫ ɪɫnoɫk'idji xaɫni djɪn. ąɫtso xosbąyɛ' djɪn. e dikwi kɪn ca dołɪɫ. e
tc'iyan naxaisɪɫbanɛ e bikin at'ɛ bina'nɛl sizligo nasbąsgo kojigo dasɪɫtągo
ɑlya djɪn. ɫa'i nasbąs ɑlya djɪn. ɫa' eyi sɪtda djɪn. djak'ɛ daxoɫdɛ
xaɫni djɪn. kodɛ kɪn ɑlya djɪn. e binnago djak'ɛ axolya djɪn. bitc'idjigo
bixailgɛ djɪn. e'atc'igo ile' dadjɪllinɛ' ixa'ądji xatcilgɛ djɪn. tsɪnbɛdzɪɫ

Mush he made they say. "Five (fingers) with eat it," he told him
they say. In vain he tried to eat it up they say. He got enough | they
say. To him he gave back the dish they say. Four times he did it they
say. He dried it out they say. His pocket | he put it in they say. Small
wind he gave him, "You will know," telling him on his ear | he put it
they say. "That with it tells you you do," he told him they say. They
two arrived. | Turquoise jewels his ear putting on that to him gambling
you won't lose.   Woman Picks-up-small-things | her son very precious
turquoise he wears they talked about. "Where did he get it," talking
about it in vain | they asked. House standing nothing we do not have
that kind they said they say. | In vain they bargained for it they say.
Food in vain they offered in exchange they say.   Paper bread in vain they
offered, | they say, "All right, one (person) I will bet," in vain he said
to him they say. "Woman I will give you that with you | two will
live together she will marry you Chief said it they say. "No," he said
they say. "I will bet," | he said they say. "All right, paper bread with
on top of each other. We will bet. Seven dice sticks those with we will
play," | saying to him he took them out they say.   Box (?) I will
weave (?) two feet high that full paper bread | with one on the other we
will bet," he said they say. "All right," he said they say. "How many
this will be?" | "Once," he said they say. He put down a basket they
say. Between them he put it they say. Up he threw them.   Basket | he
took out they say. "I will throw them in vain," he said they say.
    Dice he put in they say. "I first," in vain he said they say. "No," |
he said they say. "My dice they are, I first," he said they say. "All
right," he said | they say. He threw them they say. White they fell
they say. He won they say. That paper bread | putting it away tur-
quoise he bet him again they say. Same way their goods he beat him
continually.   Food much | he won they say. After that goods he began
to win they say. Their houses | all he won they say. "These houses I
have won from you, goods too, food too all | woman one with I bet," he
said to him they say. Woman one he won they say. Then he began to
win | they say. "People all those of you I have won turquoise jewel all
of you | with I bet," he said they say. All he won they say. "Those here
house for me you build. This | food which I have won that their lunch all
his slaves having become round one there lies on | was made they say. One
round was made they say. That in he lived they say. "Race track
make," | he said they say. There house was made they say. That around it
race track | they made they say. On his side they came in they say. From
the west the people east they came up they say.   Tree push against |

xolgε εtsi· bεtc'idji'. bits'ądji' ałdo axwot'i ła' εtsi? djɨn. najǫci ilalαd djɨn. bił'ai xolge yąxidinεskallαd djɨn. ats'abilαcgan nαcdoi bilαcgan dadidji bilαcgan yandαtdεsnilαd djɨn. dεnε dazdisconci nεsna xabą daxisnillαd djɨn. ilgɨcgo wαnnaltc'illi wolgεgo biji' αlya djini. djoł αlya djɨn. nladji kɨn dasittαnnε baγaxodzago αlya 'εnda baγaxαlgεgo candaixołbįllε. nεhεttsigo e ci naxannicbinlε ni djɨn. kɨntεl do' kɨn doł'ij do' tsεdεs'ą do' 'ąłtso baiyat'igo bayεldε djɨn. dį·go binaltci· xolonlαd djɨn. xadaidεs'į'i bayildε' wεxε ci'ilε' ni djɨn. nixεsdzą axi'inɨl ni djɨn.


nilą bidjɨni djɨn. xa'osba djɨn. wεxε' sεsdzą da'ała' cido' inct'ago e danokain dεnεdo' inłtago ała'dε naidobinł xałni djɨn. xana'osba djɨn. nakida xanaosba djɨn. k'αt e nixikeya dici cina'nɨl at'ε cido' inɨctago naiłkidji' naxodon'ni djɨn. xana'osba djɨn. xadat'ε'ε 'e itdzi djɨn. e cǫ'andjɨn. t'a at'ε nixidzɨłbanigε' dode cido' inɨctago bɨł ɨłk'idji' xałni djɨn. lą' isli djɨn. sa·isołbago sεłnizdołxαł αłni djɨn. αłγa didit'αc ni djɨn. lą izli djɨn. di· tsin etsiyę aiyoi nzago εtsilαd djɨn. ła' dabaka djɨn. bidjiabika dɨnnε axadɨnnεstcą djɨn. kɨnnεn binną axεxijnnεltca djɨn. bits'ɨki ndjɨlgo djɨn. xatc'ojgonε' xacγacla djɨn. xak'aigonε' xacγacla djɨn. xasitt'agonε' xacγaclε djɨn. xatsiyagonε' xajγajlε djɨn. ado' taxats'ągo tcideya djɨn. xwilγa dahitε djɨn. ndεdilgołni ciilε' xałni djɨn. kodji bitc'idji bits'adji ndjikaidjɨl'a djɨn. adjiyę' tcahaiya djɨn. bitc'idjiyę' adɨlni' daxεzdil djɨn. tsinεnnε' da'ilk'εsgo djɨn. xwo'ąnε' adεdjoł'ε djɨn. tsinnε' tc'ε hidjɨłi djɨn. kodε' djoxona'ai dαcdiya djɨn. doł'ijε xadat'ε 'asdzigo ba'ądɨlni' axocɨłε bε ni'inibani ciγε' xastaniya djɨnni djɨn. ciilε' nłį xago bαgai ninaką nɨłdicni naya'ai xałni djɨn. xαnnε'a djɨnnε. danazdidza djɨn. noxwɨłbį xwosgε djɨn. ba'adji sili djɨn.

called they put up. His side opposite side too, same way one they put up they say. Pole game they found he had made | they say. Its base hips called they found he had put on they say. Eagle claws, panther claws | all that scratch their claws he had put on they found they say. People those who know ten its border | they put on they say. Lightning (like measuring worm) being named its name was made they say. Ball | was made they say. Over there house which stands hole through it was made. "Now if it goes through it | you win from me. If you miss it that I win from you," he said they say. *kintel* (Aztec ruin) too house | blue too *tsedea'ạ* too all talking about it they went to him they say. Four places | guards they found he had they say. Those who watched went to him "wehe, my opponent," he said they say. "Our wives we bet each other," | he said they say.

"All right," he said they say. He won they say. "Wehe my wives both, me too myself | those who came to you too altogether at one throw you bet," he said they say. He won again | they say. Twice he won they say. Now that your land these my slaves all me too myself | I bet again," he said they say. He won again they say. (The turquoise) that was left | they say. "That bet me. Just all I have won from you me too myself with it I bet," | he said to him they say. "All right," became they say. "If you beat me you may kill me," he said they say. "Beside each other we will run," | he said they say. Consent became they say. This tree that he stuck in that one deep he had put in they say. The other shallow | they say. His side after him (?) people ran they say. That house around it they ran | they say. Ahead of him he ran they say. Muscle of his lower leg he bewitched they say. In his thigh | he bewitched they say. Between his shoulders he bewitched him they say. In under his head he bewitched him they say. | Then having spasms he walked they say. By him he ran they say. "Well, you run, my opponent," he said | they say. Here his side, the other side they cried out they say. On that side they cried they say. | On his side they shouted they say. That tree he knocked over they say. The other one | ran slowly they say. That tree in vain he worked at they say. There sun came they say. | Turquoise standing by one put their hands on that belongs to him (?) "You won my son I have come for," | he said they say. "My opponent you become. Well, white come down I tell you," (meaningless) he said to him they say. | He felt badly they say. He went back they say. *nohwilbị* was his name they say. His wives became they say.

xanni'ago danazdidza djɩn. ts'ɩtda t'a'ani cidołɛlɛ dzɩnizɩn djɩn.
atsądɩtcijɛ xolgɛ' alillɛ bik'i naxodjidlitla djɩn. xananiltsąlɑd djɩn.
naxast'ai yiskago ɑctci djɩn. ebą naxast'aigo naxadidzigo oltc'ɩł djɩn.
acdlada yiskago dɛnɛ sɩlli djɩn. ɛsdzą ditcijɛ e laxat'ɛgi dɩnnɛ istcinla
naɣa xodo'ni djɩn. ła'ayuidɛ dɩnɛy adɛtcittɛhi cila' cigɛn dahijdɛnigo
bąnadahidji'nɩł djɩn. kodɛyɛ' dontso dacdiya djɩn. cɩ'nnallɛ xodjini
djɩn. nijɛ' xagonłni xodjini djɩn. doxołbɛxozinda xajɛ docinnɛlbɛxozinda
cinallɛ djoxona'ai njɛ' xałni djɩn. kodɛ łakgaigo ididį sili djɩn. di
bik'ijdadɛna xałni djɩn. cabił'ol ɑtt'ɛlɑd djɩn. ts'ɛt'adji xolnxildɛl.
xastįle kǫ siti djɩn. dolk'ole djɩn. wosik'idilɑd djɩn. nta' ateli dobisodo-
bɛjda. nat'o yɛniłxigo di'tcɛdɩłɩł. dɛzkwi xaina'a djɩn. bikwiy ɛ' bitc'-
ɛdadji xwołnɩxndɛl djɩn. dobisodɛ̨'ida. no'iłbį ątso noxosbą'. ebą
ntc'i' tco'isɩł'įt. doł'ijɛ nat'o nadotsɛ' yɩłndilgo djɩn. xaiyixizi djɩn.
ałtso ndjɩłt'o djɩn. yinaztsi djɩn. xanaibɛłbi djɩn. ątso nadjɩłt'o djɩn.
t'oyoxołxɑsmɑs djɩn. yinatsi djɩn. akwila djɩn. xanallɛ bikwiyɛ̨'
aza tcota djɩn. ątso nadjɩłt'o djɩn. yinaztsi djɩn. yinaiyizi djɩn.
ątson nadjɩłt'o djɩn. t'adoxollaida djɩn. t'alɑanni cigɛ' nli xałni djɩn.
wexɛ' sittsi' ni djɩn. doł'ijɛ ts'ą' bi taxodɛsgiz djɩn. yołgai ts'ą' bi
taxodisgiz djɩn. ditciłɛ ts'ą' bi taxodisgiz djɩn. bacini ts'ą' bi
taxodɛsgiz djɩn.

noxiłbįhi bitsi do'ɑnnolnɛngɛt'ɛgo xwo''dɛsk'ąz djɩn. xadisi dɩłxiłɛ
tahiką xattsi'ɛn yɩł dɛdɛsni' xatc'ojgo. yɩł ndɛni. doł'ijɛ xadat'ɛ bɛnɛinł-
banɛ doociłɛ ciɣɛ' ebą act'ɛ. lą' bidjini djɩn. yałnidji' xwołnɑtt'aj
ndixiila djɩn. yago yɛdɛyol djɩn. dįdɛ yɛdɛyol djɩn. noxoiłbįhi bik'idji
bɛ' hididałɛ da'adɛ xolonni do'. xactc'ɛoɣan bandidał. akondɛ' bɛjo'
nanɛskaldjɛ'. ciɣɛl xadadɛj'įł. ditciłɛ ciɣɛl do'. di dibɛnɩł'ɛxozon do'.
nɩłtc'ibiyajɛ nɩłxalnelɛdo. xadjat'agi daiɩszit da'adɛ bɩł'ɛdaxozinni
xolonido' ciɣɛ' xołni'nk'i nɑtt'aj tsɛsgɩt. bilatadji ni' nkinɑtt'aj.
xactc'ɛ'oɣan yinilad djɑn. daxoniɣinnigɛ' ątso xanɛnsaz'ą djɩn.

Being angry he started back they say. "Certainly it was to be mine," he thought they say. | *atsaditcije* was named magically on her he had intercourse they say. She found she was pregnant they say. | Nine days she gave birth they say. Because of that nine months will give birth they say. | Fifteen days man he became they say. "*esdaditcije* where man she gave birth | living?" they said they say. Several, "Man he is good my son," saying | they claimed him they say. There large fly came they say. "My son's son," he said | they say. "Your father wants you," he said to him they say. He didn't know his father. "You do not know him, | my grandson, the sun your father," he said to him they say. There white stripes became they say. "These | step on," he told him they say. Sunbeams they were they say. *ts'et'adji* it landed | they say. Old man there lay they say. Corrugated they say. Caterpillar was they say. "Your father is dangerous. | Tobacco killing with this use." He vomited that he gave him they say. The vomit outside the door | it landed with him they say. "It is hard. *nohwilbi* all won from us. That is why | to you I came (?). Turquoise tobacco pipe he picked out they say. He filled it they say. | All he smoked they say. He cleaned it they say. He filled it again they say. All he smoked again they say. | He became dizzy they say. He cleaned it they say. Then it was they say. His grandfather his vomit | in his mouth he put they say. All he smoked they say. He cleaned it out again they say. He filled it again they say. | All he smoked they say. It did nothing to him they say. "Truly my son you are," he said to him they say. | "Wehe my daughter," he said they say. Turquoise basket with she washed him they say. White shell basket with | she washed him they say. Abalone basket with she washed him they say. Jet basket with | she washed him they say.

*nohwilbi* his hair looking like he stretched it they say. Medicine black | he put in water. His hair with it he stroked. His lower leg muscle with it he stroked. "Turquoise the last you win | will be mine my son because of that I am." "All right," he said to him they say. Center of sky they two went. | He made a smoke they say. Down he blew they say. Four times he blew they say. *nohwilbi* on him | with you bet over there you will have. *hactc'eogan* you go to. There brush | he circled around. Pay (my pay?) he looked for. Abalone pay will be. This with this you will know. | Small wind will keep you informed. On his ear he placed it. From here (now) he will inform | he has (?). "My son," he called him. On the ground they two came down. High point on its top they landed. | *hactc'eogan* he found he knew. They say. All the spirit people all he took a message to they say. |

niɬtc'ibiyajɛ e xannɛ'nziz'a djin. xoɣą xodizsǫs xolgegɛ' 'ała'dzisli djin. daka'ts'osts'iddɛ ɑlya djin. ładɛ' daldjigo ładɛ łakgaigo ɑlya djin. djabɑnnɛ ayaj iłtsoi bakagi xaiiłtsoz djin. di niɣɛldo xodon'nit'. xont'ąa dinał xodon'nit'. daka' xont'a dinał xadjinni djin. dɛgodikał djabɑnnɛ dabɛbiyadikat xodjinɛ bidinadɛ' daxidjihɛ bidadiłkał. adodzi' kodo bidakaa adahitdjido dego anadiłkał biya nadikał. noxiłbi bidaka bida-adiłkał bɛ ba'iidobinł. najoncɛ bąs ł'istso' ni' bidinał xadjini djin. tcɛłtci'i niɣɛl do'. ntsitagɛ' dadotał. tsinłkałɛ bɛ'ɛsni' bidinał xodjini djin. yołgai xaiɣɛl ɑlya djin. djołɛnnɛ nat'ɛni' bidinał xodjinni djin. ditciłɛ xaiɣɛl ɑlya djin. ts'inbɛk'ai wonaltc'illɛ bidinał xodjinni djin. nł'ijbize' xaiɣɛl ɑlya djin. ts'inbɛdził niłtc'i nł'ij xaiɣɛl ɑlya djin. bɛtc'idji i'axa' xoyago adigis xodon'nit' djin. kodji bits'adji yoyago itsiyɛ' tsinnaya'i bacinɛ xaiɣɛl ɑlya djin. tsinbɛł'ol hidigac xodon'ni djin.


xadinnɛ djin. nadɛk'at xaiłkago xaxodilnɛ' djinnɛ. dadildɛ djin. nacdjadini djin. kodji' at'ɛgo docinołni'da ni djinni. nacdja niɣɛl xodollɛl citcai xodjini djin. dodago xadati sitsokɛ t'aanaǫdalkał ɑlni djin. ba xadadɛs'į łą ni djin. xaicbɛ bɛni' dolgic ni djin. xaz'it djin. 'ałni'ago djoxona'ai xaiɣɛl ɑlya djin. bɛjo' annɑskaldji' ditcił ts'ą' nł'ij bɛnika djin. xiłidjį djin. ado sin' didɛsta djin. bɛxodɛnonɛli nadɛ' xaiyiłka djin. xaicbɛ binni' dolgic xaicbɛ binni' naki dolɛl nlą k'at xodon'ni' djin. badillɛ' nla' bɛsdza to djitdɛya adjilgo djin xodɛ' dadiya djin. ba'at to yila djin. ła' canka bidjini djin. to yaiika haiyika ai doda inlai djodlą djinnɛ. bɛ'ǫ xadjodlą bitsitagɛ yadzizit djin. bidji' dasdiya djin. nijinłk'o djin. zizkɛ djin. ndjilgo djin. badilla' ni djin. k'atla' ɛsdzɑnnɛ nɑtdza djin. xat'ila xaxɛ nainlgot xaxaxaxa ni djin. xat'ila cɛlt'e ci cadinlago adinnɛ ni djin. yadila' olye ciką' xazlįc djinnɛ tonigit'ɛli nlai djoɣał eba adicni. axaxa didji, cidot'ɛl ni ¡ djin.

Small wind that took the message they say. Hogan yellow shining where it is called they gathered they say. | Stick dice they made they say. One side black, one side white they made they say. | Bat small yellow skin gave him they say. This will be your pay they told him. "In the roof | you go," they told him. They told him, they say. They throw up bat | with down throw? another in its place one he had he throw down. He throws so his card | he throws up. Up he threw, down he threw again. *nohwilbį* his dice down he threw | with he will beat him. "Pole hoop large snake you go in," he told him they say. | Red shell your pay will be. On your firehead put it. "Woodpecker mud balls, you go in," he told him | they say. White shell his pay he made they say. "That ball rat go in," he told him they say. | Abalone his pay me made they say. "Bent stick measuring worm go in," he told they say. | Hard jewels his pay he made they say. Trees set in whirlwind screw down hard his pay was made they say. | "On his side deep down screw it in," they told him they say. Here the other side deep | it is set wood worm jet his pay he made they say. "True roots you gnaw off," he told him they say.

They are ready they say. Now morning they dress him they say. They start off they say. | They started (?) they say. "Here being didn't you tell me," he said they say. "All your pay | will be, my mother's father," he said to him they say. "No, not go today, my grandchildren, just another day," he said | they say. "For him those watchers are many," he said they say. "What with his mind you make forked," he said they say. It was morning they say. | Middle sun his pay he made they say. Brush circling around abalone basket | hard material he put in they say. It got dark they say. Then songs they started they say. With those they will beat him. | Early it is dawn they say. "That with his mind forked, that with his mind two will be there now," | he said to him they say. "Play with her over there." His wife water she went for, there he came| they say. His wife water was getting they say. "Some give me," he said to her they say. Water she took up, she gave him | which she made him drink they say. What was left after drinking on his head he put they say. To her | he stepped they say. He played with her they say. He finished playing they say. He came back they say. "I played with his woman," he said they say. | Soon woman returned they say. "What so soon you come back xaxaxaxa," he said they say. | "Someone looked like me you played with you say," he said they say. "I was false to him called my husband | I became looked like you over there walked because I say it." "Axaxa, today I will know," he said they say. It was light. |

xos'int doł'ijε. yołgai ditciłε bacinε nł'ijbizai ałai acdlago hai'inil. niłtc'i
łεj bε tcadołxił. hai daidεs'į ałtso bink'ε dadoyoł. t'ado danhidołtsεłε
yaxadika. nlo actε'. k'at ntc'į nihiniya. eya'i bida'ildε'. yahadjogai
xadjilla adahisnεzlidε. xadjat'adε niłtc'ibiyajεyε' eγa' cadoilala no'ni'
xotcinni djin. asdzannε yεni nladi kasidą'. yidlǫi. kodji kodza eγa'.
ciką' silila nǫ'nį' xodjinni djin. xa sik'is xastaniya bidjinni djin. ciilε
nlį ni djin. daka' naidikąni' yiłmazilli ciilε' nlį. xago bagai ninika
niłdicni ya'ai ni djin. wexε' xεεsdzą axi'’nił ahwinni'εsjigε' nεsdzado'
kodjido' akojnelt'εgo sests'ądo' ała dεidobinł xałni djin. lą'' t'ado dego
dinnii nlį. sadi bεsdasgo akodε ca'idobinł bidjinni djin. dεgo inaγalgo
e doda bidjini djin. nla azka djinnε. kwiłi djin. bakgai bakgai
bakgai bakgai ni djinni, ni' naintą tsą'a nla djabannε dasitda xa xat'a
bε biyadjika djin. bεdinnadεdał at'ε bitda adjiłka djin. tsa bigidji yitc'į
dilgo djin. adzi ci'ilε doda ci'ilε' atdzi cikat adjickat. bizaxotcį djin.
badolya aditdi sikεs xodjinni djin. akǫ ci'ilε doxodjoba adjinnida
bidjika djin.


djabannεyε' xatt'a bε biya nadjika djin. noxiłbįε bidaka adjiłka
djin. naisiłbaci ci'ilε daka' yitc'i' dadilgot biya xatsilγaj djin. ndilgo
djin. naxwonaγa. bizaxotci'. wela' ł'odji aidi dinnε nannε'ecigi na'ado'
'ała cido' axonnelt'ego ci'ado' ała nadεni djin. ałk'idji. ł'ogi tcicna'aj.
nbąsε ciadεsbąs ni djin. doda djini djin. cibąc ict'i bidjinni djin. ciisełba.
babąsε naγoi'iłxa djin. ł'istso bąs axoditya' adjinni djin. dįnledε
axεdiłxał najǫnc ado bεt'adε bεt'adεdinił cił'inεlgo ado bεłndεdεcna
bεt'adnnigo nnajoncε bεkoninεctεl. ako ciłnajdilgo nixi sidadolsk'is
sitc'a doldo ako ciłnaj dilgo. diłł'oi olge yidiccǫnclad djin. xadja'inad
djin. adεcǫncgo yiłinil djin. ł'adε yεkinnazł'ogo nledi adjiiłka djin.
asat'i bεta sabąs ko'odo najdinabąssi bik'iznεestį. yitc'itdilgo djin.

Turquoise, white shell, abalone, jet, hard jewels together five he
gave him. Whirlwind | dust with will make it dark. Those watch-
ing all their eyes will blow. Not they will see us | we go in-
side. Over there I am. Now to you he is walking. I am (?) (No
meaning.) They came by the door. They came inside | where they were
watching. On his ear that small wind that one, "He went with my wife
let him think about," | he told him they say. That woman her face
other way nearly she sat. She laughed. This way she turned. | "That
one my husband he became she thought," it told him they say. "Well,
my friend, I came for something," he said they say. "My opponent |
you become," he said they say. Dice which he took up he swung back
and forth. My opponent you become. "Well, white come down | I
tell you he said they say. "Wexe, our wives we bet ? your wife too |
this side just as many my wives too one time we will win," he said to him
they say. "All right, not up | you look you are. House timbers you
throw against then you will win from me," he said to him they say.
"Up if you look that not," | he said to him they say. There ? they say.
He made motions they say. "White, white, | white, white," he said
they say. Ground he put down again basket. There bat sat on it his
feathers | with he took up they say. In the place of them all down he
threw they say. Basket to it | he jumped they say. His missed.
"You my opponent. No. My opponent you missed. On me I play."
He swore they say. | "Some one was with his wife he thinks about," he
said to him they say. There my opponent I am going to skin you | he
played they say.

That bat his feathers with up he took again they say. *nohwilbi*
his cards he threw down | they say. "I win from you, my opponent."
Dice toward he jumped he threw them one side they say. He jumped up |
they say. | He ran around. He swore. "Well, outside these people
you won from me your wife too | I too as many my wife too once ? I
bet." Outside they two went. | "Hoop I roll," he said they say. "No,"
he said they say. "My hoop I have," he said to him they say. "I won." |
His hoop he rolled they say. Large snake hoop I made myself," he said
they say. "Over there | you throw pole then near it it falls throwing
on it then I will get up. | Close you go your pole I will lie down on it.
Then when I lie down hard he will slam down, my belly will burst. |
Then when I lie down." *dił'oi* called he finds it wiggles they say. He went
in front of him | they say. Running with the pole he put it down they say.
Under it it being tied on over there he threw it they say. | ? close to it
it rolled so far it rolled along on it it lay. He jumped toward it they say. |

zizsił djɩn. xalanlɛ sabas ci'ilɛ dodjobadjɩnadjɩnnida na'isɛłbala ni djɩn.
ti' wannɛdji wannatcillɛ k'at dɛsazniłbanigɛ' at'ɛ nałk'idji aładɛ naidobinł
nadini djɩn. e ts'ɩn daicdlojige nakɛzgo nidjidaihildlojgo caxodinniłnɛł
cidjɛ naikɛsgo lą djɩnni djɩn. haiitą djɩn. e doda. ciłdoxolǫ. xadjitą djɩn.


    la' ni djɩn. ako ciilɛ doxwodjobaadjɩnnida. ciilɛ' wǫtca' yadjiłdɛł
djɩn. njonigo dalildloj djɩn. wannɛtciliyɛ. xatcidilwot' djɩn. xalannɛ'?
nasiłbacɛ ciilɛ. lą' ni djɩn. di ca'isɩnłbangɛ cido' at'ɛ nałk'idji'. lą
djɩnni djɩn. ti'' ł'ogi ni djɩn. ado idɛze djɩn. banaltsiddjɛ e ci nadɛcbɩnł
bittis ɛltsɩdjɛ e ni' caiidiłbinł. lą' djɩnni djɩn. idɛz'ez djɩn. kodo annaz-
diltałgo sinłkaliyɛnɛ dandji'a' hwilγa hilgo djɩn. bittis ɛltsɩd djɩn.
na'isiłbą ciilɛ bidjɩnni djɩn. lą'a ni djɩn. e k'at sididat'ɛdinɛgɛ dabin-
nɛltɛgo aładɛ naidobinł ni djɩn. xakoci xonɛdjɩn ni djɩn. tcoidiłił
xodininnɛ djɩn. ñɩłtc'ibiyaj sɛsdali djɩn editila djɩn. wonɛ kwi tosa dasa'-
ala djɩn. nli' xat'it'ɛ xałni? djɩn. nli tosa at'ɛ k'osdɩłxɩł bixolǫ djini djɩn.
naγai łakgai dasa'angi xat'it'ɛ tosaat'ɛ. nłtsaba'at bixolǫ nli'. xaditɛ?
xałni djɩn. nli' acki tc'ilidɛlan djɩn. naγai dasizingɛ xadit'ɛ ni djɩn.
at'ɛd tcilidɛ naγailą sitdiłdǫɛ najdonigo xadjiya djɩn. nt'ɛxadjigi djɩn.
k'acbɛnt'ina djɩn. anłaciγɛ' docetdidotinłda djɩnnigo na'issɛłbaci ciuli.
lą ni djɩn. ai k'at saisinłbanigɛ at'ɛ nɛdo' nanɛcigɛ' t'atɛ na'ado' altągo
daładɛ na'idobinł. lą djɩnni djɩn. ł'ogi ni djɩn. djoład djɩn. nanokɩn
nasitąlad djɩn. baγa' xotsąlad djɩn. dɩdi yidokał hits'isgo baγaxotsą
itsigo cidɛcbinł. baγakatgo ca'idobinł. djoł bigidji yixadaka nacidołxał
djɩnni djɩn. nledi edjɩnłxał djɩn. adɛ xadjołgo djɩn. xasts'oxa'agɛ.
ndjill'ą djɩn. xanedjɩłła djɩn. adjɛdjolgoła baγadjilgo djɩn. na'isɛłbą
ci'ilɛ djɩnni djɩn. agotsa ni djɩn. aidi at'ɛ niłtsą biką niłtsą ba'adɛ
kinnɛ' da'at'ɛ keyaxan xadat'ɛxɛ nixido' anilk'idji saisinłbago
ciłnazdinłnił.

He pulled it aside they say. "What you do? My hoop my oppo-
nent I win," he said to him | "I win from you," he said they say.
"Come, inside measuring worm. Now you won from me all I bet on one
another at one time we will bet," | he said to him they say. That stick
arched where it falls off (?) curved    ?        ?    | "All right," he said they
say. He took it up they say. "That not I have one." He took it out
they say.

"All right," he said they say. "Now my opponent. He didn't
say let him win." "My opponent," you cry. He threw it up | they say.
Well it curled up they say. Measuring worm it was. He tried to throw
it down they say. "What you do? | I won from you, my opponent."
"All right," he said they say. "These you won from me I myself too all I
bet." "All right," | he said they say. "Come outside," he said they say.
"Now football they say. "If it drops these I win from you. | Over if it
falls these you win from me." "All right," he said they say. They
began to kick they say. So far (two feet) when he kicked | that wood-
pecker flew (?) beside it he went they say. Over it he threw it they say. |
"I win from you, opponent," he said they say. "Yes," he said they say.
These now    ?    even | one time we bet again," he said they say. "All
right," he said they say. "Substitute," | he said they say, Small Wind.
What they will use they guess | they say. Inside this water basket what
it stands on | they say. "That one what is it?" he asked they say.
"That one water basket it is black cloud is inside," he said they say. |
"Beside white the one that stands what?" "Water basket it is. Female
rain is in it." "That one what?" | he asked they say. "That boy
image," they say. "Beside it stands it is," he said they say. | "Girl
image." Beside bird singing (?) came up they say. He had poison
they say. | He is poisoning people they say. He watches me. You will
catch me saying I win from you |    ?    "All right," he said they say.
"That now those you won from me all you too yourself your wife too
besides | one time let us bet." "All right," he said they say. "Outside,"
he said they say. Ball they say. House stood | long way they say.
Through it a hole was they say. Four times he kicks, missing it | hole
through if he misses I win. If it goes through you win from me." "Ball
one inside    ?    he will hit me," | he said they say. That he pretended
to hit it they say. Then it ran they say, mink. | He arrived running they
say. He ran to the line they say. He ran after him. It went through
they say. "I won from you, | my opponent," he said they say.    ?    he
said they say. "These all rain male rain female | houses all farms all
we too I bet you win from me | you kill me."

nɛdo' naisɛɬbago niɬnɛzdezniɬ xaɬni djin. ti·' bidjini djin. aɬɣa
didit'ac di bina aɬɣadiditac xaɬni djin. dinnɛ daixiddiniltcą' nlc binnadɛ
hwilɣa dadelgo djin. ndidilgoɬni' ci'ilɛ. bittc'in najdilgo ndidilgoɬnɛ'
noxoɬbixi ci'ilɛ. k'at nsanxinswat xatc'i'. nadilgo djin. doxodjobadjin-
nida? k'at nts'ą nxinsɣat ciilɛ. bitc'in' najdilgot. noxiɬbixɛ k'at nts'a
nxinswat. bitsin ndjilɣot. ako' k'at ntcojgonɛ' isi yudago xadjinni
djin. yudago yadjiltalgo bɛdaɣącɛ. yudago siznsi biɬnajdilgo djin. ako
nak'aigonɛ' isi. nadilgɛs xadjinnɛ djin. nanigo adɛ' idjolɣal djolɣaɬego.
siznsi biɬnajdilɣoɬ. ako nzitta isi nixiɬdja ade djolɣal xaka adzissi'
biɬnadilɣoɬ. ako nitsi'yagonɛ' isi nixiɬdja. adɛ djolɣal. xaka adzissi'
biɬnajdilɣoɬ. xoxaɬkanizi' hwilɣadadilɣot. doxodjobaatc'innida ciilɛ
ntsąn nixinsɣot naxadjobai. dɛjogo njoɬɬ'ɛllɛ. xatsin nilɣot. bitcocgonɛ'
bik'a bɛ indjinɣac. bɛk'aigonɛ' bɛ nadjicɣac. basita'gonɛ bɛ nadjicɣaj.
bitsi'yagonɛ bɛ nadjicɣaj. k'at biɣa dadilgɛt t'andzadɛ ntc'i' dɛdolɣoɬ
xodjinni djin. niɬtc'ibiyaj xadjataɣɛ dasidayɛnnɛ' aixoɬxolni djin.
t'andza dacdilgo djin. xatc'i' dadilgo djin. oxanaɣacn k'at ntsą'
nxansɣot. noxiɬbihi nadjobai xajogo njodaɬ'ɛle noxiɬbixi. xabitinɛdji
xadzisgo djin. xadjoni· djinin'a djin. bidjoni· dawocxaya djin. xajonɛ-
xedji tca·xaiya djin. xa'andjolɣot xajonɛxɛdji' diwocxaya djin. dlǫda-
hisdɛ djin. bidjonɛxɛdji' tcaxaya djin. naildlǫɛ xolge djin. tsini'a
biɬgitdiswot djin. tsįbɛdjiɬ xolge djin. kodɛ ilɬ'ɛ djin. nadida djin
tsinɛnnɛ yaiilɬ'a djin. xayiɬxan idjin. tc'ɛ 'iɬ'i djin. yiɬiɬiɣą. ɬɛj nibɛjgo
xa· ciilɛ baɬkitla nijdɛlti bidjinni ni. nadji xadzidzį djin. xagoci
adoxasoɬ'ą. di bɛ siɬniɬnɛ nigo sɛniɬ dizɛhi kodji, nina'a djin. xadjatadɛ
aidɛ dinnɛ yɛ diɬndadzilnɛ xajinni djin. doda· niltcilinnɛ bidjini djin.
bitsɛniɬɛ kanadji' kodjila. daxwoxattsɛnnɛɬ k'at bɛ biɬnidjiɬnɛ kodɛ·
djuxona'ai dasdiya djin. t'a cigɛ' adicdo't'a bɛxolni'. adicdo't'adadjolɛɬ
ciɣɛ'.

"You too I win I kill you," he said to him they say. "Go ahead," he said they say. | "We will foot race, this around we will race," he said to him they say. He started around. That around | beside him he ran they say. "You run my opponent." After him he ran ? | "*noh-wilbihi* my opponent. Now I leave you." After him he ran they say. | "I will skin you." "Now from you I run, my opponent." After him he ran. *nohwilbihi*, now from you | I run. "Ahead he ran. Then now in your leg muscle he shoots up," he told him | they say. Up when he jumped he witched him. Up that he shot he ran with it they say. "Now | in your hip he shoots. Jump sidewise he told him they say. Across he threw himself when he ran. That he shot with it | he ran. "Now between your shoulders he shoots." He threw himself when he shot him. "Throw yourself down." He ran with it. "Now base of your head | he shoots." "Throw yourself down. He threw himself down. That he nearly | shot him with he ran with it. Along side him he ran. "I will skin you, my opponent. | From you I run. You poor fellow. Easy you run." Ahead of him he ran. In his leg muscle | in his thigh with he witched him. In his back with he witched him. In the base of his head with he witched him. | Now beside him he ran. "Far away after you he will run," | he told him they say, Small Wind, on his ear that sat told him that they say. | Far away he ran they say. After him he ran they say. He nearly caught him. "Now from you | I ran *nohwilbihi* poor easy you run, *nohwilbihi*." On his side of the trail | he ran they say. His partisans were deceived they say. His partisans shouting went up they say. From the partisans | of the other crying went up they say. He came up over the hill from his side shouting went up they say. They were laughing they say. From his side | crying went up they say. Laugh now and then it is named they say. Tree standing | with it he ran they say. *tsibedjil* is called they say. Here he ran they say. He walked they say. | That tree he ran to they say. He tried to pull it out they say. In vain he did it they say. He fought with it. Earth he trod down | "Well, my opponent, why too long you stay," he said to him. (?) he pulled it out they say. "Come, | I am out of wind. This with kill me" saying ax his name there he put they say. His ear, "That person with they kill themselves," he said they say. "No shut your eyes," he told him they say. | His ax he put. His own ax now with he was going to kill him here | sun came they say. "Wait, my son, he is not boss of anything," he told him. "He will be boss of something | my son.

nnai it'ε dεgo ałtį diłxił biłdildǫ xodjinni djin kǫ nijnt'a djin.
di bik'i. daxizinε tcinnai bidjinni djin. yik'i dadahizį' djin. dεgo bił
tsiddεst'ǫ djin. dała daihijł'ijdan ałkidą ni'bidjegε' sizzε xazlinε nt'ε
dananajł'ijdan yołkałgo niłnidjε t'asinsikεs andot'i ni djin. tadi
daxazłij niłni'dji' sensikεz annat'igo yat'ε dasiłłε dodatsiyacǫdallε dεgo
dįdε daxijłij alyos ni djin. xotdza djin. bitdjonεhεn xagoci tca'xa'a
djin. tcaxaįła djin. xadic badatcadi' noxiłbihi binanilnałinnε ci doda kat
akonhisłada djinni djin. nihila' tąnixįdannosįgo. xawicci kinnałdą
tanhidanosigo niγanεnnε' nikεyaxa t'ałtsǫ nixi akola xodjinniłε. εxε
tsildixwannεlandi ąłtso naztci djin. akola xwodjinniłε, danniłtagε
xagoci dinnε dita djin. ta'oci dicnini' ciγε' djinni djin. djoxona'ai.
xadat'ε akonε' xodjinni djin. εxε ciγε'. dįdi biji djijic djinnε. ajanεła'
bigidji' dadiyadi. tsidcidolεł nzį djini djin.


kadzozdεl djin. kintεl xolge adji dadidεl. t'akwε kintεl adjin nijnna
djin. ado' yogodji ma'idεsgijdjε' bananεstą. kεya'iyo xotεlla. ąkǫlε
xwondonnit'. tinε daxicdonnit di' nixε. disεtdaγε t'ą'xai'ina. dεtcindi'
ądji tsεdεs'adji adε nadiną'. di yuiyεdji tawokoxwogε ninna djin. dakwi
xwinnaxacacçį' ado nadina'. tsεdεgonεnεgε' nainą''. acdlą xonaxai djin.
dziłnaodiłε bilatado' atsεxastin atsεεsdzą dinnε xodollεłegi' yaxadziεn
xatdji naibitdεγi łaxaban sinnanεskεs nεxεnε, eyanditsala djin. ni'
bidje disdjolgε' dinnε xwodolεł nizįlad djin. tc'ol'į biyagi yiłxazlε'εnnε
yołgai nadą ditdjol doxonot'innε dinnεyistcįn alya. atsεεsdzą yiłxazlε
ditcił nadanłtsoi doxonot'innε εsdzą yεstcįn alya. kodε' djuxona'ai
dasdiya djin. doł'ijε icki tciliñgo di' bik'idji' atiddati eba' dinnε biyo'
yε xadaditt'ε elya. bik'ilkat sisnadjinnε bεgistįn alyan' yitis dεya.
tsodził bigistin alyanε bik'idji' nniya. yitis dεya. doγosłid bεgistin
alyanyε bik'idji nniya. bitis dεya. dεbεntsa' bigistin alyanε' bik'idji
nniya. bitis dεya ado' adε dεst'ą xaiiłką dadεzną'. ndεsditdzi' xazlį'.
dondit'acda daxodiyinγi tc'ε xannε'nast'ą. ya'acgo xannε'nast'ą. γεl
xazlį' nł'iz xadągigonε' niłtc'ibiyajε ałna xa'aj xat'acł'o alya. xaγa alya.
xadaztci'go alya. εsdza xastą dinnε xastą nakidzatago nadildε'. kodo
dinnε' xododεslin.

Your elder brother up bow black you shoot him," he told him they say. Here they two went they say. | This on it you step my brother he said to him they say. On it he stood they say. Up with him | he shot they say. Half way where he landed long time at the earth's heart standing (?) became | where he stopped again always center of earth my thoughts you will come back," he said they say. Third time | he landed center of the earth "My thought will come back it may be good it may be bad." | Up fourth time he went "Adios," he said they say. That happened they say. His friends they cried | they say. They hollered they say. "Why do you cry. *nohwɪlbihi* his slaves. I not I do that,"|he said they say. "Go ahead wherever you please. ? ? your houses | your lands all you that way tell them." "Thanks,"| they all said all they embraced they say. That way they tell it. | Every way people went they say. "Will be always I say, my son," he said they say, Sun. | "All all right," they said they say. "Thanks, my son." Four times his breath he breathed they say. One that stays | inside I went in. "It will be mine you think," he said they say.

They all scattered out they say. Pueblo Bonito called there they went. | Right there Pueblo Bonito there they moved they say. Then this way, Jemez they investigated. Farms were wide they found. "There it will be," | they said. "All right this ours," they told each other. Back they moved. | Foot of red hill *tsedes'adji* there they moved. This way where salt cañon flows they moved they say. How many | years I do not know then they moved. *tsedegonenege'* they moved. Five years they say. | *dzɪlnaodɪle* its top First Man, First Woman people going to be they came up. | First time they came up they study about it he said (?). They found he had started to make they say. Earth | its heart where it is round Navajo will be he had thought they say. *tc'olɪ* under with it he became | white shell corn round can not be seen person's image he made. First Woman with it she became | abalone yellow corn can't be seen woman image she made. Here sun | came they say. Turquoise boy he was this on it make more because of that people their beads | with they will have he made. They covered them. Pelado Peak who lives in was made | over them he stepped. Mt. Taylor who lives in was made on it arrived. Over it he stepped. San Francisco in it | was made. On it he arrived. Over it he stepped. La Plata Mt. in it he was made on it|arrived. Over it he stepped. Then there he began to sing. In the morning they began to move. They began to breathe it happened. | They two can't get up. The holy ones in vain they invited. To the sky they sent messengers. Pay | became. Hard jewels in his mouth Small Wind passing each other they two came out. Body hairs were made. | Their hair became. Air comes out was made. Woman six, men six twelve got up. So | Navajo came to be.

## ORIGIN OF SOME NAVAJO CUSTOMS

dobisoxodɛbɛjda.   dɛnɛde·ldɛli t'anitɛ.   tc'ol'į· bilatagi k'osdɨłxɨł
dasa'ɑn silį djɨn.   nakiskago ɑłni dabitc'igo dahiltǫnł.   tayiskago ɑłni
bilago k'osdɨłxɨł yįnol'ą·.   dį yiskągo k'osdɨłxɨł nats'idask'igo nixinigi
silį djɨn.   k'ɑt dzɨłna'odɨłi bilatado djiltɛ djɨn.   dalit'ɛgo att'ela ɛsdzą·?
tc'olį bilatagi dį yiskɑnda bilatagi k'os dɨłxɨł dasa'ɑnni· k'ɑt t'at'ɛ
nixiniɣi didɛcįnł xat'ila?   akǫyɛ' yadɛda dɛldɛli t'ohayo.   yadica xadina?
djinnɛ djɨn.   atsɛɛsdzą dosdo'xonsadɑlla djinni djɨn.   atsɛxastin ado
nixidjilɣo djin.   kodo· djolɣołgo di· xajdį'a djɨn.

baniya baniyoowiyɛ.
bɨł yaixołkal cinnicłįgo atsɛxastin cinniclį.
k'ɑt dzɨł tc'ol'i baniyau wiyɛ.
k'osdɨłxɨł bɛ atsadasxɛldji' baniyauwiyɛ.
atsɑnnɨɬ'ic adaxazladji baniyauwiyɛ.
nadzillit adaxasladji' baniyayuwiyɛ·
to bijol nɛst'įdji' baniyauwiyɛ.
tsa'anaɣai bikɛxojon nicłigo baniyaowiyɛ.
sɛtsiddji' xojogo
cikɛ'dɛ xojogo
ciyagɛ xojogo baniya.
cik'ɛ'gɛ xojogo baniya.
cina t'aąłtso xojogo baniya.
sizatxa xojǫgo baniya.

2nd
xasiya | in place of baniya.
3d
nadɛsdza.
4th
naicdał.
5th
nɑnicdza.
6th
nɑnisda.

kodji bilatadji xadjiyadɛ kodji awɛ yitcatsa djɨn.   ats'innɨɬ'ic
atsąxot'i djɨn.   t'ado'ɛxozinnɛ to jolɛ nɛsti djɨn.   bɛ dobiyɛt'ida.   kodjigo
sɛtįlad djɨn.   'ɛ'adjigo bitsi'lɑd djɨn.   xa'ądji dɛsɛ·zlɑd djɨn.   nadzilit
agodɛ biya sɑllalɑd djɨn.   cabɨɬ'adjɨłtci bidjɛ nana'alɑd djɨn.   ła' bikɛɬ'a
dasɑlalɑd djɨn.   binik'idį· nadzillit at'ɛla djɨn.   k'osdɨłxɨł k'osdoɬ'ij

## ORIGIN OF SOME NAVAJO CUSTOMS

Times were not good. Those which ate people were everywhere. *tc'oli* on its top cloud dark | resting became they say. The next day middle toward it there was rain. The third day middle | beyond cloud dark it reached. Four days cloud dark base of mountain water | standing became they say. Now *dzulno'odili* from its top he ran they say. "What has happened, old woman | *tc'oli* on its top four days since on its top cloud dark rested. Now all | is cloud-covered. I will look what it is." "There is danger. Devouring ones there are many. What you go for?" | she said they say, First Woman. "Nothing will go wrong," he said they say, First Man then | he started running they say. So far when he had run this (?) he began to sing they say:— |

I come to it, I come close to it,
With him dawn I being, First Man I am
Now Mountain *tc'oli* I am approaching.
Cloud dark with where it is black I come close.
Lightning where it lies I come close,
Rainbow where it lies I come close,
Water its rebounding where it is I come close
Old age good fortune I being I come close to it,
Before me with good fortune,
Behind me with good fortune,
Under me with good fortune, I come to it
Above me with good fortune I come to it
All around me with good fortune I come to it,
My speech with good fortune I come to it.

Repetition of above song but instead of "I come to it, I come close" substitute the following:—

2nd: I start up
3d:  I start back
4th: I go along back
5th: I arrive back
6th: I sit down again

Here on top when he came up here baby he heard cry they say. Lightning | was striking everywhere they say. He did not know. Water its rebounding lay they say with one could not see. There | he found it lying they say. Toward the west its head he found they say. Toward the east its feet he found they say. Rainbow's | short under it he found two lay they say. Rays of the rising sun its chest he found lay across they say. Another the soles of its feet | he found they say. Above its face rainbow he found it was they say. Dark cloud, blue cloud, |

k'osłittso k'osłigai bε łitcį'te la bεkaγε ats'innił'ic ałts'adji nitila djɪn.
cabił'ol bε iłtc'i dasdlǫla djɪn. dobεxozinda djinnε. azdolíłegε t'o
nixɪj niłti dεya djɪn. nazniłtį djɪn. awelε ndiłtį εsdzą disitįgε' k'os bε
tcaxałγełla djina djɪn. idjɪnni djɪn. atsεεsdza adjɪnni djɪn. kodεyε
xawu· xawu· xawu· xawu· ists'ą djɪn. bikεdε xuuuxu xuuuxu wuwuoo
nixanigε' xactc'εoγanla djɪn. nixanigε' xactc'εłti'la djɪn. dadi'aj djɪn.
bizε dadεlni'la djɪn. axεzkat xindjika djɪn. yayaγe axadzala sɪttsokε
djɪnnε djɪn. xactc'εłti nixε bayεłti'at'ε yołkałgo binni' bik'εgo axotεłεgo
bini'gε' bayεłti'. ako nilti djɪnni yonigε isǫsgo bεsł'ǫgo at'εla djɪn. ado·
naiyoz'ago 'ałtsą naiyǫz'a djɪn. nixaniγε xactc'εłti adjit'i djɪn.
axot'εgo adołεł.

tsɪn 'alt'ąigo biya donnił. ł'oł do' bockijnt'i ako xolǫn. awεtsal
xolgε aidi didosǫzgo dεnoxxicci biya ndołdja. at'εd la. atsεεsdza
i· djɪnni djɪn. citc'ε dolεł. atsεxastin sitsi'. dolεł djɪnni djɪn. dałai
yiska djɪn. naxai dolεł djɪnnε. akogo nεzda djɪn. nanεska djɪn
ndiltido naki yɪska djɪn. naγal sallį djɪn. katka k'atca yołgai εsdzą'
dεcgεj yołgai bikεgo dεcgεj. yołgai bikεbą nasdjin dεcgεj yołgai
bεkεł'ol dεcgεj yołgai bisł'ε dεcgεj yołgai bitsisγą' didjic yołgai
biłakałgo dεcgεj yołgai bitsisła·t dεcgεj yołgai bi'ε dεcgεj yołgai bini'
dεcgεj yołgai binε decgεj yołgai bits'os dεcgεj bilatagε iyacdoł'ij biza
naxodlεc binε' nijǫ tsa'anaγai bikεxojo nligo dεcgεc bitsi xojo bikε'
xojogo dεcgεc biyage' xojogo dεcgεc bik'igε' xojoge dεcgεc bina ąłtso
xojogo dεcgεc bizat xa xojogo dεcgεc ako nakiskago anaγa djɪn. kwε
nanaiska djɪn.

kogo akwidi yiyiccic djɪn. ndiltido dį yɪskago daγandilgo' djɪnnε.
asdlą yɪskago xast'ą yɪskago bił tajda'ac djɪn. citc'ε bidjinigo. sastc'it
yiska djɪn. tsεbi yiska djɪn. nast'ai yiska djɪn. nεsna yiska djɪn.
nεsna biskago yołkai εsdza yε daxokałgo olji djɪn. ładzada' naneska djɪn.

yellow cloud, white cloud with it was wrapped. Its loops lightning on both outer edges he found were they say. | Sunbeams with toward each other he found it was laced they say. He didn't understand it they say. ? altogether | he took he started they say. He arrived home with it they say. "Baby it is I found ( I picked it up), old woman, where it lay cloud with it | was dark he said they say. "Ee!" she said they say, First Woman said it they say. Then | "*xawu' xawu' xawu' xawu'*" was heard they say. After him *xuuuxu xuuuuxu wuwuoo* | Mirage *xactc'ɛoɣan* it was they say. Mirage *xactc'ɛlti'* it was they say. They two came in they say. | His mouth he put his hand over they say. Against each other he struck them they say. "Something great has happened it seems, my daughter's children," | he said they say. *xactc'ɛlti* "We talked about it. In the future her mind ruling | will be her mind we talked about. Here he put it down they say. Behind the fire string it was tied with he found it was they say. Then | when he pulled it both ways it came open they say. Mirage *xactc'ɛlti'* did it they say. | This way it will be.

Wood thin under it will be put. String too a line on both sides here will be many. Cliff rose | called that when it has been shredded the rubbed fine under it will be placed. Girl it was. First Woman | "Ee!" said they say. "My daughter she will be." First Man, "My daughter she will be," he said they say. One | day was they say. A year it will be they say then it sat up they say. Second day was they say | since she was taken up two days were they say. She looked around it happened they say. Surprise White Shell Woman | gazed white shell her moccasins she gazed. White shell border of her moccasins embroidered black she gazed. White shell | her moccasin lace she gazed. White shell her legging she gazed. White shell her legging decoration she gazed. White shell | her skirt she gazed. White shell her belt she gazed. White shell her shirt she gazed. White shell her face | she gazed. White shell her mind she gazed. White shell her soft feather she gazed. On the crown of her head bird blue its mouth | white across it whistles nice. Old age, good fortune being she gazed. Ahead of her good. Her feet | good she gazed. Below her good she gazed. Above her good she gazed. Around her all | good she gazed. Her speech good she gazed. Then when two days passed she walked they say. Then | another day passed they say. So there | she danced they say.

After she was found four when days were she ran a little way they say. | Five when days passed. Six when days passed with her they two walked they say. "My daughter," saying to her. Seven | days passed they say. Eight days passed they say. Nine days passed they say. Ten days passed they say. | Tenth when day was White Shell Woman with when it dawned she was named they say. Eleven days were they say. |

tadai yiska djɪn. kwɛ ɛs'ago at'ɛago najdiłti ts'idi ąkwɛ nɑnna'ago tcoɣin sillila djɪn. xat'ici ciɣangola cima' ni djɪn. ailą tsidɛsdlą xolgɛ' citc'ɛ ni djɪn.

atsɛɛsdza aidi at'ɛkɛ tadzadą bɛnaxago kɪnnaldą'lɛgo. dako ts'idiłts'ogo daxodinigi hi'ni' ako yołgai ts'ą bi' tanazgiz. doł'ijɛ ts'ą ditcił ts'ą bi tɑnɑsgiz. bacinni ts'ą bitɑnnɑgiz. biyajɛ ilagɛ k'axacdɛlɛc. k'at yolgai at'ɛt xacdɛlɛł. atsɛxastin bɛxoɣan yaxałnigɛ' xact'ɛlɛł. yołgai bikɛgo xact'ɛlɛł. yołgai bikɛbą nacdjɪngo xact'ɛlɛł. yołgai bɛł'ol xact'ɛ'lɛ yołgai bisł'ɛ xact'ɛ'lɛ' yołgai bɛdzɛsɣa didjɪcgo xact'ɛlɛ yołgai bił'akałgo xact'ɛlɛ yołgai bitisłałgo xact'ɛlɛ yołgai bi'ɛgo xact'ɛlɛ yołgai bini'go xact'ɛlɛ yołgai binɛ'go xact'ɛlɛ yołgai bɛts'osgo xact'ɛlɛ yodɛ ałtasai bidɑ'xazlago xact'ɛlɛ bidaxaslago xact'ɛlɛ dintc'ɛ ałtasai bidaxazlago xact'ɛlɛ nɑnsɛ' ałtasai bidaxazlago xact'ɛlɛ niłtsabik'ą bidaxaclɛgo xact'ɛlɛ niłtsąba'ad bidaxazlago xact'ɛlɛ aiyacdoł'ij bitsidji' sołts'inłgo xact'ɛlɛ tsa'anaɣai bik'ɛxojon at'ɛd nligo xact'ɛlɛ bitsidji xojogo xact'ɛlɛ bikɛdɛ xojogo xact'ɛlɛ biyagɛ xojogo xact'ɛlɛ bik'igɛ' xojogo xact'ɛlɛ binat'ałtso xojogo xact'ɛlɛ bizatxa xojogo xact'ɛlɛ xact'ɛla djɪn.


nilka djɪn. bįsołłakgai xał'atdɛ nilka djɪn. tc'it łagai nilka djɪn. diłxił naską nilka djɪn. tagonɛ' maitc'itłagai dį bɑkka bɛdisk'ąz djɪn. kodo ndilgɛ't' cittc'ɛ. dacabikɛgo nandilgoł adonnɪnł. ado' yunidji' nixidilɣoł. 'adji' nihisɪnłgoł. yudɛ bił nihisɪnłgoł cittc'ɛ. yołgai bił nihisɪnłgoł citc'ɛ ni djɪn. ta yiską bidjį nahonlįdji daxodiɣinigi 'ąłtso ałaadolɛł ni djɪn atsɛxastin. binibik'ɛgo ndilt'inɛnɛ nixanigɛ' xɑ'ctc'ɛłti' nixanigɛ' xactc'ɛoɣan dziłnɑ'odiłi nakidzadą' ałki nɑnt'i godɛni djɪn. akwi adonnił xoɣɑn xadzǫnt xoɣan xodissǫs olgɛgi' akwi adonnił ni djɪn. atsɛxastį nagwiya iyago ałaollɛł xoɣɑn xattsǫnt holgɛgi xoɣɑn hodisǫns olgɛgi'. nixanigɛ dinɛ nixanigɛ xactc'ɛłti dinnɛ annɛdi' nhɛcnt'i silį djɪn. nixanigɛ xactc'ɛoɣɑn nhɛcnt'i nanasdli djɪn. tagonɛ' xactc'ɛłti dinnɛ axɛnacct'i nanasdlį'. xactc'ɛoɣan axɛnt'i dį ɣonɛ'. acdłągonɛ' daxodiɣindɛ' dził bi danɛzbinɛ axɛcnt'i xasta gonɛ' ɣąaskidi dinnɛ danɛzbinɛ

Thirteen days were they say. Here when sun was being when she was found exactly there when it came menstruation | happened it was found they say. "Something passed from me, mother," she said they say. "What is it run a race is called, my daughter," | she said they say.

First Woman then girl thirteen years old will be adolescent then | so all (?) (message is taken) having passed. Then white shell basket in she washes. Turquoise basket, | abalone basket in she washes. Jet basket in she washes. Her child (?) she dressed. | Now White Shell girl she dresses. First Man his hogan back from the center he prepared. | White shell her moccasins he prepared (I am apparelled?). White shell border of her moccasins being black he prepared. White shell | its string he fixed. White shell her leggings he prepared. White shell her legging decoration he prepared. | White shell her skirt he prepared. White shell her belt he prepared. White shell her shirt he prepared. | White shell her face he prepared. White shell her mind he prepared. White shell her soft feather he prepared. | Clothing all kinds will go to her he prepared. Quadrupeds all kinds | go to her he prepared. Vegetables all kinds go to her he prepared. Male rain | go to her he prepared. Female rain go to her he prepared. Bluebird in front of her | calling he prepared. Long life good fortune girl being he prepared. In front of her good | he prepared. Behind her good he prepared. Below her good | he prepared. Above her good he prepared he prepared they say.

It was spread they say. White buckskin on the bottom was spread they say. Blanket (cotton) white was spread they say. Black | embroidered was spread they say. Third on it a white coyote blanket. Four on it she was stretched (and molded) they say. "From here | one runs my daughter. Just sunwise one runs around," she told her. "Then inside one jumps over. | There you finish running. Soft goods with you finish running, my daughter. White shell with you will finish running, | my daughter," she said it thus they say. Then it was day. "It's day where they live where the holy ones all let come together," | he said they say First Man. Leader they made you Mirage *xactc'elti'*. Mirage *xactc'eoɣan dziɫna'odiɫi* twelve one after the other circles he drew they say. | "There," he said, "hogan spread Hogan-Iridescent | where it is called there," he said | they say. First Man when sun goes down they come together Hogan Pink called, Hogan-Iridescent where it is called. Mirage People, Mirage Talking God People behind in a line | became they say. Mirage *xactc'eoɣan* in a line became again they say. Third Talking God | People a line side by side became again. *xactc'eoɣan* a line side by side four in. Five | in Holy Mountain People mountains in who sit line beside. Six in Hunchback People who sit |

axɛnt'i.    xactc'ɛltci dɩnnɛ dɩnnɛzbin djɩn.    tsots'ɩt gonɛ' aniłtąni
dɩnnɛ dɩnnɛzbin k'adolɛł xwodo'nit djɩn.    'adjila djɩn.    dadnbal adjila djɩn.

xat'ɛgo donixinołnida djɩnnɛ djɩn.    niɣɛł xwodollɛł xodjɩnni djɩn.
donit'inłt'i djɩnni djɩn.    yołgai ałkɛ na'acila djɩn.    doł'ijɛ ałkɛ na'acila
djɩn.    xadat'ɛ ałkɛ na'acila djɩn.    yocbij ałkɛ na'acila djɩn.    yałitci wolgɛ-
djila djɩn.    yocbic wolgɛla djɩn.    maitc'itłagai wolgɛla djɩn.    dɩłxɩł naska
wolgɛla djɩn.    kɛɛstcin wolgɛla djɩn.    t'ats'ɛnxɛnnɛ nakidzadago ałki
najnt'i dzilį djɩn.    k'at 'ado xojondji dadit'i dolɛłgo binigɛla djɩn.
tadɩtdin xaltsoz djɩn.    xoɣan bɛ da'odlic xodonni' djɩn.    dacabik'ɛgo
tadɩtdin axɛltsosgo tadɩtdin dadjodɛl djɩnnɛ annɛdi' nixiniɣɛ xactc'ɛlti'
dadjiligo axɛnt'i wɛxɛ xwodonni djɩn.    xadɛz'ą djɩn adɛdɛsta djɩn.    dzadɛ
xoɣan nila.    xojo xoɣan xa'abiyadji.    xojo xoɣan xactc'ɛlti bixoɣan nila.
xayołkał bɛ bɛxoɣan nila.    nadanłgai bɛbɛxoɣannila xojo xoɣan yodɛ
ąłtasai bɛ bɛxoɣannila.    xojo xoɣan tołanactcin bɛ bɛxoɣannila.    xojo
xoɣan tadɩtdin bɛ bɛxoɣan nila.    xojo xoɣan ɛ'a biyadji bɛxoɣan
nila xojo xoɣan xactc'eoɣan bɛxoɣan nila xojo xoɣan naxotsoi
bɛxoɣan nila xojo xoɣan nadanłtsoi bɛxoɣannila xojo    xoɣan
nł'ij ałtasai bɛxoɣannila tobiyajbɛ bɛxoɣannila tadidinbɛ bɛxoɣannila
xojo    xoɣan    daxwɛt'ɛgo    nakindɛta    djɩn.    akogo    bik'ɛdoilɣaci
xat'ɛgola' adadonił xastui nakigo axadin.    nakidzada axɛznt'i dadoyɛd-
ntanda djɩnnɛ.    xat'idodaxołyadalla.    haicabɛ' tsanacalɛ?    haisbɛ bikɛxo-
jonnictilɛ?    lą xodonnit'.    akwɛ nda naki' bik'idaisnil djɩn.    tsa'anaɣai
bikɛxojon.    ado adadɛsta djɩn.    nakidzada ndɛta djɩn.    bik'i dasillai
do' naki ako dįdzada sili djɩn.    k'at xaiłkago aniłtanni dadɛdɛz'a djɩn.
tsilo yisa' djɩn.    yits'ago djɩnni.    xat'ɛgo donixinołnida.    ła' yaxajnolnɛ'
djɩn.    niɣɛl xodolɛł? xodjɩnni djɩn.    xayołkał adjiłt'ila djɩn.    ako xadadɛsta
djɩn.    nanat'innila.    xactc'ɛlti nandinla.

formed a line by the side of. Red God People sat around they say.
Seven in Grasshopper | People sat around. "Now it will be," he said
they say. It happened they say. Curtain blanket was lifted they say.
   "Why we were not satisfied," he said they say. "Your offering will
be provided," he said to him they say. | They made a long line he said
they say. White shell one after the other came in pairs they say. Tur-
quoise one after the other came in pairs | they say. Ring of haliotis one
after the other came in pairs they say. Braided beads one after the
other came in pairs they say. Red shells they were called | they say.
Braided beads they were called they say. Coyote blanket white they
were called they say. Black fabric | was called they say. Figured fabric
was called they say. *t'ats'ɛnxɛnnɛ* twelve one after the other | lines be-
came they say. Now then *hojondji* we begin will be because they say. |
Pollen he drew out a sack they say. "Hogan with it paint," he said they
say. Sunwise | pollen being yellow one after the other pollen they ate
they say. Last row Mirage Talking Gods | being were in line. "Wehe,"
he said they say. He started to sing they say. He began to sing they
say. Here | hogans stand. Good hogans from the east. Good hogans
Talking Gods their hogans stand. | Dawn with their hogans stand. White
corn with their hogans stand. Good hogans soft goods | all kinds with
their hogans stand. Good hogans water of all kinds their hogans stand.
Good | hogans pollen with their hogans stand. Good hogans from the
west, their hogans | stand. Good Hogan Talking God their hogans stand.
Good hogans stand. Horizontal yellow light | their hogans stand. Good
hogans yellow corn their hogans stand. Good hogans | hard property
of all kinds their hogans stand. Water's child their hogans stand.
Pollen their hogans | stand. Good hogans. That way twice they say.
They the one then sing over. | "Why do you say that men two are lack-
ing?" Twelve there were lines. They didn't know | they say. "Some-
thing you do not know. With what shall I live forever? With what shall
I have good luck?" | "All right," he said. There two they put on top,
long life, | good fortune. Then they began to sing they say. Twelve
they sang they say. On it there | lie also two. Then fourteen became
they say. How nearly day grasshoppers began to sing they say. |
Woman's song was heard they say. When it was heard they say.
"Why didn't you notify us?" one put his head in | they say. "Your
face will be (provided)," he said to him they say. Dawn they found
did it they say. There they began to sing | they say. They stood in line.
Talking Gods were in line.

kɛlagai a̧ltso binɛlt'ɛgo nandinla.
yisł'ɛ łakgai a̧ltso binɛlt'ɛgo nandinla.
bi̧tso łakgai a̧ltso binɛlt'ɛgo yuda.
xadzɛlgai a̧ltso bɛnɛlt'ɛgo nandinla.
bɛlatagɛ' ayacdoł'ij a̧ltso bɛnɛlt'ɛgo nandinla.
biza naxodlɛlgo binɛ' nijogo nandɛnla.
ts'anaɣai bikɛxojonniligo nandɛnla.
bitsidji xojogo nandɛnla.
bikɛdɛ xojogo nandɛnla.
tc'itdja' xacta ałaigɛt'ɛ yikaiłɣin wolgɛ'.
di̧ nanɛska djin. xat'ici ciɣa nangola cma nazdini djin. ela
kindzisda' olgɛ dinni djin. ɑsdzą̧. t'agot t'ɛgo bana·sde djin. ałts'a'
xosigo diɣi dɛnɛ yɛ k'at donɛdolsɛlda xodonni djin. ałts'a tɛ·sda djinnɛ.
xactc'ɛlti' xadzi djin.   xadɛta xactc'ɛlti yiłts'ąci djinnigo ɑnnai'i binigɛ
adɛcnił. djuxona'ai xadzi djinnɛ.   t'atdzaigɛ acdidonił doyaconi biniɣɛ
accicdidonił eba nat'ɛ ɑst'e djin.


'ado ałai yiska djinnɛ. xat'ica ciɣannagola ni djin. ela tcedji'na'·
holgɛ. di̧ yiskago ɑsdi djin ebą̧ ɑsdzannɛ tcoɣin ilɛgo.   dinłkago ɑdi̧
djin. tcoɣinnɛ nabidiltcą djin.   djuhona'ai tondiłkǫns bidado' sizk'aigo
hatł'ɛ didi̧ngo djuhona'ai bitc'igo dadilɣago ɑltc'i' ɑndjint'i̧go djinnɛ
djuhona'ai ts'idɛlnigi niɣago haiya ts'ats'isɣi' niɣago tondiłkǫnsɣɛ'
biyado nadzizk'ai ha'ɛdji tonahɛltcąnł kodjit'ila djin.   akwotdzidzado
'ado tc'ide'ac djin.   cada'a bitc'idji bidadji'ac djin.   ł'ots'ozɛ bandji'ac
djin.   t'ado ałts'ą̧ (probably ałtso) nazniłdeda najdit'ac djin.   ładakon-
cidjolgo k'addɛ ałnɛ'ago tsinłgo ntc'itt'aj djin.   t'acitdjolɛ baldecɣoł.
dodɑndjin'ɑsdza doda cittc'ɛ nɛ djin. ts'inłgo ndɛcɣoł. akoyɛ yadan-
tcągɛ. daldɛlɛ łągo ilwoł ni djin ɛsdza. doda cima ts'inłgo yɛ̧ dinnɛsdahi
hadɛcɣoł cicdo dohonsadalla hasigoyɛ. lą̧'a tinɛ citc'ɛ ni djin.   ɛsdza
atcinila djin.   adjilla.   ts'iddaiyɛnɛ 'a̧ltso' nazniłdɛgo kwɛhact'ɛdjilago
t'anitɛ. konɛ łi̧' łakgailɛ sizi djin.   azzatt'i łakgai djin.   hakɛ łakgai djin.

White moccasins all being dressed with they were in line.
Leggings white all being dressed with they were in line.
Buckskin white all being dressed with.
White eagle feathers all being dressed with they were in line.
On top bluebirds all being dressed with they were in line.
Their mouths singing, their voice pleasing they were in line.
Long life, good fortune with they were in line.
In front of them with good fortune they were in line.
Behind them with good fortune they were in line.

Six were all alike dawn songs called.

Four days passed they say. "Something from me flows again, mother," she told her they say. "That | *kindzisda'* is named," she said they say woman. The same way it is done they say. From each side | at daylight holy people. "Now we will never see again," he said they say. From both sides they depart they say. | Talking God spoke they say. "After this Talking God he saw when he says wartime he will be killed on account of it | I say." Sun spoke they say. "Not so they see me. It is not right (bad luck) on account of it | they see me." On account of that they dismissed the gathering they say.

Then one day was they say. "Something from me flows again," she said they say. "That *tcedji'na"* | is called." Four when days pass it ceases they say because of that women menses have. Four days it ceases | they say. One having menses was lustful they say. Sun water drips on top spreading her legs | her crotch shining Sun toward when it rose toward each other. | Sun in the center (name of a place in the sky) when he reached there where he feeds his horse when he reached water dripping place | under she spread her legs again in her crotch water sprinkled. They found she did that they say. After she did that | then they two started away they say. South toward they went down they say. Rush grass they two came to | they say. Not all (from each other) threshed they two started back they say. Some | lying in a heap. Nearly noon quickly they two arrived back they say. "That lying there I will run for." | "Do not do it. No, my daughter," she said they say. "Quickly I will run back." "There | it is dangerous those who eat people many run about," she said they say woman. "No, mother, quickly the threshed seeds | I run for. I too, I am not ignorant, I will be wary." "All right, go on, my daughter," she said they say. Woman | said it they say. She did that. Those seeds all when she had threshed when she was arranging | (her load) with surprise here horse white stood they say. Bridle was white they say. His moccasins were white they say.

at'e ɑlgaigi hazdɛt'ɛ djın. łį' t'aiyodago dɑssizzi. hatc'i hadzi djın.
doci adoniłgo' ɑnt'i nladɛ hacago citc'į' sɛnak'aiłɛ. yałnigɛ haiya ts'aha-
dzisgi nicago t'ondilkǫnsdji' ts'inłk'aiłɛ to nł'ɛ hɛdiltc'onłɛ docidoniłgo
'ɑnt'i. ha'adji njɛ iłnidołti bɛhɛdolzinłinnɛ̨' ni djın. k'ɑttcą' djuhona'ai
ɑtt'ila djın. t'oyɛ kodji kodzidzaigɛ ɑtdin djın. danazdildza djın. ndzit-
dzago xat'icilɛ yiłtsą cima· djınnɛ djın. t'aładizɛ łakgai łį łakgai
t'at'ɛdjilgai. docidolniłgo 'ɑnt'i. nla hacago sittc'į' tsiniłk'aiłɛ. yałnigɛ
nicago hayats'ahadzisgɛ tondiłkǫnzgɛ tsinłk'aiłɛ ciłni djınnɛ djın. dako
t'ani ɑnt'i djınnɛ djın atsɛasdza. t'ani ɑct'i atsɛ hastin ntsitdza djınnɛ.
hat'ici ntsi' yiłts'ąla djınnɛ djın. t'ałądizɛ' tcilgailɛ yiłtsala. t'ayadago
łį' dasizzi. donigɛ sizzida ni· ntsi'. docidoniłgo 'ɑnt'i. nladɛ hacago
citc'į' tsinłk'aiłɛ. inda· yałnigɛ nicago tondiłkǫnsdji tsinłk'aiłɛ. ako
t'ani ɑct'i ni ntsi'. ha'adji njɛ iłnɛdołti tc'ɛtigɛ nago xoɣan ahodoldził.
tcicts'osdo' ła' nidodji' ninni'. ł'ots'ozɛ kinnɛcbiji łanidokał nintsi'
ɑnni cannɛ annidalla bɛ ta'osdɛ' diɣin dinnɛ. donɛdoltsɛla doxodonnit
'ałtso diɣinni. yu hat'ilaba adinnɛ hastin 'iłndiłtinɛ. nla 'iłndzist'i
do tc'ɛtigɛ naɣo axwots'idził tcijts'osɛ do' łanijniłdjit djin. i'a djın.
xiłi djın. tc'itłakgai nizinłkat. naska t'o nizinłtsoz il (n)ɛcbijɛ nijnɑtka·.
nicnadjigo ɑskat do' tsɛzda djın. nicładji'go atsɛhastin dzɛsda djın.
ginnɛcbijɛ edjɛska' djın. xojǫ yiłxɛlgo atsɛ hastin nanazditsa. yołgai
at'ɛd yidolɣɛlgo akǫ ho'iska djın. hosįdnt'ɛ̨ tc'ɛtigɛ. nicnadjibɛ· t'ałaigo
da'ak'ɛ. kinɛjbijɛ t'ałai ɑtdɛn djınnɛ. ndzitdza djın. daxot'ɛ sɛtsi'.
niyotcila dicni ni djın atsɛ hastin. cijɛ tc'ɛtigɛ t'ałaigo dakɛ nicnadjibɛ
ginnɛcbijɛ do' t'ałai ɛtdį. ha'adjigo xiłnanɛdji tcɛnadziskɛ. wojo
ciłłidji djın. ndzitdza djın. daxot'ɛ· sitsi' donaɣaida. niyotc'ila dicnin.

All white he was dressed they say. Horse so high (two foot) stood above the ground. To her he spoke they say. | "Not anything you accomplish. Over there I come up toward me you spread your legs. At the center of the sky there I come up at *ts'ahatzisgi* | when I arrive place of dripping water you spread your legs. Water your crotch drips will accomplish nothing | you are. East your father let him make a brush house. We will see what will happen," he said they say. That one (surprise) Sun | she found it was they say. Away here while she looked he was gone they say. She walked back they say. When she got | back, "Something I saw, mother," she said they say. "All over white horse white entirely white. | Nothing will happen you are. There when I rise toward me you spread your legs. Middle of sky | when I arrive at the feeding place at water dripping you spread your legs' he said to me," she said they say. "Thus | truly you did?" she asked they say First Woman. "Truly I did." First Man came back they say. | "Something your daughter saw it seems," she said they say. "All over white it seems she saw. Right up here (gesture) | horse stood above the ground. Not on the ground he stood, she said, your daughter. 'Nothing will happen you do. There when I come up | toward me you spread your legs. There middle of the sky when I arrive where water drips you spread your legs.' 'That | truly I do,' she said, your daughter. 'Toward the east your father let him build a brush shelter across hogan let him rake the ground. | Chips too pile up in a pile. Rush grass seed that boiled place in a vessel.'" "Your daughter | said with they went away Holy People. 'They wont see us again,' they said, | all the Holy Ones." "Yu! for something you say that." The man built a brush shelter over there. He built brush shelter. | Before door he swept, chips too they piled up they say. The sun set they say. | It became dark they say. White blanket he spread down. Fabric she put down. Cooked food he put one side. | On the right side on it too she sat they say. On the left side First Man sat they say. | The cooked food stood there they say. Quite when it was dark, First Man went away. White Shell | Girl being named there passed the night they say. When it was light in doorway on the right side one side only | was a track. The cooked food one was gone they say. He came back they say. "How it is my daughter? | You lied I said," he said they say First Man. "My father, in the doorway just one was footprint. On the right side | cooked food too just one was gone toward east." When it was night again they sat there again. Quite | it was dark they say. He came back they say. "How is it, my daughter?" He didn't come. You lied I said. |

k'adde hailkago ciedenac nizį. akonde nakigo dahak'e tc'etige. inec-
bicyę kodjigo la' dji' 'ala. ako nakidi xilnanidji djin. tc'enadziske
djin. naxosi djin. nadzitdza djin. dahot'e? sitsi' ni djin. atsehastin dako
nacdonit donaγaida djinne djin. niyotc'ila dicnin. hat'ala kojinltcągo
ndzistago diγį haki'hole'. yu! hat'i dadodinido' k'at bedolzinline ni djin.
'atseasdzą.


di dinecbiceyę ha'adjigo la nanatdi nda' tago dahak'e. gene'
dinnilil cije. tį akǫ tooyoyego citahadjiyago xojo hayilka nizi.
xilnahidjįgo l'eilnidjin danidza djin. ndzitdza djin. nahokǫsdjigo
ginecbije ladi akodi dįgo dake daigisiyego hayilkago cidadjiya ndi
adaholtsada, cil'e adaditle'lago ts'endzit ni djin. ebą asdzanne hailt'ego
t'adobaxintine dįnlka. denedji akot'e k'at akotdza. dįn yiską djin
hakwinist'indo dį yiska djin. cama' kweγa' hat'ici danaltal hailkago
djini djin. cittc'e niltsągo awe. hidesna'go dinnila. ebą di bigi' xahwin-
nisti ada dį yiskago xayilkago awe hedesna. diyene' nahidizide silį
djin ebą dį' nahidizigo awe hidi'na djin. di djingo xahwinnist'ido nast'ai
yiskago adjistcį djin. naki yistcį djin. nahididzidi silį djin. ebą nast'ai
nahidizigo ni'itci. t'alai yiska sike djin. naxai dolel lako djin. djictcido
nayiskągo tada'ac djin. naki naxadolel. djistcido nezna' yiskago
atsehastį k'a badjila djin. ts'iddi banidje djin. djistcido acdlą'ada
yiskago dzilnaodili bilatagi na'ac nde dontso baniya djin. hat'ila xa'ac
cinalle. dokwi biniγe nixidestcida cinalle. noxeke ako hwonnilt'el nt'i
altso bilexozin e ahalne djin. nixije bitc'įn' do'ac. nlį djohona'ai yikaleγe
nixijego at'e hat'ila nije hwededǫnil nixima dįdi nahododolk'il 'adinda
nije bitc'in det'aj hwodedǫnil. alade xatc'į' xadodzi. naxineltc'a djin.
cma hat'ila nixije. hotacke noli naxadonago cma hat'ila nixije kabije
nixijen ebą. nihitsi dadecya. nahodonnago naidelk'it djin. xwocsetda'hi
lą nixijen. nahodana djin. yadeca'. djinnido' tsetacke noli. hwattacke

"Now when it was light someone touched me I felt." Then two there were tracks in the doorway. The cooked food | here one is gone. Then the second time it was dark they say. They two sat again they say. | It was daylight they say. He came back they say. "How is it my daughter?" he said they say First Man. "Here | I said he didn't come," he said they say. "You lied I said. Why being ragged | we live Holy Ones will not come." "Oh! That do not say. Now we will see," she said they say | First Woman.

This cooked food east side one was gone again. There three there were tracks. | "Go look my father. Go on here this side I him go away quite it was daylight I felt."|When it was night again midnight he went away they say. He came back they say. North | food one there was gone. Four were tracks sides someone left in. "At dawn went from me but I didn't see him. My crotch | being damp I woke up," she said they say. On account of this woman why she is married | they do not touch four days. Navajo now that way they do. Four days they say | they have intercourse. Four days are they say. "Mother here something pulsates at dawn," | she said they say. "My daughter being pregnant baby it moves you mean. On account of that in you have intercourse. | Four days when were when dawn it was baby moved that month became they say. Because of that four when months are | baby moves they say. That day after they had intercourse. Nine | when days were it was born they say. Two she gave birth to they say. Months became they say. Because of that nine | when months it is born. Just one day they two set up they say. A year will be they say. After she gave birth after | two days they two waked they say. Two years will be. After she gives birth ten when days | were First Man arrow made for them they say. Birds they hunted they say. After she gave birth fifteen | when days were *dzilna'odili* its top they walked about then large fly came to them they say. "What you two walk after | my son's sons. Not here the reason you were born, my grandsons. Out here the wide earth it is | all he knows that he told them they say. Your father to him you two go. That one Sun he walks | your father he is. What your father you will ask your mother. Four times you ask her. Then | your father to him we go you tell her. One time to her you speak." They ran back they say. | "Mother, who is our father?" "Everybody's kin you are." After a while "Mother who is our father?" | "Barrel Cactus is your father. | For that reason your hands are bushy." When time had passed they asked again they say. "Standing Cactus, | yes was your father." When time had passed they say. "What about you ask? Anyone's kin you are." "Somebody's kin |

nolins tcindac tcilɛ kabijɛ njɛc 'ɑsda' tcindac xacjɛ hwocsɛdahi njɛc
tcindac xajɛ hwocsɛdaihi tsɛtackɛ ɛsda' tcindac tcolɛ k'at nijɛ
bitc'į dɛt'aj.
  djuhona'ai nixijɛ. cma ctco ctcai dį yiskago naxandint'ac. dadi'as
kodo tc'ɛtido na'aj. łakgaigo nadzillit at'ɛla djin. eyɛ dadi'aj
ndaxadɛsɛz eyɛ djin. bidisk'az djini. bini' dalgaigo adalya djin. dik'at
dalaolyɛ dolɛł la xodontni djin. nixanigɛ' xactc'ɛltiyɛnnɛ' bilni'. nixanigɛ
xactc'ɛoyan xactc'ɛlti hwilni djinnɛ. xactc'ɛoyan hwilni djinnɛ. tsɛ'-
ąxaldjin holyɛdo xactc'ɛsjinnɛ hwilni djinnɛ. djuhona'ai bidaiya djin.
k'at didaolgedolɛł hwina'aj djin. nayɛ'nɛzyanɛ aladji naya' hwodon'ni
djin. tobadjistcinɛ akɛdɛ tcili xwodon'ni djin. k'at biji ołłɛ hwodon'ni
djin. 'ałła xodilya habadocjij djin. k'at ni' iji anlɛ xwodontni djin.
xactc'ɛcjinnɛ. hat'ila 'ałsą dohalyadąlla ni djin. cunaiyɛ' ałtso atdizdit.
ala djilinɛ nayɛ'nɛzyannɛ djolyɛlɛ. akɛdo djillini xama' 'att'ini tobadj-
ictcinɛ djolyɛlɛ. hadji' dacdido'ac hwodont'ni djin. ya diłxił bit'ɛj bɛ
hodict'ɛj. dlɛc bɛ ałti bɛlyago hak'i ninil djin. bɛ xatsaniyɛdo tobadjist-
inɛ ni' bitc'i bɛ hodijtci djinnɛ. dlɛc bɛ tsiyɛł nt'ɛl holyɛ hak'i ninil djin.
bɛ xatsahastido.


  to axɛdlę xolyedjɛ' dacdidɛ'ac ni djin djuhona'ai tsitdi ałts'a
xonnałtsogi sik'ɛdo ałtcicdɛ' bɛ nixił ɛxozindo nɛɛlniyɛ sikɛdo.
didɛ atsɛxastin didɛ atsaɛsdzą xanacda' biladɛ todots'oz xolgɛdɛ
hodjillọlɛ. diikwiya dacdidoyał. nlidi nnacdadɛ hodjillondo' yołgai
ɛsdzan. djuhona'ai anni djin. t'ałtsọi bił dacdido'yał xałtcidɛ bɛyani
naxok'a dinnɛ bił dacdidoyał. bahwodjilyado. t'atsinnadozgasgɛ.
axwot'eli ci 'iado cini'ohogɛda bik'i diya adji niłtsa' ba'ad bɛhwokolnido
ci'i niłtsą' baką' bɛcoholnido nansɛ' ni'honlidji' bɛhwoholnido nahok'-
adinnɛ ba datcollɛlɛ. nle bił'adɛ mai'i toyidjiłɛ idilyodɛ aladji nanniya
djin. bikɛdɛ atsɛhastin niniya djin. bikɛdi atsɛɛsdza djin. bikɛdi
atsɛxack'ɛ. xa'adji dadildɛ' atsɛɛsdza xatdzi djin. bitc'ɛya siyadɛsti'.
tsindiskosgo naxodiłnido tsindiskosgo dakos ndiłnido. tsindiskosgo
ałta anohonniłdo. tsindiskosgo atsɛxack'ɛ hwɛɛxozingo. ahoalɛ tsiyadɛsti

we are without none he has Barrel Cactus your father.   Now his father
Standing Cactus your father | none his father.   Standing Cactus anyone's
kin.   Now he will be.   Now our father | to him we two start."

"The Sun is our father.   Mother grandmother grandfather four days
we will come back to you."   They two started. | So far in front of the
door they came.   White rainbow it was they say.   That with they two
went. | They stepped on it that with they say.   They formed them they
say.   Their faces white they were made they say.   Now | names will be
given he said they say.   Mirage Talking God that one invite.   Mirage |
*xactc'ɛoɣan* Talking God he invited they say.   *xactc'ɛoɣan* he invited
they say.   Hole in black rock | it is called from Black God was invited
they say.   Sun came down they say. | Now those who will be named they
two stood in front they say.   *naɣɛ'nɛzɣanɛ* ahead he went he addressed |
they say.   *tobadjistcinɛ* second he is he addressed they say.   "Now his
name make," he said | they say.   They came for it.   They do not know
(?) they say.   "Now you name give," he said to him they say | Black God.
"What ? he doesn't know," he said they say.   "Monsters all they killed.|"
The first one *naɣɛ'nɛzɣanɛ* will be named.   Second who is his mother
who did it *tobadjictcinɛ* | will be called.   Where will they two go?" he
asked him they say.   Sky dark its coals with | I made them black.   Clay
with bow sign of on him he put they say.   With it will be no danger.
*tobadjistcinɛ* | earth red with they red made they say.   Clay with hair
from wide called on him they put they say. | With it he will be protected.

"Water-flows-together where it is called they two go," he said they
say Sun.   "From each other | there is a yellow flat (?) they will live ?
with us we will know center of earth they will live. | Here First Man here
First Woman where I rise beyond narrow water where it is called |
they will be.   This way she will go.   Over there where I set she will live
White Shell | Woman," Sun said it they say.   "Everything with she will
go her children their food | on the earth people with she will go.   She will
look after.   She will study about it there. | It will be that way.   I (?)
everywhere on it I go there rain female with she will be boss. | I rain male
will be controlled by me.   Vegetation where ever it is | will be bossed by
her.   People of the earth for them she will keep it."   Over there on the
other side Water Coyote he ran first she stepped out | they say.   After
him First Man stepped out they say.   After him First Woman they say.
After her | First Warrior (Coyote).   East they went First Woman spoke
they say.   Her daughter began to talk bad. | "When I think it will be
bad.   When I think cough will be.   When I think | different things will
be bad.   When I think Coyote will know it."   Forever she talks bad |

djin. atseɛsdza t'ado dinnɛ dokwi holondallɛ biniγɛ baiyɛłtii att'ɛ ni djinnɛ. nixaniγɛ xactc'ɛłti nixaniγɛ xactc'ɛoγan.
t'ado dinninɛ ałtcicdjɛ nɛxɛ xozinlɛhi do'. xactc'ɛłti xadjinni djin. k'at yołgaiɛsdzą' yɛdadiγahi kǫ k'at hadelya. dɛnɛ nakidzada nakaidi bił dadedɛska ne djinnɛ. biladji' bikąi nikai djin. bikɛdi ba'adi nikai djin. biladji' niłtsą biką djinnɛ. bikɛdɛ niłtsą ba'ad djinnɛ. biladji' k'os diłxił bikɛdɛ a· diłxił. bitsidji' k'os doł'id djin. bikɛdɛ a· doł'ij djin bitsidji k'os łitso djin. bikɛdɛ 'a· łitso djin. bitsidji k'os łakgai djin. bikɛdɛ a· łakgai djin. nansɛ' noholidji' tcɛlɛhojon' bɛ hadelya yił diya djin. yołgai tsą'annɛ doł'ijɛ tsą'annɛ ditcili tsą'anɛ bacinɛ tsą'anɛ t'oaosγindɛ bił dadildo djin. tadiłxił sɛstą xolgedi yił nniya·. k'ata sitda djin.


ninniyadɛ łį hodollɛlgi dɛnɛ ya yątsinkɛlad djin. bɛtsinniłkęz yołgaiɛsdza ci nicli caxoγan ałnigi bitsi'niłkɛz yodɛ. baxaztɛl bakaγɛ bik'iγɛ bɛtsiniłkɛz. yołgai ts'ą yołgai łį· bigi silla kabɛ silla bitsinłkęz. tc'ilataxojon bɛxaditdin biγi' silla kabi silla ts'iddaaigicdɛ k'ɛ'ądiljij dondinnɛc kabɛsilla biγi silla.

they say. "First Woman not you talk not here you will live because we talked about it is," he said | they say, Mirage *xactc' elti* Mirage *xactc'eoγan.*

"Not you talk each other we will know," Talking God he said to they say. | "Now White Shell Woman get ready (?)." Here now was decorated. People twelve they lived | with her they started they say. In front males came they say. After them females came | they say. In front of her rain male they say. Behind her rain female they say. In front of her | cloud dark. Behind her mist dark. Before her cloud blue they say. Behind her mist blue | they say. Before her cloud yellow they say. Behind her mist yellow they say. Before her cloud white | they say. Behind her mist white they say. Herbage wherever it was, flowers with | she was decorated with she started they say. White shell that basket, turquoise that basket, abalone that basket, jet that basket | everything with she rose up they say. Black cloud it lies where it is called with she arrived. Now | she lives there they say.

Where she arrived horses will exist people for she thought they say. She was thinking, | "White Shell Woman I am. My hogan in the center I think about. Goods spread out on | on them I think about. White shell basket white shell horses in it lay. ? with it lies I think about. | Flowers their pollen in it lies. Come to me they increase they will not die. | ? in lie."

## Pot Woman Teaches Witchcraft

xaclicdelja holgedji' dasdidɛl. asa datcillɛ xaclic asa.   akwidi di
yoₑ nohistci. banatinłɛ holge at'i djin.   yołgai gic doł'ijɛ gic ditcili gic
bacinɛ gic.  nohiztc'i djin.   diła kiya'an tcilindɛ tsɛdatda asdza ayoi
aldel.  bayan 'ɛsdzą tsɛdadagi bayannigɛ' akwibį naztsɛtla.  dohwonnida
ado doɛsdzą bit'ąni hodontni djin.   di kiya'anɛ dotą' kiya'a holgedji'
anana' djin.  listso biligo ył ninnamɛ. e alyagi.

dɛnɛta tohɛdlį cada'a bidji'go habizko'a' holge djin.   dinnɛta'
nodai dahazlingo djinnɛ.  adɛ nodai hanaba' hana'a djin.  akwi yiskago
naxanadiba' dani djin.  ako nli tsɛ naz'ą bilatago tsɛndazdjittigo akǫnda
hayą djin tsɛkɛ holge.  nakai 'isnanɛ nakai dinnɛ bɛditci.  nakidzadą
dinnɛ ako nakidzadą iltego dinnɛ' badazdillɛ djin.  ako bahat'a djin.
adese djin bizi baisinna.  ado djinba djin.  nakai dinnɛyę dį tc'ilt'ɛgo
hwodooya djin.  nodai axałe djin.  naildɛ djin.  akɛ naniba djin.
nakaidinɛyₑ nabidoyą djin.  t'axanaba'bikɛ nakai dinnɛdi naxwotdittset.
ładzada xodoyą djin.  dałai idzi djin.  ladjobai holgedi billa' t'ayiłdilt'ɛgo
asdzanyₑ' binanits'a djin.  tcɛ́ azɛ' baaligo daztsa djin.  hatal djin.
ha'adassannɛ taidą' atzisgɛlad djin.  akwi niya djin.  latcoba olge daka
olge tsin honiłtsogo gɛcgijgo bɛ'isdaką' sa'abigi djin.  dɛgo yadjitka e
bɛzdaka djin.  bɛilti' hwonnilnɛ djin.  koj dikago djuxona'ai bitc'į'
ałts'anagic.  djuxona'ai bitabi bidjo'ał dadɛc hwodonilni djin.  anai
djinne di bił anaiłɛ' ni djinne.  ayanya adizts'i djin ado hadadeya djin.

k'a ałtsi yidɛst'o djin.  bɛlt'ɛtsigo ył datdilgo djin.  k'ayɛl dį
ała dahisgi got'ila djin.  k'a ąłtso naidɛst'o djin.  t'a bił djitdjɛgo ła'
yiłxananadɛl ałts'a naidɛst'o djin.  dį k'ayɛl isdingo indan sizzɛ haslįla
nigo dahɛts'os yilyoł djin.  hadatįgo tsɛ dɛsł'on.  adatdin nahaigo
nanelts'a.  naxananda hat'ilabą ant'i.  djik'ɛanninandai nlį.  adohat'atci
dɛya djinnɛ.  hat'alad djin.  akǫ ałtso bɛyiisdella djin.  asdzale assai

### Pot Woman Teaches Witchcraft

Mountain-of-Mud where it is called they went. Pots they made,
clay pots. There these | beads they hid. *banatinte* who was called did it
they say. White Shell cane turquoise cane abalone cane | jet cane he
hid they say. This one *kiya'an* clan stands on a rock woman large |
live. Her hogan woman where it stands on a rock where her house is
there deer it seems they killed. She didn't say | anything then not
woman hand on her side she spoke they say. These *kiya'ane* ? *kiy'a*
where it was called | they moved back they say. Snake being his pet
with they moved back. That happened to it.

Navajo country streams unite south on that side where cañons come
up it is called they say. Navajo country | Ute where they lived they say.
Then Ute made war. "(Some) days | pass here we will come back to fight,"
they said they say. There it was rock stands up on its top they built
stones around there | they killed them they say. *tseke* he was called.
Mexican captives Mexican clan they bred. Twelve | men there twelve
were men they commit adultery against them they say. | Then they went
to war they say. ? his name I forget. Then they went to war they say.
Mexican those men four | were all killed they say. Utes did it they
say. They came back they say. | Afterward they came to fight again
they say. The Mexicans were killed they say. | Every time they make
war Mexicans they killed. Eleven were killed they say. One was left they
say. *latc'obai* he was named his sister only there was. | That woman was
sick they say. In vain medicine being made for her she died they say.
A sing was they say. | The one whose wife died already he was married
again they say. There he arrived they say. *latc'obai* named, cards |
name sticks yellow being cut with them gambled basket in they say. Up
they threw them those | they gambled with they say. His bow he had
in his hand, they say. Here he was walking sun toward | he made
signs to shoot. "Sun ? I might hit I wish," he said they say. (?) This |
with (?) he said they say. Between the shoulders he shot him they
say. Then they ran after him they say.

Arrows all (?) he shot they say. His bow with he ran they say. Quiver
four, | one hanging he had they say. Arrows all he shot again they
say. Just with they overtook him. | Another with he took down all
he shot they say. Four quivers when were gone, | "Now I die it befalls
me," singing big peaks he ran to they say. Where the road comes out
stones he tied on. Four when years had passed | he was seen
again. "Come back to us why no use you do that. You chief of us
you be." Not close | he went they say. There was singing it seems
they say. There all went to the sing they say. Old woman pot |

dzisdali' haniya djin. hat'iyɛ' cąiɣą cittco'? bidjini djin. asdzą hadicdoleł sitsoi naɣe hannehilą binɛ'bik'ɛgo annadji xannihila ye i xastinnikɛgo cackɛgo xannihila ant'ihila daxanatsiahwot'i. dabinidji bada'dołéłxɛ ailan binina. hat'ic bidɛlnɛ. bɛdɛłnihi. holǫn· hat'ic bidɛlni. bɛdɛlni ał'ic nactcinla naco nacidoł'ij ahinago asdzan tcikɛ yits'ą· dogic bił'ij hadolgeł nacoyɛ ndɛdolt'as tcikɛhɛ do' naco inalnodɛ ahinago bittsa nadolgic naditdolt'as bił'ic hanadollɛ dinnɛdo' nadidolt'as. adoinda atsąnat'aggi bił'ij at'ɛ naldloci at'ɛ bił'ij tc'il tsinnadlɛ bilatagɛ hɛstsi' di biłɛ nɛsdljhɛ inda adił'ał naki didolɣeł. acci ts'idałts'o babɛdadinnił hogɛlahatcitigo. hanadjgo. hawo atdjgo. hwɛgela lą'a citco. ahwɛt'ela ciłhwinlni'. yaik'ą. its'ąila. iyą. yoɛn haidigɛ. djał'oł idjagainiłt'i. k'at dibihandiclagɛ t'abɛhadant'ɛgo inałɛ. k'at niłnicxał lą sitsoi. ako cile bitsiya yitsiłxał djin. ado dadiya djin. hat'alɛ ndaildɛ dandekago nełtsɛ djin. hadɛl'į hadadeya. hadilɣot. dobɛnohozinda. ado binadobinnɛst'ą hadellɛgo dokwiji nakai. kisanɛ tcɛkɛ yisna·la djin. kisanɛ ɛcki yisna·la djin. nacodoł'ijɛ ya ilnindɛi. yitts'ą ngij.

nacoinalnǫdɛ yiłnandɛl. ackiyɛ nadɛlt'az. ał'ij bina binɛdɛstą tsidałtso ila djin. acdɛdilyago. dinnɛ' xadzi hat'ilaba ant'į. nadanhinį'. nahananda. djik'ɛnihinandai nli. la'ą dacdoit'ɛ. al'attso doɣał tsitdɛ dat'a ałładołeł tananniyajdji' nihe 'asa' ni tosdjɛ dat'ɛ dainadjago. ako hadza djin. haɣoci atsa dasnil. ado bąk'idolyago kot'ɛgo assa dɛst'i. ts'in yoiłnes daiditą djin. di bi naką hot'ɛgo nigo axxɛholdjij djin. ado dicį binił nigo axxɛnaholdjij djin. k'at dinnitc'į' hasdzi djinnɛ ladjobaigo la dicdɛnnɛ ninandai nlį dacidonni. hadji yałtigo k'at dosą hwidinni djin. ado dacniya·. t'o nahodannildjigo adacdannidjit. ła' sɛtdi' adjigo· łądad djin. ado dadazdijɛ xaɣannɛ bidji. tohayonłtį'lad djin. bahigɛ' adat'i. ałtso' naztse djin. t'ado binnaxossinda djinnɛ. andɛ tohɛdlingɛyago dabidikɛ djin. adɛyago ałts'ądji' ildɛ totagɛ' toxɛdidlingi yago danabikɛ djin. kwiya ałts'ądji ildɛ toontsosoko ididlįgi dɛgo dana-

was living alone. He came to her they say. "Why did they kill all my
people grandmother?" he said they say.    Woman | "Something will
happen my grandson witchcraft his way witchcraft that man | bear track
who knows turn into coyote who knows how to talk. | His brother's wife
that they kill." "What is its medicine?" "I have medicine for it. There
is what is its medicine. | Its medicine gall bladder lizard blue while alive
girl its belly let her cut open its gall let her take out. | That lizard when
it dies the girl too.   Lizard long one while alive its belly let cut let it die
its gall let take out man too let die quick. | Then hawk its gall that
quadruped that its gall brush tree mistletoe become its flower | break
to pieces this with frozen then ask to help you two let them plant corn.
All bring cooking vessels | will have hard time. Her eyes none. Her teeth
none too. I have hard time." "All right grandmother. | That way you
tell me." He ground corn for her.  He fed her. She ate. Beads he
took off.   Earrings | in her ears he put. "Now the way I am dressed
just that way you will be dressed you will go. Now | I hit you all right
my grandson." Then (?) behind her head he hit her they say. Then he
started away they say.   The singers | they came home every one he
killed they say. They saw him. He chased him. He ran. They did not
know where. | Then that she taught him he prepared, how many years.
Pueblo girl | it seems he captured they say. Pueblo boy it seems he
captured they say.   Blue lizard he caught for her. "Its belly you cut."
    Lizard he caught.  That boy he died. Its gall what she taught him |
all he did they say. He dressed himself. Man spoke, "What you do.
We are sorry for you. | Come back to us. Be our chief you be." All
right I will do that. Something big I ask | just think you will do little
children your pots your water baskets all carrying them along." | Then
they did that they say. ? pots they put. Then for him planting this way
pots | were placed in a line. Stick six feet long he took up they say.
These in vessels he put this way saying he went around (dancing) |
they say.  Then salt I put in saying he danced around they say.  Now
to the people he made a speech they say | *ladjobaigo,* "One I myself your
boss you be you told me."  To them when he spoke, "Now you eat," |
he said to them they say.  Then they began to eat. After a while they
began to itch.  One backward fell. | ? they say.  Then they ran back
their homes to.  They were bad people | they say, warlike they were.
All he killed they say.  Then they couldn't find him again they say.
Then | junction of Las Animas and San Juan they tracked him they say.
Then down stream on both sides they went Farmington | water flows
together below they tracked him they say.  This way both sides they
walked a creek Mancos where it flows in up they tracked him again. |

bidikɛ. ai tontsoko tsɪnnabąs nbidɛtį biyɛgi danidɛ. k'ɪccingonabikɛ.
dɛgo olda· djinɛcdji djɪn. ado t'o dazdɛz'įgo o'ał tsɪdda ałninnaago tsɛ·
yowodjɛ i'agɛ adɛ bidaihiɣał djɪn. tontsosko kwiya iya kodo nazdidjɛ
daznɛsɣal. haiya djɪn. hoɣądą nahoɣał djɪn. bit·ɛldji dobɛxozɪnda.
bitsiyadɛ hildjɛ. binidji' dobɛxozɪnda. ałtc'ɪcdɛ' bini yi'ila yɪctci.
annɛdza djɪn. kaxanidaznizi tse'ya nadaznɛsɣal. hananesdja djɪn.
ako nanatdza djɪn. akwiya annadza. tca· yatsinla djɪn. kodɛ bɛł'a
datsalba djɪn. bikɛ zɪssi djɪn. ładji'do' nazdilt'e djɪn. xaxaa ni djɪn
ndanɛsɪz'ɛ hazlila. t'aci haca. ako bɪnnilta hwodonnit. koho nɪz'ntdzizgo
ł'oł binį'go na ł'oł bɛ bizizł'o'. ako dį djɪlt'ɛgo ałtc'idji biɣan nadzizsit.
hastą djɪlt'ɛ dadjotą'. hwocgij ndjiłk·al bitsi' igij nłnɛ'. bitsi'iya naltal.
bɪnkɛto' dɛzgo'iyɛ. adinsinda naigo·. ado dadildɛ bɪtda hwonniłdilgo
ts'asdzi' itsɛdgo yɛ nana' nala djɪn. hwodji ladjobai at'įgɛ adji nt'i.

That Mancos creek wagon ford below they saw (?). It had rained on the tracks some days before. | Up they walked they slept they say. Then just while they were watching the sun rose just midday rock | beyond where it stands then he climbed down they say. Mancos creek down he went. So far they ran they lay down and watched. | He came up they say. On the hill he turned around they say. His front they couldn't tell. | His hair was cut on top. Where his face was they couldn't tell. Toward both directions his face he had made red. | He started back they say. They thought he went in rock under they lay down again. He came back up again they say. | Then he got back they say. Down stream he went back. Beaver he was digging for they say. Then soles of his feet | were brown they say. His feet they seized they say. Other side too two of them they say. "*xaxaa,*" he said they say. | "Today I die I find it happens. By myself I will come up." "Then let him do it never mind him," he said. So much when they pulled him up | rope half of him rope with they tied him. Then four of them each side his arms they took hold. | Six there were they held him. They cut him in two (?) they split him his head they cut off (?). His head jumped off. | His tears ran down. After that he fell over. Then they started off (?) | soap weeds when they pounded with it he had climbed they say. Here *ladjobai* what he did its end.

## WIZARD STORY

łitsoi tsınnadɛzkɛz łakgan. yıł nakigo ts'iddanɛ' nts'ıztsɛ digɛ' haladɛ at'ɛgo. tinadaxoj. dǫ'nɛ' hojongɛ dįdɛ adolt'o łа dɛst'ogo łakgai dolɛł. ła nadɛst'ogo kodo doł'ij dolɛł ni djın. ła nadolt'o kwi łitsoilɛ. ła nadolt'o. nadanłbai t'a ałt'ahi k'ididolgɛł ni djın. k'at daik'ɛgɛ nildɛ ąłtso'. k'idolya'. ła dolt'ogo doł'ijɛ k'idolya. kwɛ di łitsoi donɛznıłts'izdalα djın. kwɛ daik'ɛ naoldɛgo nadanłtsoi ɑtdın łitsoi i ɑtdın. lu'' łitsoiyɛnnɛ' ɑtdın. łitsoi olgego bik'ɛ bınni'ąlαd djın. ła nadolt'ogo nadanłbai akǫ do' ałtsǫ'' k'idolya doyałtigo. tadaγa djın. yuwɛdo cidonit'. łitsoi ɑtdın cidǫnnit'. k'at bahini' cinıłłi. nalgɛhɛyɛ' yo'ɛ' hat'ila bilɛla nsį'go. k'ɑt baini' cinıłxi. kot'ɛgo tsɛndɛzbala djın. nalgɛhiyɛ' yoɛn ąłtso au ałtsǫ nit'adɛcni. ɛ daki hot'ındɛ ałtso' aładołɛł nixidinnołna dątsɛ. dadαnnoxt'ɛ. ałtso la'la' dajdinni'. kodo dɛjɛj kodo kwott'ɛgo tsidɛzt'i''. yits'a hwonnil kodo nildɛ'. nahǫdadiya ndɛ tsın dajyago tcɛtc'il. tsɛ sa'an bɛł'adɛ konzago xahwisnilla djın. tsɛ' biya da'bitdazdiłtsi'. bąs adɛ. haiigɛ nǫdał'oligɛ nahalɛgo bą nınnilla djın. tc'ɛtc'il ndaz bąs tsaztsi' ałnɛgo. bant'i kwonndilgo. k'ɑt nladɛ nnano'ka. kwi' tsɛ łɛsa'ala djın. binask'ajgo diyɛnɛ' hinaist'ii kwɛya bida' iłdɛł. ninhindɛl. kodo idjınnɛzda' ado atsodɛnilzin taji' nilγat diyɛnɛ' kǫ' ndadiltałgo yahiγał. nats'ıdiya tsɛndɛzba yɛ dɛ tsɛ isdasla djın. adji iya djın. adɛ sonnadilzın yits'a djın. adɛ ayui hahɑst'a djın. iłkɛnaaci xactc'ɛłti' (ınyibitcai) at'ɛhigɛ. kɛt'ɛgo bitsi yinot'ala djın.


nadanłgai dohwonot'ınnɛ la djın. nadanłtsoi dohwonot'ınnɛ yistcį la djın. ɛ nailgɛ nita donni' hałninɛ. hak'i dɛ ɛyui ahwodonniłgo hołnila djın. dici ałkɛnaaci aładɛ haitsigo bik'ɛgo ahwonnıłi yıłila djın. ɛ ya hinot'ąla djın. adɛ hwot'ɛgo dahizį. bidjoni ts'idałt'i dinɛł ałnido sizįla djın. łakgai hwolge. nadą hatc'i daidila. dine co ałaidɛ ndaołtsɛ

WIZARD STORY

Yellow (man's name) was thinking about something. White (man's name) with him being two exactly he killed people there | more than beyond he did. There was a hard time. At *hojon* four places he shot arrows one when he shot | white corn will be. One when he shot again, "So much blue will be," he said they say. One he shot again there | yellow will be. One he shot again. "Brown spotted corn just all kinds will be planted," he said they say. Now | garden place they arrived all. They planted. One bow shot blue they planted. There this | Yellow he had not put they say. There garden they were standing. Yellow corn is not, yellow is not. Lu (prolonged) the yellow | is not. Yellow he being named he was sad about it they say. | One where he had shot brown corn there too all they planted. Not speaking he walked around they say. | "Very bad I have been called. Yellow is dead they said about me. Now grieving to death I am. That property, | beads who will possess it I am thinking. Now I am grieving to death I am." This way (so thinking) they say. | "Property beads all, yes all I divided among you. Those your people live here all come together | I will give you all of it maybe. What do you say about it?" All, "Yes, yes," they said. So much he led them off | so far this way they lined up. From them he selected some. Here they went up. He walked a little way then | stick curved oak. Stone lay there under it so deep when he prized it he dug under it they say. That stone | under he prized. Hoop it was. He took out yucca rope like on it he tied | they say. Oak made into circles soapweed through the center made a line so large (five inches). Now over there | you go. There stones were in a circle (?) they say. Where there was a low place | that he had fastened around (the stone) down over the rim he threw it. It reached the ground. Here there he sat down then he said a prayer. Back he turned. | This one here stepping in the rings he came down. He arrived at the bottom that curved rock there stones lay | they say. There he came they say. Then he prayed they heard they say. Then large he put on a mask | they say. The ones who follow in a pair Talking God the one like. This way his head | he had put in it they say.

White corn perfectly kernelled they say. Yellow corn perfectly kernelled image (?) | they say. "Those goods I will issue you think," he told them. On it there some thing great he would do he told them they say. | This one follows the other one word when he said this way he would do he had they say. | That was why he put it on they say. Then this way he stood. His partner lined up people in middle | he stood they say. "White" he was named. Ears of corn toward him he held up. People stood once more see this |

tsɛbin dodlił. ałnido sizinɛ xadzi łakgai. nakidzadaci hat'i. ałkɛ'naaciyɛ
t'aiyi nɛsago hak'idji bida' tcɛłγot. di tsɛbin ndodlɛlnɛxɛgi'. tsɛbin
ndǫ'haii e aiłnila djɪn. di hadzi nakidzadaci hat'inixɛ'gɛ nakidzadą
ndohaii ahiłnila djɪn. k'idolya'ha' k'asidą nestągo ąłtson nɛsdlita.
k'inadolya di nadą ba'ad siłigo ditci' djɪn. kwigɛ k'inadolya. natcaggi
ałtso dɛiyą. kǫnɛ k'inadolya. t'adohanisada djɪnnɛ. dįdi tc'ɛ k'idolya
niłtsą hwɛ'nį'. nansɛ' 'atdin. hadjiyą' atdin. tsɛbi ndoha nɛhɛdo'
ałtcinnɛ biyayɛ axɛdajnt'igo dadjildɛł. nakidzada nɛxɛdo' xatsit'
nahodɛzti. nakidzadacį' xat'ɛnɛxɛ e 'a' hiłnila djɪn. kwi ada'bidjɪnni.
nadahidjoldelda. adoinda'' dacont nałtin nahasdli'. tc'il binąda
k'inadodɛlya da dɛnɛtagi' ahwottint. e bik'ɛ dinnɛ' ąłtso' hadjina dziłdji'
hojǫgo k'ɛdɛzdiłłego nle niłtsą' dzil na'ągo bits'adɛ to tc'ɛdagogo. k'ɛda-
didle ełɛ xa'nigo ąłtso dziłdji' kodzidza. di łitsoi ts'iddɛzkɛzgi' kodji'
ąłtso. k'addi.

eight will be. In middle one standing he spoke to White. Twelve I guess it is. | That mask he had on from the top down he ran. This eight will be. Eight | years will be that he meant they say. This spoke twelve I guess it is twelve | years will be he meant they say. They planted, nearly it was ripe, all was frozen. | They planted again this corn kernel became burned out they say. Here they planted again. Grasshopper | all eat up. Here they planted again. It didn't come up they say. Four times in vain they planted. | Rain was not. Vegetation was none. Their food was none. Eight years from that year | children their young they stole from each other they ate them. Twelve from that year a little better | it became. Twelve summers (?) that year that he meant they say. This he mentioned. They ate (?) each other. | Then it rained it happened again. Vegetation its seeds | they planted again at Navajo country it happened. That one their leader people all moved away to the mountain | a good place they planted corn he rain (?) mountain lies from it water runs down. | We will plant saying all to the mountains they moved. This Yellow he thought this | that's all.

## Game Story

bąs be dak'atts'os ts'idde be xaɣan ayoi ahwot'e nt'e ąłtso xawozba'.
hadjekę' dabiyo'ę ąłtso xanehezba. binina haze'dest'a djɩn. tadeldja
hwolge djɩn. hwonnige' daidenil djɩnne. xatda' hwołholne aidį nanedo'-
bɩnł djɩnne cit'ai. ląą citda'. yołgaiyeene doł'ijyeenne ditcɩłe tsełtci
bacine asdlago bitts'ajninnil djɩn. destci· djɩn. tadadɩn doł'ij djɩn.
tadɩtdin te'l bitadɩtdin ado dacdiya djɩn. tseł'agone' nadą hadezbin
axidadɩttągo acdlago bits'a djɩnnitnel djɩn. e 'ałtso· axanbɩcbi·kad. djo·
sɩzze' destala. citda' naxidiltseł dats'e. cimayaji halane'. 'ę ado ts'in
adɩł tadjota djɩn. hołni'el djɩnne. tontel bitc'ide tontel lįdi ts'ittsadjiya
djɩn. tajdaɣą yiye djɩn. nadą dałai na'annego atdatdziz'ą djɩn. ałna
bidi'ą bidadidjil djɩn. nakidzadago ałna' bidadidjil djɩnne.


yalado· dists'ai nadątco nakidzadago ałna bidi'ago dists'ą. dziłdiłxił
bik'aɣe ałna bidi'ago dists'a. tc'illataxojon ałna bidi'ago dists'ą' dintc'e
baką bize' sinosiñdo' dists'ą. akwi dį· xwonaxai dį naxaiyįgo nixe-
dzitdza. dakwiincą' hwiską a·bingo nadzitdza djɩn. tc'inask'it xwolgegi
ndzitdza djɩn. abɩngo ndzitzago nadą' annegone' tcįdiįnde łai'nde·
dosa'ada nadą dįgo akǫne andjonil. dįdi dzissoł adonda xadjekę bantsi·
dza. hadjekę· sɩtdala djɩn. ditcį silį sɩttsą' i'ilį cimayaji djini djɩn. atdį.
dadinniya. ado dįda yiskago nadą dobehozinda at'ed xadjiniye djɩn.
tc'ał ts'innezda djɩn. t'ado nsą ocłeda cit'ai djɩnni djɩn. dɩnnęį ła nandja.
t'adoatdinnine djɩnni djɩn. atdɩn cit'ai. ałtc'įtdji dįdi axicdonni.
t'ett'e akǫ dadeya. ade'· xadebįla. citdai axxe e biłxojongo ndan bits'in-
naindja djɩnne. at'ede dadilɣot' citdai natdza. nadądo' xadadebinla.
ade biłxadjɩtdje' yahɩtdje. haląne dałnigo hazedatcįgo ndandannel kałła
daxałnigo t'aɣannidi nehet'i na'· sits'ili yalabinnige yadannahizdɩn'nido'.
dɩnni'ennę tc'e bika det'i. xadjici silį'. hat'edjidoleł. ts'inizį djɩn.
tc'e ndjildjego dacinnelą· yiska djɩn. tc'inesgit bida xadjiyadet'ande'
akǫ bį sizid djɩn. kwot'ego tsexent'i kǫdet'au najdilɣot' bandjin'na'
nt'e bį xet'i 'atdin. tc'e heatidjitait (?) dadoni'xasdiłda. yiskanne

## GAME STORY

Hoop with dice seven with his house very good it was all he lost.
His niece her beads all he lost. | Because of that they were going to kill
him they say. Necklace of mixed beads | was called they say. In center
of the house they were hanging they say. His niece her uncle she told
him, "This you will lose," | she said, "my uncle." "All right, my niece."
Those white shell beads those turquoise, abalone, coral, | jet, five he took
one by one they say. Iron ore they say. Pollen blue, they say. | Pollen
water reed its pollen then he walked on they say. Corn pits corn full | of
mixed colors five from he took they say. That all he patted together.
"Well, | kill me they talk about. My niece we see each other again it
may be. My small mother goodbye." Then tree | with himself he put in
water they say. It floated with him they say. Colorado river toward it
ocean where it flows he got out | they say. He walked along the beach
lonesome they say. Corn one hill where he planted cross (?) | he put
one by one they say. On either side | its ear projects they say. Twelve
of them on either side ears are they say.

I hear large corn twelve on either side being ears I hear. Mountain
black | on it on either side its ears I hear. Flowers on either side being
ears I hear. | Deer male I kill, he will like me I hear. There four years
after he returned home. | Unknown number days passed early morning he
returned they say. *tc'inask'it* where it is called | he arrived home they say.
Early when he arrived corn its pits (he looked) but one | does not lie there.
Corn four inside he put. Four times he blew then his niece he came to. |
His niece he found sitting there they say. Famine had become. "My food
prepare, my niece," he said they say. "Is none. | You went away. Then
four days were corn I don't know," girl said to him they say. | She cried
she sat there they say. "Not you food I cook, my uncle," she said they
say. "You look, some bring." | "Do not say that," she said they say.
"None, none, my uncle." Toward each side four times they said to each
other. | It was then when she walked away. It was full she found. "My
uncle thanks," being joyful | corn she brought they say. Girl ran "My
uncle has come back. Corn too, I find is full." | Then his brothers came
in. Greetings saying around his neck they put their arms | saying, "You
only you are my younger brother in the future we will not say bad things. |
The game animals in vain after we hunt." Something happened. "What
is to be done." "He thinks they say. | In vain while he hunted many days
passed they say. *tc'inesgit* its top when he walked | the deer stood they say.
That my cliff this way he ran around. He had crept up | to it when deer that
was it was gone. In vain he looked not earth was disturbed. Next day |

xanadzizdza andε bį nanεzį' djin ado bitc'į nihijni.    ya tcε djinnił'įgo
t'ą'ądji asdįnt djin.    andε' bį bitcan sa'a djin.    e at'ila djin.    kodo sizįgo
tc'o' adaz'aha.    acą' k'adja' xactc'εłti att'ila djin.    xwhoooo ni djin.
ba'jdiγalnt'ε kodε' xactc'εłti sizzį djin.    xat'ila sitsoi?    xałni djin.    adi
kodji bį'ε sizįdε asdint bidjinε.    dai yołgai hwilǫ sitsoi.    t'a'ałtso hwilǫ
citc'ai t'a'ałtso hwillǫla.    sitsoi adonniłla sitsoi.    tcąłxεł bidadinlala
djin xayołkał bidadinlala djin.    ł'εhona'ai bida'dinlala djin djohona'ai
bida'dinlala djin.    xactc'εłti xactc'εjinnε yił ałdadε sikεla djin.
wεhεnε' sitsoi.


akǫnε nicnadji dadidilεs dįdi yisołgo danaka silį djin.    xactc'εłti
bilįla djin.    ya'a nayonilla djin.    xodists'ąla djin.    yonigo ho noxoka
dinnε xactc'ą.    xast'i bahwit'i.    k'at nohoka dinnε yił hiłγałnε.    t'ado
atdo noninε.    t'ałtso hwillo djinnε.    yunigε' dintc'ε bakką' atsεbεst'an
bεk'az bidastcigo bit'ajdjigo dasit'a djin.    annit'da' ba'xaxasdozli.
hwoniłdo' ts'innεsda djin.    yołgaiyε nijna'a djin.    doł'ij nijna'a djin.
tsεłtsi ditciłido bacinε dεstcido' taditdin doł'ij taditdin tεłbaxaditdin
bik'iilkat.    dįdi yaxatis dεyago kogo dadats'os silį djin.    baxwonnε'go
nts'itts'εkεz (ts'izεskεz).    doizinda sitsoi bik'ε nahwoditdiljon.    k'atc'ą'
dįngi yiskago at'εla djin.    dinnε bεγa gonε' la djin nł'iz dεsni'.
acdlaadągo dεsni' tadzada silį nahast'ai sostsit acdla ta k'at di ąłtso
adji nasni'.    xactc'εłti xactc'εjinnε ąłtso' bεniłna.    hwot'εgo nal'ądo
xwodonit'.    kǫ axadalwodlε bitsit' abant'igo bįtcįn abahεdjitdjingo.
binayaγε xojogo xaxaldzonlε.    t'adobaγagεci.    bilij do'badiγatdjigεcda.
t'adjigo bakaγε bikεnastido'.    kodε' dinε' sozsalε, bitsi'ts'in yunidjigo
bitsigo yit'εsdo bina dodillidallε.    bowodo' dodillidallε.    inda dołεstci
binnatago yit'εsdalla.    dobεlkwidalla dinni'i sittsoi.    nle kajdjε'.    e di
xawo' dadillidε hwołndanεłγa noxokadinnε xannidjin.    xacdedεlε sitsoi
xałni djin.    ałtso xact'εdjila.    adji' ałtso' xact'εdjila.    xat'i xaniya sitsoi?
nle axεnzinnεgε ąłtso dinnε' yεstcin dede tct'ε xałdjinnε niłtc'ibiyajε

he went up again then deer stood again they say then to it he walked.
Not looking where it had been | it was gone they say. Then deer its
dung lay there they say. That was it they say. So far from where he
stood | spruce stood. Now *xactc'ɛlti* it was they say. "Xwhoooo," he
said they say. | "When he looked around at him there *xactc'ɛlti* stood they
say. "What is it, my grandchild?" he said to him, they say. "Then |
here deer that stood it has vanished," he said to him. "White Shell you
have my grandson." "Just all I have | my grandfather. Everything I
have." "My grandson, we will do it, my grandson." Darkness he found
his door post | they say. Dawn he found his door post they say. Moon
he found his door post they say. Sun | he found his door post they say.
*xactc'ɛlti xactc'ɛjinne* with facing each other he found they sat they say. |
"Begin, my grandson."

  Here right side he stepped, four times when he blew footprints (?)
became they say *xactc'ɛlti* | he found he had a pet they say. He had taken
them inside he found they say. He heard a noise they say. Way inside
"Ho, earth | people I smell." Polite man he brings guests. Now earth
people with he brings. Not say | that. All he has he said. Behind the
fire deer male feathered arrow | his arrow being red back end to lay on
him they say. Recently for him he had pulled it out. | In the center he
sat down they say. White Shell he put down they say. Turquoise he
put down they say. | Red stone abalone too, jet too, iron ore too, pollen,
blue pollen, water reed pollen | over them he spread a blanket. Four
times over them when he stepped so much a pile it became they say.
Sorrowful | he felt. "I do not think, my grandson in return for it we will
give you enough." Surprise | four days being he found it was they say.
Game animals their house inside it was he found they say. Jewels he
distributed. | Fifteen apiece, he distributed, thirteen became nine, seven,
five, three, now this all | he had distributed. *xactc'ɛlti, xactc'ɛdjinne* all
they distributed. "This way it will be skinned," | he told him. "Here
(wrist joint) break it apart its sinew let hold it. Its nose (lips) leave
skin on. | Under its eyes carefully pull them out. Do not cut through.
Its bladder do not cut through. | Toward the rear its hide will lie on.
So, game kill all the time. Its head toward the center | its nose, cook
roast, its eyes do not burn. Its teeth too do not burn. And not ashes |
putting around it you cook it. Do not throw away the game animals my
grandson. There it | lies sickness. That this his teeth if were burned
they will hurt him. You earth people tell about it. They make well, my
grandson," | he said to him they say. All he made well (?). There all
he fixed again. "What you come for, my grandson?" | There they stand
side by side. All game images (?) they are," he told him, small whirlwind. |

nle xa'adε abidε konε sị holọ.  bik'ijdilni djịn.  yatsą djịn lą sịttsoi hai niyaγala· ni djịn.

xaniya xactc'εlti niclingo xaniya dεntc'ε ba·γanlagi.

xaniya xactc'ałγεł dadinlagε.

xaniya xayołkał dadinlagε.

xaniya łʼεna'ai dadinlagε.

xaniya djuhona'ai dadinlagε.

xaniya xactc'εlti xactc'εjin yił ałdacdε sikεdji nilaγε.

xaniya ałtin dịłxịł atsεbεst'an bik·az bidactcigo ałbił ałdε na sila.

yuwεdji dεntc'ε bika bizadił xatcigo bił ałdεlnasila.

yowodji' bizε sinosi.

bin dałai dindi dzągεgo holonli.    tc'ε hεct'i tsinizị djịnnε.    didi bε' tsịnsdazi bisdissi xwodonnit'.    tsąñaladi holon.


k'a xactc'εlti ciniclinεgo.  dzịł dịłxịł bika dantindε tc'illεtaxajon bitadi dạntindε dεntc'ε biką holọ, tcil xadịtdin bizε· naiilε.  tc'il bidato yidiłis dεntc'ε biką bizε sinosin dzaiala di holon.  tsịnzdązi bihidissi k'a' yił tsịnnamaz bị dastc'il bị hidistsi' biyactcint' k'a yił tsịnnamaz.  tcidą' bihidzissi bikọ' k'a yił tsịnnamaz.  tcidanłtsissigε bihidzistsi' tc·atalgai k'a yił tsịnnamaz.

adji' yuwε cεyit'int tsinzεgo t'andjiltεndε. 'ałtso nahidildjεla djịn. e ba biłacdildo' nt'i nahidika yohika t'ohaiyui singo αt'ε dinnεdji' sịn. dobεxotsịnsịngo dondjildjεda.  nixi bεneltsit got'ε.  xactc'εlti bili' e bą abaxadzịt.  k'αddi.

There east side paunch in songs are. He pointed to them they say. "All right, my grandson those | you came for," he said they say.

I came up, *xactc'ɛlti*, I being, I came up to the abode of the deer

I came for darkness where are the door posts.

I came for dawn, where are the door posts

I came for moon, where are the door posts.

I came for sun, where are the door posts

I came for *xactc'ɛlti xactc'ɛdjin* with facing each other where they two sat ?

I came for bow black, feathered arrows his shaft being red with crossing each other they lie.

Over there deer male his mouth blood red with across each other they lie.

Over there I kill it he likes me.

Deer just one he sang (?) (were four of them). "Here is where they are. In vain I hunted them," he thought they say. This | with brush shooting he told him. Here they are.

Now *xactc'ɛlti* I being. Black mountain its top trail up from flowers | among from its trail deer male there are. Herbs its pollen its mouth put in. Herbs | its dew he washes in, deer male I kill he likes me? they are. Brush | he shot in arrow with deer rolls deer brush he shoots in fawn arrow | with it rolls over. Brush he shoots in yearling arrow with it rolls over. Brush | he shoots in yearling arrow with he rolls over.

Here something big I did when he thought he ran back. All he killed | they say. That because they get away when they get well (?) very many songs there are. | Game songs if one doesn't know he doesn't hunt. We are afraid that way. *xactc'ɛlti* his pets those | because we are afraid. All finished.

## THE CREATION OF THE HORSE

bik'i ilkad djɪn. daihidɛzna djɪn. adadinnit djɪn. t'ałaigo nadidji.
nakii idaci ałtsą bahidɛ idɛ bik'idizo. łị· daidɛznaz djɪn. atdadịnit
djɪnnɛ. xadjiłt'i djɪn. disɪttsa'ą.

asdzanadlɛ cincłigo disitts'ą
caxoγan ya'ałnigi disɪtts'ą
nł'iz bazt'e'l bikaγɛ ts'idda bik'igɛ di·sitts'ą
bacinɛ ts'ą' bacinɛ 'łị ts'idda bigigɛ k'at bił silla.
tc'il bidat'o ts'idda bigigɛ bił silla.
ts'iddai gijt'ɛ kɛ'ąn.
ndiljij dǫ dinnɛ k'a biłsilla bigi silla
haxonniγɛ' bikɛ ɑlya djɪn.
e bą bikɛ nodǫz djɪn.
nadzillit bigal ɑlya.

cabitł'ol bizat'igo ɑlya· ɑnda tots'aiiłtci bidji ɑlya djɪn. to łanactci·n
bitci· ɑlya ɑnda nɪłts'a nadjin bitsɛ' ɑlya. yɑn nɪłtcin bitsiγa ɑlya. hadjɪl-
gic bidja ɑlya. son'ts'o dɛsya bina' ɑlya t'ae bɛ bit'a ndzokaigo ɑlya. bita'
hwisgaigo ɑlya. ł'ɛgo bɛ billadji ditdlat. biniγɛ· nɑnsɛ' bini' ɑlya. yotso
bidɑ·' ɑlya. yołgai biwo ɑlya e dodizyacda hwodont'ni·t djɪn. łị dilni·
dɪłxił yɛennillɛ. xayołkał bibit ɑlya ładji' k'itłakgai ładji' łijɪnnɛ' gądji
łakgai olgɛ. yołgai ts'a bɛnika djɪn. atc'itto nastcin hwolgɛ bɛnika djɪn.
doł'ijɛ ts'ą bɛnika djɪn. atcito nika ditcɪłi ts'ą 'ąγɛnji nastcin bɛnika
djɪn. bacinɛ ts'ą aγɛnji nastcin bɛnika djɪn. dikodo yołgai ts'ą doł'ijɛ
ts'ą di nakigo naldloci bɛ bɑnnika djɪn. ditcɪłi ts'ą bacinɛ ts'ą
aiγɛnji nastcin bɛnika ai nat'ɑggi noxonlịdji' hɑnnika.

kodo k'ɑt adɛdɛsta djɪn. kodɛ denno·t' aładɛ ła' naikiddɛ denno·t' e
bą łị' łat'a naki idołtcił djɪnnɛ. kodɛ ła nadesdza djɪn t'ado siznodɛ k'ɛ'ą.
hadjolgo·t'. nadɛsdza djɪn. abitc'indo k'ɛą hanadjolgot' djɪn. naz-
dɛsdza djɪn. k'ɛą hanadjolgo·t' djɪn. naałdo' nadɛzdza djɪn. c· ni djɪn.
ni·i yaltal djɪn. dodɪłtcɪłda. djanɛs yinłγɛlɛ hwodon'ni·t' djɪn. kodjɛ
aγɛnji nastcin bɛsakɑnnɛ łądɛ dezno djɪn. nat'ai dinnɛ e bą dats'izł'ɛ
djɪn ditcɪłɛ bacinnɛ ts'ą bi datziznot' e bą ła dadɛzdɪłxił.

## THE CREATION OF THE HORSE

On them it was spread they say.  It moved became alive, they say.
He whinnied, they say.  Of one sort the songs are. | Two first and last
these you write.  Horse moved they say.  It whinnied | they say.  She
began to sing, they say.  This she hears.

> *esdzanadle* I am, I hear
> My house in the center behind fire I hear
> Jewels spread wide on it sitting on I hear
> Jet basket, jet house there in it now with it it lies.
> Vegetation its dew there in it with it lies.
> Over there come ? more.
> It increases the house now with it it lies, inside it lies,
> Mirage his feet are made they say.
> That because its feet have stripes they say.
> Rainbow his gait was made.

Sun strings its bridle is made and red stone its heart is made they
say.  Water all kinds its intestines | is made and rain black its tail was
made.  Cloud with little rain its mane is made.  Distant lightning | its
ears are made.  Big star spreading twinkling its eyes are made just
that with its face white striped is made.  Its lower legs | white are made.
At night with in front of it it gives light.  Because of that vegetation its
face was made.  Large beads | its lips were made.  White shell its teeth
are made those not wear out quickly they said they say.  Horse trumpet |
(flute) black was put in.  Dawn its belly was made, one side white one
side black.  Half white | it is named.  White shell basket stands they say.
Water of afterbirth from mare it is called is in it they say. | Turquoise
basket stands they say.  Afterbirth water stands abalone basket eggs
different places stand in it | they say.  Jet basket eggs from different places
stand they say.  This many white shell basket, turquoise | basket these
two quadrupeds with it stands for they say.  Abalone basket, jet basket |
eggs from many places stand in it these birds all it stands for.

So now she began to sing they say.  Here taste once some twice
tasted that | because horse sometimes two will give birth to they say.
Here one ran back they say not tasting | he ran back.  He went again
they say.  He stopped he ran back they say.  He came again they say. |
He ran back they say.  Once again he came they say.  "Sh!" he said
they say. | He walked back they say.  "She won't give birth.  Long ears
you will be called," she said they say.  Here | eggs from many places that
stood in baskets many times he tasted they say.  Feathered people that
because (?) | abalone jet basket in they taste that because some are black.

## WANDERINGS OF THE NAVAJO

tala dadigaindɛ tc'aɫtcinnɛ ndiddo'ɫt'inɫ xwɛdjinni djin. nixaniɣɛ'
xactc'ɛɫti nixaniɣɛ xactc'ɛoɣan e axwodjinni djin. ado' dɑndilde djin.
yoɫgai dzil dasitt'a djin. doɫ'ijɛ dzil dasitt'a djin. ditcili dzil dasitta
djin. bacinnɛ dzil dasitta djin. yoɫgai dzil bilatadji' dadildego adjinni
djin. xazdi'ą djin. xactc'ɛɫti yoɫgai dzil bilataɣɛ dahasdego. halan
nzadɛ (hanil asdɛ) hadzil

sisnadjinnɛ e bidjinnɛ
sisnadjinnɛ ha'a.
yoɫgai dzil ha'a
dziɫ nandai ha'a.
sa'anaɣai ha'a.
bikɛhojon ha'a
halonlacdɛ ha'a.
tsodziɫ ha'a.
doɫ'ijɛ dzil ha'a.
dziɫ nand'ai ha'a.
sa'annaɣai ha'a.
bikɛhojon ha'a.
halannzacdɛ la ha'a.
doɣoosli'd ha'a.
ditciɫɛ dzil ha'a.
dziɫnand'ai ha'a.
sa'annaɣai ha'a.
bikɛhojon ha'a.
halonlocdila ha'a.
dɛbɛntsa' ha'a.
bacinnɛ dzil ha'a.
dziɫ nand'ai ha'a.
sa'an naɣai ha'a.
bikɛxojon ha'a.
holonnɛlo'cdɛla ha'ɛ
dziɫna'odiɫɛ ha'a.
yoditdzil ha'a.
dziɫ nand'ai ha'a.
sa'annaɣai ha'a.
bikɛhojon ha'a.
halonlocdɛla ha'a.
tcol'į ha'a.

## Wanderings of the Navajo

My children go back to look she told them they say. Mirage |
*xactc'elti,* mirage *xactc'e'oγan* those she told they say. Then they started
back they say. | White Shell mountain it lies they say. Turquoise moun-
tain it lies they say. Abalone mountain it lies | they say. Jet mountain
lies they say. White Shell mountain on its top when they come he spoke |
they say. We begin to sing they say. *xactc'elti* White Shell mountain
its top when they come. | Greetings way off stick up | *sisnadjinne* that
they sing about |

> *sisnadjinne* sticks up.
> White Shell mountain sticks up.
> Mountain peak sticks up.
> Old age sticks up.
> Good fortune sticks up.
> Greetings way off stick up.
> Mount Taylor sticks up.
> Turquoise mountain sticks up.
> Mountain peak sticks up.
> Old age sticks up.
> Good fortune sticks up.
> Greeting far away sticks up.
> San Francisco sticks up.
> Abalone mountain sticks up.
> Mountain peak sticks up.
> Old age sticks up.
> Good fortune sticks up.
> Greetings far away stick up.
> La Plata sticks up.
> Jet mountain sticks up.
> Mountain peak sticks up.
> Old age sticks up.
> Good fortune sticks up.
> Greeting far away sticks up.
> Huerfano sticks up.
> Soft goods mountain sticks up.
> Mountain peak sticks up.
> Old age sticks up.
> Good fortune sticks up.
> Trail of Beauty far away sticks up.
> *tc'ol'i* sticks up.

k'at dzil djoli ha'a.
nł'ij dzil ha'a.
dził nand'ai ha'a.
sa'annaγai ha'a.
bikɛhojon ha'a.
halanlo·cdɛla ha'a.
bits'ɪddji hojon ha'a.
bikɛdɛ hojon ha'a.
biyaγɛ hojon ha'a.
bik'iγi hojon ha'a.
cɪnna·t'ałtso hojon ha'a.
halonlocdɛla ha'a.
iyai i haha'a ha'a·heyo.
dził ałai dasɪttan bilatadji dahasde''.
nadzillit bɛ· doł'ijɛ dzil ǫ bilatadji danasdɛ.
iladɛ nijonnigo hadjil
nijonnigo ha'a.
k'at k'anniłnijoni ha'a.
ditcił djil bilatadji' danadilde
ɑnda at'ɛ bitsigo hit'i silị' djɪnnɛ.
djokǫn t'abi at'ɛ t'a diγingo ha'a.
k'anniłdiγingo ha'a.
kodji danadilde.
bacɪnnɛ djil bilatadji' nixinaildɛ.
nlela k'at bitc'ɪnndikai
djokon t'abit'ɛ sɪsnadjɪnnɛ bidjɪn'diyaihi
xactc'ɛłti. cɪnnɪcłigo bitc'ɪndiya.
sɪsnadjɪnnɛ bitc'ɪn diya.
yołgai dzil bitc'ɪn diya.
dził nand'ai bitc'ɪ diya.
sa'annaγai bikɛxojon bitc'ɪ diya bitc'ɪ' diyaiyɛ.
xactc'ɛyałti k'ac cɪnnɪcłigo bitc'ɪn diya.
tsodził bitc'ɪn diya
dził nand'ai bitc'ɪn diya.
sa'ąanaγai bikɛhojon bitc'ị' diya. bitc'ɪn diya·yɛ bitc'ɪn'diya.
xactc'ɛłti cɪnnɪcłigo bitc'ị' diya.
daγo'osłid bitc'ɪ' diya.
ditcɪłɛ dzil bitc'ị' diya.
dził nand'ai bitc'ị' diya.
sa'annaγai bikɛhojon bitc'ị' diya. bitc'ɪn diyaiyɛ.

Now mountain round sticks up.
Jewels mountain sticks up.
Mountain peak sticks up.
Old age sticks up.
Good fortune sticks up.
Trail of Beauty far away sticks up.
Before good sticks up.
Behind good sticks up.
Under good sticks up,
Above good sticks up.
All around me good sticks up.
Greetings far away stick up
Refrain
Mountain one lies its top they stepped on.
Rainbow with turquoise mountain its top they came.
Way there beautifully it sticks up.
Beautifully it sticks up.
Now now with you it sticks up
Abalone mountain on its top they alighted.
Now its hind foot is seen it happens they say.
See that one it is very holy sticks up.
Now holy with you it sticks up.
Here they came.
Jet mountain its top they arrived.
That now to it we (pl.) go
Look just that, *sisnadjinnε* the one I go to.
*xactc'εlti* I being to it I go.
*sisnadjinnε* to it I go.
White Shell mountain to it I go.
Mountain peak to it I go.
Old age good fortune to it I go, to it I go.
*xactc'εlti* I being to it I go.
Mount Taylor to it I go.
Mountain peak to it I go.
Old age, good fortune to it I go, to it I go to it I go.
*xactc'εlti* I being to it I go.
San Francisco peaks to it I go.
Abalone mountain to it I go.
Mountain peak to it I go.
Old age, good fortune to it I go, to it I go.

xactc'ɛti ciniclịgo bitc'ɩn diya.
dɛbɛntsạ bitc'ị' diya.
bacinnɛ dzil bitc'ị' diya.
dziɫ nand'ai bitc'ị' diya.
sa'annaɣai bikɛhojon bitc'ị' diya. bitc'ɩn diyaiyɛ
xactc'ɛti cinnicɫi bitc'ị diya.
dziɫnah'odiɫi bitc'ị' diya.
yoditdzil bitc'ị' diya.
dziɫ nand'ai bitc'ɩn diya.
sa'annaɣai bik'ɛhojon bitc'ɩn diya. bitc'ɩn diyaiyɛ
xactc'ɛti cinniclịgo bitc'ị' diya.
tc'ol'ị bitc'ị' diya.
nɫ'iz dzil bitc'ị' diya.
dziɫ nand'ai bitc'ɩn diya.
sa'annaɣai bik'ɛhojon bitc'ɩn diya.
bitc'ɩn diyaiyɛ. bitc'ɩn diyaiyɛ
sits'iddji' hojon.
cikɛcdi hojon.
ciyaɣɛ hojon.
cik'iɣi hojongo
cinadɛ aɫtso hojongo
bitc'ị' diyaiyɛ
sizatdɛ hojongo bitc'ɩn' diyahiyi bitc'ɩn diyaheya
'adji dziɫ diɛnnɛ aɫtso biba
dosdɛ' biya oldɛ
dziɫ baniyahi
sisnadjɩn bilatagi' nhildɛ' bik'iiyahi.
tsodziɫ bilatadji nixinaildɛ'.
ciɫdɛnilahɛ. ciɫdɛnɛlahɛ
doɣo'oslid bilatadji' nixi naildɛ'
k'at nadɛsdzahi
dɛbɛntsa bilatadji nixinaildɛ.
k'anaisdaɫ k'annaisdaɫ
dziɫna'odiɫɛ bilatadji' nixinaildɛ'.
tc'ol'i bilatadji' nixinaildɛ'
bananisdzahi naildɛ.
yoɫgai isdza bạdɛ k'ananacdahi.

*xactc'ɛlti* I being, to it I go.

La Plata Mountain to it I go.

Jet mountain to it I go.

Mountain peak stands upright to it I go.

Old age, good fortune to it I go, to it I go

*xactc'ɛlti* I being, to it I go.

Huerfano to it I go.

Soft Goods mountain to it I go.

Mountain peak to it I go.

Old age, good fortune to it I go, to it I go.

*xactc'ɛlti* I being, to it I go.

*tc'oli* to it I go.

Jewels Mountain to it I go.

Mountain peaks to it I go.

Old age good fortune to it I go.

To it I go.

To it I go

Before me good

Behind me good.

Below me good.

Above me good

All around me good

Toward it I go |

My speech good

To it I go

These mountains those four all they pass.

Under it they pass

Mountain the one I come to.

*sisnadjinnɛ* its top we get on the one I come to.

Mount Taylor its top we arrive.

With me it lies well, with me it lies well.

San Francisco peaks its top we arrive

Now I start back

La Plata mountain its top we arrive.

Now I am coming back, now I am coming back

Huerfano its top we arrive.

*tc'oli* its top we arrive

The one I came back to we arrive

White Shell Woman shore on I sit.

dakohodela? yahot'ego haz'ala k'at yahot'ego haz'ala tcaɫtcin
ni djin. yoɫgai asdzą tc'illatahojon adasallɛ tobitdzilgo hadazlilɛ.
haḷ'ągo biinallɛ caɫtcin ni djin. kodji dziɫ na'agɛ' yoditdzil
niɫts'ą dzil nɫ'iz dzil tadɨtdɨn dzil holge'go na'ado. nokadɨnnɛ
aɫts'adji' hil'ąlɛ. k'at di yoɫgai dzil na'ai bigigɛ. niɫtc'i disǫns atsąbiyaz
binigo ndi niłɛ ndi'nido. nansɛ' hidiɫnalɛ, niɫtc'idisons adiɫnaγɛ. tc'il
bitc'i' daditdisǫnslɛ. doɫ'ijɛdzil dasittannɛ bigiγɛ niɫtc'i doɫ'ij adiɫnalɛ.
tc'il doɫ'ij hit'inlɛ. dolɛɫ ditciłɛ dzil dasittannɛ bigigɛ niɫtc'idiɫxiɫ nansɛ'hi
diɫnatɫ'ɛ. tc'il diɫxiɫgo adasalɛ. bacinnɛdzil dasittannɛgɛ niɫtc'i łitso·
yidiɫnalɛ. tc'illatajon hidiɫna haγɛ' ła' daɫtcigo ła' daɫgaigo ła' dadoɫ'ijgo
bilata aɫta ahwot'elɛ. kodji' dįdi ndi'nido. sitdatsɛ' ndi ni'hiγɛ cac
ts'edadzitdzidlɛ. hatcą bɛ ndadjildehiγi. adadɛzk'ąnslɛ. tc'act'ɛzɛ
atsɛ' haznesłɛ e hanɛ' nadji'alɛ 'adɛ aɫtsǫ nadadɛsdɛ' tcinnilɛ. akwɛ
nat'aγɛ doli dɛbɛni tsico' hasbiddɛ dɛɫ aɫtsǫ nadjikalɛ.

yoɫgai yik'ą djin nadą axɛditągo biɫ yik'a djin. hwɛt'ɛgo yisdiz
bidjegɛ. hwonniɫsaza nanit'e djin. k'os diɫxiɫ biɫ yisdis djin. dįdɛ yitis
deya djin. cini doda. e bi nɛ'hincna cini biɫ nct'ɛ. ndilde djin t'a dinnɛgo.
cada'ą bitc'į'dji'go dado·ka sitsokɛ hałni djin. 'adjɛ sittsokɛ ła' nahastą
hałni djin. k'acą' dinnɛ nakidzada nakai ahiɫnilɛ djin. di to hinigini
ababągɛ adji hoγan akwi aɫtcinnɛ dahazlį djin. t'a nezdali djin taba
hondanɛ toilko·łgo yoɫgai biɫ sits'alkoɫ indɛlago yɛndanɛ. dinnɛ nakidzada
nakai. hako hidinnɛla djin. e di sittsokɛ akǫ ekaigɛ yoɫgai sittsa'ą ndela.
bacini' at'ɛ. citdąt'ɛ t'ado datindo banictci' yidinilad djin. t'a yogoigɛ
dziɫdiɫxiɫ bitsįngi nitco nhiɫnɛ edɛ yoɫgai bacinnidɛ. cidą't'ɛ t'ado ndelailɛ.
t'aiyogohigɛ nahaztalɛ dziɫxiɫdiɫ bitsingɛ nį'hiɫni nhitco. dinnɛ nakidzada
nakai nigo nadza djin. ako adji nilde. dziɫ tcałγɛɫ holge djin. cac kǫniɫ-
tsogo handilt'i djin. halinlɛgo djin. hatco'· binnibik'ɛ gola djin. dziɫłitsoi

"How is it over there?" "Beautiful it is, now beautiful it is, my children," | she says they say. White Shell Woman flowers spread everywhere water strong will flow up. | "Hereafter they will live with it, my children," she said they say. Here mountain lies horizontal. Soft goods mountain, | rain mountain, jewels mountain, pollen mountain being called named it will lie. Navajo | on both sides (Navajo mountain) will be many. Now thus White Shell mountain lies inside of it. Wind spotted eagle young | month thunder first makes a noise. Vegetation will come to life move. Wind spotted will move with itself. Vegetation | toward will be spotted. Turquoise mountain one that lies inside wind blue makes it move. | Vegetation blue will appear. Abalone mountain one lying inside of it wind black vegetation | will come to life. Vegetation black can be seen. Jet mountain one that lies wind yellow | will make come to life. Flowers will wake up there some will be red some white some blue | flowers all kinds will be seen. Here four times it will thunder. First its thunder bear | will wake up. His belly with he travels. He will stretch himself. A plant | first comes up that the news will carry back. "Now all come," he will tell. Then | birds blue, Say's phoebe, buzzard, dove, crane all will come.

White shell she ground up they say corn mixed colors with she ground they say. This way she rubbed | her breast. This size (match stick) fell down they say. Cloud dark with she rolled it they say. Four times over it | she stepped they say. The song not. That with I live, songs with I am. They got up they say just like persons. | "South toward go my grandchildren," she said to them they say. "There my grandchildren some live," | she told them they say. Besides (?) people twelve live she meant they say. This water ocean | along the shore there hogan, there children they became they say. (?) they say. On the shore | they played when the waves came White Shell which the waves left then they played with them. Persons twelve | live. "Come," they sent word they say. "These, my grandchildren, there those where they went white shell from me they pick up. | I like to have it is. My corn my food not they will do that I like to have it," they found she said they say. Just beyond | Black Mountain near your grandmother tells you, "Those white shells I like. My corn it is, not pick it up." | Just beyond a little further "You will live Black Mountain near," she told you your grandmother. Persons twelve | live saying returned they say. Then there they moved. Mountain darkness called they say. Bear so large | they picked up they say. It was their pet they say. Their grandmother according to her plan it was they say. Mountain yellow |

holgɛdo˙ nɑcdetso nadɛsdiłti (najdiłti) djin. hatco' binibik'ɛgo cac alilɛ
neya djin. nɛsdoitso alilɛ neya djin. ała bikąla djin. dį yiską djin.
dį binaxai sili djin. dinnɛ nakidzada nakai hago nabidǫnni't la djin.
ako niya djin. ai sittsokɛ iczłagɛ do kwɛbinihɛ'. iczłada nixitco˙ hogo
nixinizłni. bąni djolgɛ djin baiłnikǫsɛ djolgɛ djin. banatinł djolgɛ djin.
gicdo djolge djin. e hago hodonni't djin. adjikai djin. do kwidɛ biniγɛ
nhiczłada sittsokɛ. dinnɛkɛyago daditdoka. niłtsądzilna'ągo dinnɛkɛyago
dikwi yołgai dzil holge dasittanɛ bitis do˙ka doł'ijɛ dzil dasittą bitis
nado˙ka ditcizłedzil dasittą bitis nadoka. bacinnɛ dzil dasitą bitis nadoka.
adji' dį nixidokał. ako nlįdɛ' dził ła' ha'a dolɛł. dził bini łakgai holgɛ
biyago nahokǫs bitc'į djigo hǫkałɛ. dził ła' hanasokaigo ho'o'honɛstįngo
dził sa'ąłɛ aidi nadziz'ą holge ts'iddi biyago nato da ndetin holge akonnna
tsetna' ai dził t'a na'ągo dził yidjin holgɛ nna'adɛ hazt'ɛl holgɛ yiwotc'ɛ
ła' sa'ą balok'ai holgɛ. akona tsɛtna' ndo˙ka. yiwodji' tsɛtna' dził
dasa'anɛ holgɛ e biyago ai hasokaigo yiwodji' dził sa'ądolɛł.
dziłditł'oi holgɛ.


cada'a bitc'idji' daditdoka binnɛdɛ' bahast'a holgɛ adji' akwi
nahoka'dinnɛ kɛho(a[?])t'i. niłtsą dzil ninna'ą akonɛ nahadinnɛstą'
adɛ'. ts'innadza. ł'oł dɛya adɛ' tcinniłti ł'ołdɛ. yołgai t'a dį bą tasinnil.
kodjigo ananadza. adɛ t'a kwott'ɛgo ł'ołt'ɛ e tcinnanɛgi e adɛ e 'a bitcicdɛ
dadį' badananasnil. nahokǫsgo ananadza adɛ' ahwot'ɛgo ł'ołdɛ tcinanɛgi
djin. ha'adji ɑnanadza yołgai gic tc'intą. kodji ɑnanadza. doł'ijɛ gic
tcintą. ɛ'adji ɑnnanadza. ditcizłi gic tcintą. nahokǫsdji ɑnnanadza.
bacinni gic tcinnaintą. haditdą di bą' nixiniγągo ahwodilką gwiyaadał-
γał t'a cabik'ɛgo ndołhis adɛ to hadonna. doł'ijɛ gicɛ haida dibą'˙ nixiniγągo adołγoł t'a cabik'ɛgo ndołhis. adɛ to hadonna. dabą˙ nadisoliñgo
ahwot'ɛgo ɑnnadołγwoł t'a cabik'ɛgo nadołhis. todona. haditda dabą
nadosiłłingo anadałγwoł adɛ to hadoγo. t'acabik'ɛgo nadołhis todogo
bacini gic hainil. ł'oł aziz dį bɛ haigi djin. dį yiskago inda dził dį dasittą
bitis okaigo adiinda daditdo'ął. bɛdadotaigɛ banictcin dodidittsinł.

it will be named farther they found they say. Their grandmother by her
control bear by magic | grew they say. Panther by magic grew they say
Both were males they say. Four days passed they say. | Four years be-
came they say. Persons twelve walk, come, they told them they say. |
There he came they say. "Those my grandchildren which I made not for
this place. I made them: your grandmother, cone | I told you." *baṇi*
was named they say *baiłnokǫse* was named they say. *banatinł* was named
they say. | *gicdo* was named they say. Those "Cone" he told they say.
They went they say. "Not here for | I made you my grandchildren.
Navajo country you go. Where rain mountain lies Navajo country |
there White Shell mountain called where it lies beyond go. Turquoise
mountain where it lies beyond | go. Abalone mountain where it lies beyond
go. Jet mountain where it lies beyond go. | There four days will pass
with you. Then way over mountain one sticks up will be. Mountain
its face white called | under north toward you keep going. Mountain
one when you go up just a little can be seen | mountain lies there crescent
called in front its base under water you cross (crossing) called there |
across that mountain just lies mountain black called at the end of it
flat called on it | one stands *balok'ai* named. There across you go. This
way across mountain | stands called that below that when you go this
way mountain will be standing. | Brushy mountain called.

South toward side of it you will pass (?) line (?) called there then |
Navajo live. Rain mountain. *tohatci* there you will live | it is. He
went back. String he stepped over, then he picked up string. White
shell just four for her (?) lay in the water. | Here she went in. Then just
same way string she brings that there west toward | just four lay on it.
North she went there same way string she brought | they say. East she
went in White shell cane she brought out. Here she went. Turquoise
cane | she brought out. West she went. Abalone shell cane she brought
out. North she went. | Jet cane she brought. "These you are thirsty
is killing you set them on ground, | stick it in the ground just sunwise
twist it then water will flow out. Turquoise cane that one thirst | is
killing you stick in ground just sunwise turn it. Then water will flow
out. Thirst when it becomes | put in the ground just sunwise turn it.
Water will flow. That one thirst | put in the ground then water (?).
Just sunwise twist it. | Jet cane she gave them. Strings sacks four in she
gave they say. Four days then mountains four lie | beyond when you
come then you untie it. With open it." I won't let you have (I with-
hold) the songs.

dadilde djɪn. yołgai dzillᶓ t'obitis oldego tcɪnnezdjc'. doł'ijɛ dzil
bitis naoldɛ akwi nanezdje'. dadjɪłdjidɛ t'andaz silᶖ ado' nixinaildɛ.
ditcɪł dzil bitis naoldɛ nainecdje' djɪn. wojǫ yegondaz silᶖ djɪn. yo'ąnɛ
nixinnaildɛ djɪn. bacɪnnɛ dzil bitis ayoi nɪłdac dadjɪłdjit djɪn. nanecdje
djɪn. k'at dadɪtdo'ac nixidoni·tdnɛ djɪnɛ djɪn. ban'ni' djolge adjɪnnɛ
djɪn. dadadɛz'a djɪn. t'oaxayoi yo' silᶖ djɪn. ado ɪnda ałta dzɪsni.
ɑsts'olgo nixidadɪsdjit. ado akwi yɪska. dobɛxozɪnda kwodjigo adɛsdc.
dɑsdɪnnɛsbin djɪn. nle datsɛ ha'agɛ dzɪł binᶖ' łakgai nɪnɛ djikɛkodjigo
akǫnɛ dadadika. nahokǫs bitc'i'dji' ha'nɪnɛ baɣaosde djɪn. nt'c kǫ· ła'
ndjiyala djɪn. cilᶖ' kǫla łą djiyala bidjɪnni. cac bidjini djɪn. adji kodza
djɪn. nt'ɛ kwotdza djɪn. hat'inca' ɑt'i? k'ɑt dahwidilts'ɛlci' cilᶖ'. ado'
ilde djɪn. sɛnt'i djɪn. ᶖ'ą djɪn. k'ac hat'i dadidlᶖnł djɪnni djɪn. bailnikǫsɛ
djolge djɪn. adjɪnnɛ djɪn. ba'ni' e djɪnnɛ djɪn. yadella olge cą' dɛba'
nixiniɣągo di tc'ɪtdedołił. yołgai gɪci hadjita djɪn. kwott'ɛgo cabik'ɛgo
nzizɪz. adɛ'' to hadnna djɪn. dadjodlǫ djɪn. djɪnnɛzdje. djɪn nak·ɛla'.
di(bi)djɪn datsɛ dediltsɛ djɪnni djɪn. ba'ni' nat'ąni djɪllɛdji adjo'icɛ
bitdahasdɛndɛ' sɛkǫhwiya haɣoci nadą hil'ą djɪn. atsɛllade hagoci
dasakąt djɪn.

kodjigo ndadjɪcdjit. ła disson'ᶖ. hat'ila donaɣaida djɪn. hoɣandɛ
naz'ą djɪn yadji'aji tc'ɛtindo dzizi djɪn. ndᶓ' hakɛdɛgo ła' dacdi'aj
łą dinnɛgo ła' nasdit'aj djɪn. ła' ɑsdzɑngo wonnasdo· hadɛbin djɪn.
k'attca k'adɪnnɛ tc'ɛhatinla djɪn. k'ɛdahijdoni djɪn. hatɛdela adat'ᶖ?
nitcobą̊de yik·a dinnɛkeyago nixinikaigo adɛt'i'. hat'ila akǫnɛ nɪnnǫxnɛ
axɛdaidᶖnɛ· ni djɪn. k'adɪnnɛ. adjuyañgɛ ahwot'ɛ akǫ annɛst'ą dado'ął.
ndjit'aj. akǫnɛ no'nɛ nihidonni·t. dado·sinł nixidonnit'. annɛstą dadoał
nixidonni·t'. halɛgo hwodonnit. t'akǫ akǫ łą hota' adzɪskai. nadą
nadadjɪcdjit. xɪłidjin. ɑsdzannɛ bɛką dadɛngo bɪł olda hanɛ'ą̊djiłdo'
dinnɛ bestsą adadɪnnɛ ɑłtanidjela djɪn. adɛyᶓ nadą dezgɛla djɪn. kodoyᶓ

They started they say. White shell that mountain just over it when they came they slept. Turquoise mountain | beyond they came there they slept again. What they carried heavy became then they went on. | Abalone mountain beyond they came, they slept again they say. Those beads | more heavy it became they say. They went on they say. Jet mountain beyond very it was heavy they carried on their backs they say. They slept | they say. Then you opened them she had told them he said they say. *ba'ni'* named said it | they say. They opened it they say. Very many beads had become they say. Then among them he gave them. | Being light they carried them. Then there it was day. They did not know which way they were going. | They sat down on top they say. There it may be one sticking up one mountain its face white we go. | This way there we go. North toward any way they went they say. Then here some one | they found had walked they say. "My dog, here someone it appears has walked," he said to him. Bear he addressed they say. Then he looked | they say. Then he stretched they say. What kind is it? "Now we will see, my pet." Then | they went on they say. Cliff was they say. The sun set they say. "What we drink?" he said they say. *bailnikǫse* | was named they say. He said it to they say *ba'ni'*. "That," he said they say. "When thirst | is killing us this you will use." White Shell cane he took up they say. This way sunwise | he turned it. Then water flowed up they say. They drank they say. They slept, they say. Tracks lie. | "Today maybe we will see," he said they say, *ba'ni'* chief he was the leader | they were going down bottom of cañon very much corn was there they say. Tassels many | stood they say.

There they camped. One looked about. Someone did not go about they say. Just hogan | stood they say. Two went inside in doorway they stood they say. Then behind others two came, | one man, came back they say. One was woman inside (?) it was full they say. | It turned out *k'adinne* lived there they say. They made relations of them they say. "From where are you?" | "From our grandmother's shore we came Navajo country we are going we are." "(?) | here you live we get acquainted," he said they say. Arrow People. "What one eats this here is ripe you chew." | Two came back. "Here you camp," they told us. "You eat," they told us. "Getting ripe you eat," | they told us. "It is all right," he said. Then some among them went. Corn | they brought back. It got dark. Woman her man who had none with he stayed | man his wife he had none (?) together then lay they say. Over there corn they gave as marriage fee they say. Here |

yo dadzizgela djin. haγociyε axiłdadjitdlịgo. kεhodjitdε. γa binna
hoditaxogo haditdjitdje djin. naγaci holge djin hadadjildje djin. naγaci
bik̓ạγiyε dadziłtsego dadzitsεyan. aziz adatcillε'. ła' ha'ε adatcillε'.
nεcdetso halε yannigo xεł bikago t'o dasittị. mosk'εtεgo t'o allaγałgo.
kodjigo cac hahwiznil akwiya t'o sitda t'oadji baisiłtso cilị' t'ahahε
nixiditka bidjinni djin. cac bạ'ni· adjinni djin. nawodjingo bạni'·
yadjiltε djin. yik̓ạgo adεt'i hacdεda. donłnε' e nadạ' nahanasgegε dak'a.


histε' (nisdε) adałε djinni djin bạ'ni'· yo'icε ε aiłni djin. k'a
dinnεdji t'atcε ndaidεcdjela djin. tatcε hodji"' i"' tatcε hodji tatcε
hodjε ni djin. k'adinnε. ako ba'ni' djinnε baiłnik̓ọsε banatilε kicdo·t
e dịgo iłdε. tatcεgε e nat'ani datcilli yahooldε badnyanεnna. dadnnabal
yanεnna. au ni djin ba'ni· cadani cijaakε akida sinnołdεn'ca' dodac-
hwotcinnido nihila yikago adεt'i niłtsạdzil dasittạgo ak̓ọn kinnikai
nihitcon εnhiłni. nakiskago nixidika. nadạ badosoεnnigε ist'c εddclε.
k'adinnεdε t'adohadastsida djinnε. tala' aninni· axadεnhinni.    ca'ndi
cadannεkε cijaakε całtcinnε t'ado bikε adlị'. dałai ikado ako k'adinnεyε
dadina djin. nanała ałtso k'adinnεyε tc'indjc djin. t'o łεj εtditdesdja.
hadadεzdza.    εnnahaskai.    hado ndjεkai.    hoγan di dado'idzai.    nakiska
djin.    akoci nladji hayat'ila djin.    εsdazεnε njonci yiłhika.    yo do'
t'ohaiyudegε'.    dinnε ałtso ndolsis.    εsdjεni dεnhiεddlε. kwot'εgo hanasti'-
łεd djin.  ado dadilde djin.  iγεyε ałtso t'o 'εdεgo.  haja'adεn ałtso t'a'adε
dadildε.  tcinnezdje djin.  hiłnanaidjin djin.    nakiłkago iłnast'i (naxo-
djingo).    cada'ạ bitc'idji' caccε tc'oyaj haiitzịz. εłnεnε ninłdcl yikado
nεzda djin.  nnnn sos sos sos ni djin.  ba'ni· εnni hi hi cilị' at'εgo cạ'.
hwonni godnni cilị'.  nixikεdε do'εhwizzinda.  t'o hwindina'go cacε
hadi'a djinnε.  cacε hada'ạ djinnε.

beads they gave they say. Very they were hospitable to each other.
They stayed there. Rabbit arrived. | When they surrounded they
hunted them they say. Mountain sheep called they say they hunted
they say. Mountain sheep | its hide when they removed hair they
soften it. Sack they make. Some their shirts they made for them-
selves. | Panther their pet where is piled loads on it just he lies on.
Like a cat just he eats. | Here bear low place there just he sits just
there he feeds him. "My pet soon | we will start," he told him, they
say. Bear *ba'ni'* told they say. When it is dark *ba'ni'* | begins to
speak they say. Tomorrow we get ready. We go (?) that corn they
gave us, you grind.

"Your lunch you prepare," he said they say, *ba'ni'* (?) he told, they
say. The Arrow | People sweathouse they had built fire they say. "Sweat-
house come (?) . . . ," | he said they say. Arrow people. Then *ba'ni'*
*baitnikǫse banatile* | these four went. Sweathouse these chiefs they were
they went in he put curtain down. Curtain | he put down. "Yes,"
he said they say, *ba'ni'* my son-in-law, my daughter-in-law they like
each other only | I am not going to mountains you tomorrow we travel
we are Rain mountain where it likes there we go. | Our grandmother
told us. In two days we go on. Corn that you gave us lunch we made."
Arrow People did not say anything they say. (?) they said to each other. |
"My sons-in-law, my daughters-in-law, my children not (?). Just one day
will be (?). Then that arrow men (pl.?) | went away they say. Another all
Arrow People went out they say. Dirt they put on themselves. | They
dressed. They went back. Others too went home. Hogan these did not
say anything. Two days passed | they say. Then over there they talked
it was found out they say. Women good they go with. Beads too |
there are many. Men all we will kill. Women will be ours. Thus | he
spoke he found out they say. They started on they say. Men married
to women all they left. Their daughters-in-law all (left) without | they
went on. They slept they say. It was dark with them again they say.
When it was two days when it was dark again. | South toward that bear
small spruce he pulled out. Across each other he put them on top of
them | he sat they say. "n n n n sos sos sos," he said they say. *ba'ni'*
said it they say. "That one my pet I guess | is doing something. Message
you are giving my pet. Behind us we do not know." "Just a short time
the bear | began to sing they say. The bear sang they say."

ciɣañɣala ni nats'ołdizε cinnicłįgo
ciɣañɣalani caclaba· ci nicłįgo
ciɣan bεts'a djilgicgo
ciɣan bεts'a niɣεgo
ciɣan binohodzitgo
tsa'ąnaɣai binohodzitgo ci nicłį hihinyihi·.
kodji hwot'εgo ndziztago 'ądji ako haɣin dazłį djin.   nladε nεzna
nidn'ą djin tihigo hayiłkago sin nadistsą djinnε.

cinictεj kabinnεhodzit.   nadzoldis' cinnisłinεgo kabinnεhodzit
caclaba· cinicłinnεgo
cinictεj kabinnεhodzit.
cinictεj bits'a tcilgicgo.   cinictεj bits'ahinigε kabinnεhodzit.
tsa'ąnaɣai binεhodzit cinicłį.   hayinihihi· hayininini·

naki nidn'ago dako ndilgot djin.   dadolnigo t'adji ła adεdzolɣal ado
daihitε. k'adinnε hannazt'ila djin.   honiɣago.   cacξ dįdε ałkilɣot. hilkεtξ
ha'ą ahwonnilkat.   ba'ni' tcolge adjinnε djin.   cili'i ha'go cilį ha'go
djinnε djin.   nadza djin.   adε k'adinnε hadzi djin.   nahadanxinigo adit'ii
nixikε yikago adεt'i ni djin.   k'adinnε ba'ni adjinnε djin.   doda doda
nixinoɣanti· cilį' digo nihwoɣanti hahwinnε gola hat'εgo ł'εgo ndjaɣado.
djingo detε.   nihilą ndoka t'adanołt'εda.   lolo cidannεkεdoleł hadinca'
nixidεclat ni djin.   k'adinnε lolo akwila djingo nannado akwε εxozin
ni djin ba'ni'·.   e binigε handiltila djin cac.

nixikinnailde djin.   akwi yiskanei e dobεxozinda.   kodigo hwodεiłka.
ist'e dadjiłdjidε ąłtso adasdįt.   ditcį'ε hwǫniɣąoyε.   iłnadisti' djin.
haiɣεl sinni djin.   bikago nεsdoitso dasitį djin.   hala indza cilį'.   akǫyε
doadaolnε'hεda.   bidaiya djin.   adaisk'a djin.   ditc'ε djin.   bitsoą dik-
istcilgon. hwodina.   kǫdadiya djin.   dohanałdzada djin.   xεłξ yika danεzti.
bikε iłnat ndε biza·bągε dałitci djin.   hat'ila yisxila cilį' djinnε djin.   natą
nadzεzka djin.   nde kǫ djaddε yastcinlε sitį'.   bits'aɣagεt'e yiɣainaɣajla.

My hogan, | whirlwind I being
My hogan bear gray I being
My hogan from it lightning strikes
My hogan from it danger is
My hogan all are afraid of it
Old age being afraid of it I am | (blowing breath out).

Here this singing there then his songs became they say. There ten | he finished singing they say. A little when it was dawning songs he heard they say.

My black face they are afraid of.
Whirlwind I am they are afraid of
Bear gray I am.
My black face they are afraid of.
My black face from it it lightens.
My black face danger from it they are afraid of it
Old age they are afraid I am. hayinihihi, hayinihihi

Two when he had sung so he stood up they say. Putting his hand up backward he threw himself then | he ran off. Arrow People had circled around they found out they say they were going to kill them. Bear four times he ran around. The hill stands up so far he chased them. *ba'ni'* spoke they say. "My pet, come, my pet, come," | he said they say. He came back they say. The Arrow People spoke they say. "Being sorry for you we were after you we were coming we were," he said they say. Arrow person to *ba'ni'* said it they say. "No, no, | you would have killed us my pet (?) They are sorry for us. Why in the night they come. | Day time it would be. You go back before you are torn up. I will go after you, some time | I will come to you," he said, they say. "Arrow men well daytime you come then we know," | he said they say *ba'ni'*. That is why they picked him up they say bear.

They started off they say. How many days were that I do not know. So far little ways they passed the night. | Lunch they carried all was gone. Famine was killing them. They built a brush house they say.| Their loads were lying down they say. On them panther was lying they say. "Something you do, my pet. Here | is nothing to eat." He stepped down, they say. He stretched himself they say. He yawned they say. His tongue curled up | white. He went up. He passed them they say. He came back before long they say. That load on it he lay down. | His feet he licked them his lips were red they say. "Something he has killed, my pet," he said, they say. Back | they tracked him they say. Then here antelope fawn was lying. Along his side he had been cut. |

niznigε.  dadjolγal  hasda  djokai  ado  nixinailde  djin.  t'abinnigo
dananidza  djin.  dohananadzada.  bila'  dił  djinnε.  akǫ  nnasdεst'ajn
najdilt'εgo  axαnnigε  djadε  naki  nestselαd  djin.  akogo  dacǫt  ła'  hast'ε'
adadjilla.  kinnailde  djin.  naznεcdje  djinnε.  t'abinnigo·  danadidza  djin.
dohanadzada  djin.  biyatsi·n  adεdił  djinnε.  akǫ  dajniłka  djin.  ndε  kǫ
djadε ta· nistselαd djin.  akogo  αst'ε nala djin. nixinailde djin.  t'ayotda·-
αiz'ago  nilde  djin.  ndadzisna  djinnε  dadiya  djin   nesdoitso.
doxanadzada  djin.


akǫ dajniłka djin nt'ε akǫ djadε aiyoi at'ε dį sεnil djin. t'ałtso its'a·
naγajla djin.  t'o hoyuigo αttsin' bił nilde djin. ba'ni' ani djin. aidε
atcǫi dasit ndahołt'εsgo. akosolε e dakot'tgo ndaz. ai binigε nesdoitso
ndαcdiltila djin. yołgaiαsdzą bini' bik'εhola djin. ado adεstset djin.
atcǫ' t'o dadittsitgo dadjigε. dził dasa'ayε' nleγa' nasis'ąn holge ho'ninε
biyagona todandetin holge djinninnε' akodolεł djinni djin. 'adi ildε djin.
akot'εgo hilkitla djin. kwot'εgo to bitis dinnεcjε'la djin. e olgela djin.
todandetin tsinna ndjikai djin. adadilna'ha' całtcinnε djini djin. ba'nį'
kwε didoldje ndε nlai bitda dεkaiyεn dε' ła' dadaii djin djinnε djin.
ba'nį' adjinni djin. aγchiγa' nihiłkaila. ayε eγε dazlεnε tabądo· ła nizniya
adε hodjinnigo tsε'na' nildε. nahadαnxinnigo nikε' dεkai dadjinnigo.
axindadisdjit. idą doahilkitdilnida ndε'ε djinnε. ndε dohakanε dodεhaka
adat'ila djin lą djonahadαnxinnela yołkałgo t'ok'εlε djini djin ba'nį'.
kǫ sitdε da·djiyago nlidε danadaiedjin djinnε. bidadji' ła' danadizdza
adε tcinnigo tsεna' naildε. daxocłałdε. t'a yołgaiαsdzabądε naolda·lα
djin. akǫ' sittsokε łaakainε' t'abihik'εgo nixidonit'. listso dadjiłdjilla
djinnε.


ai xa'ołsiłgo taditdin badadjitdjago. e bikinla djin. daładε'it'ila
naxi cac nhilįla. nεsdoitsola nixi'. e listso nixilįla. t'okε lε, lą·'

They brought it back. They ate they were saved, then they went on go they say. Just by himself | he went (go up?) they say. Not long he came back. His front paw bloody they say. Then two went back | two of them near by antelope two they found he had killed they say. Then small some their lunch | they made for themselves. They went on they say. They slept again they say. By himself he got up they say. | He soon returned, they say. His jaw was bloody they say. Then they went, they say. Then there | antelope three found he had killed they say. Then lunch they made, they say. They went on, they say. About here | sun when was they arrived they say. They camped, they say. He went away, they say panther. | He soon came back they say.

There they tracked him they say. Then there antelope large were four lay they say. Each one guts | he had eaten, they say. Very much meat with they came back they say. *ba'ni'* spoke they say. Now | pemmican you found when you have roasted it. Not heavy you do this that way heavy. That because panther | they had they say. *yolgaiasdzą* her mind they were following, they say. Then he killed them they say. | Pemmican just when they had pounded they carried. Mountain the one that stood on that Navajo mountain (?) called, "We do not come | under it go the ford called go where she told us there it will be," he said, they say. There they arrived they say. | This way there was a bank (hill) they say. This way water beyond water flows here and there they say. That they found it was named they say. | The ford across they went they say. "We will stop to eat, my children," he said, they say. "*ba'ni*' | Here build a fire then there down where we come some is black," he said they say. | "*ba'ni*' said it," they say. Married men have come to us. Those they have become (?). By the bank one came | there the way he told them across they came. "We being sorry after you we came," they were saying. | They embraced each other. That time we did not shake hands that time. Those who came not husbands | they found they were, they say. "Well you are sorry for us, hereafter we will be friends (clansmen)," he said they say *ba'ni'*. | Then just when they started to eat over there it was black they say. Toward them one walked back | then he shouted across they came. They overtook them. Just the shore of White Shell Woman you came (they came) | they say. "Here, my grandchildren, those who walk follow," she told us. Snake they were carrying on their backs | they say.

That when you kill animals pollen they carry for. That his food they found out they say. Only one place | your bear is your pet. Panther ours this snake is our pet. Just clan one will be. "All right," |

hwoo donit' k'at t'okɛ'lɛ eladji' holda'ą dadildɛ. aɣa'łąɣɛ
ilde djin. hwɛhai djin. naɣaci ndadziłtsego bikin hwɛhai
djin. hoɣan binnago aɣa' dandantcą'. ebą aɣaą holgelɛ
hwodonni djin. k'at dąn hazlį'. nahottsoi. di dził danaago di
dził łidjin holge nihidonnitni'. ado cac tconadzott'int' tcacdɛz'i bika
ɛhisdilnigo dinnɛ bidadji adjiłkat. iłtsini do' aidi bił tadjodja'go bikin
ilde djin. ko djindjɛgo. k'at halit'elɛ? hadic toci baiłnikos cą' gici tinłni.
doł'iji gic yiłget. nakidi naisgiz adɛ tohana. bɛ datciyą' djinnɛsdjɛ'.
xosigo nɛxildɛgo tciłtcinbi'to holgedo ado ildɛ' nadɛnnestą yodjokaigo.
aigidɛ kasonsillale e bitcilladjin tsɛgi bidadela djin. tschilįdi to ts'is'ą
bihilidɛ ł'otɛł ntannɛ tsin t'oik'ądɛ ąłkɛdjoka. t'a ho lo dadzidzį'. diyɛ
tc'ɛkɛ tc'ɛdeya. nixi ako dinidja. tinɛ. kiyɛ'anyɛ' dadeldɛ'. tsinł'oik'ą holge
ako djindjɛ. kodɛ dinɛlį' dadiya. tatcinila djin. tsɛniidji'dɛ djinnɛsdjɛ
djin. ado· abingo nixinnaildɛ. ndɛ talu tcikɛ' tc'ɛdeyaha. biką hazlįla.
ba'ni· adjinni tinɛ' cadanɛ cidjɛkɛ' ca' baholyado. totso holge gonɛ'
yiłyi'aj ado totsonɛ haholtci· t'ohoyoi k'at totson'osgɛ'. ado dadildɛ'
tsɛbasozołłɛigɛ ditciłɛ gicɛ' ɛlget to doiyoi dokogo hana. dadjodla'do.
dadji yą' naɣaiɣa'. dził ditł'oi holgɛ ha'ninnɛ' djidini djinni, cada'a
bitc'idji'go ha'ninɛ' djinni djin. ba'nį· doda di do ako xot'eda. di
bagaisikaigɛt'ɛ dził na'agi nixidontnidni' ni djin. baiłnikosi koni yołgai
gic ɛlget djin. doł'iji gic elge djin. dała to hana djin. iłnaci halinɛ holgelɛ
hadonni djin. datcinyą' djin. kodɛ' tądandilde djin. nahokosigo djin.
nihoł'ijidjɛ hasde. akonɛ nledi nixidinadɛla naɣai dahots'osigɛ akwi
ndadjisdjidiyɛ. di kinnicbiji holgedo dadatsosigɛ. nle a'e basła holgɛ
haninɛ at'ɛda.


t'isntsaz i'a holgɛ biyaigɛ hojontla djin. k'idolya djin. daiitci djin.
nle dasdikadɛ ahwondonnit djin. ai yac inełdjai holgɛ bɛdontsonsgo to
bɛdałdjołdego. kodołłił kodɛyɛ cɛnahołtin didonłnił. ako inda ayaj ɑssɑ

he said. Now same clan in front being we will travel. Much wool | they
arrived they say. A year passed they say. Mountain sheep when they
killed their food a year passed | they say. Hogan around it wool they
made a pile. "Because of that wool much it will be called," | he said they
say. Now spring came. It was yellow. "This mountain we go on top, |
this mountain black is named," she told us. Then bear began to work
again *tcacdez'i* for | he dug with paws people in front he threw out. Wild
onions too that with he threw out their food | they arrived they say.
There they camped. "Now what shall we do? Where will be water *bailni?*
"Cane you have." | Turquoise cane he stuck in. Twice he twisted it
then water flowed out. With it then all they slept. | When it was light
when they went on Skunkbush-Water it will be called there arrived where
you go (perhaps addressed to me) you got lost. | Close by Two-stars-
lying those they went toward came to the edge of *tsegi* they say. Where
rocks come together water flows | they came grass is much top
covered with trees they follow each other. "Wait." They stopped.
"This woman has given out. We here will stay. Go ahead." The
*kiye'ani'* went on. *tsinl'oiką* is called | there they stayed. Here strange
man come. They found he was *tatcinila* they say. At *tseniidki'de* they
slept | they say. Then early morning they started on. Then, "Wait
woman has given out. Her husband she has." | *ba'ni'* said. "Go on
my sons-in-law, my daughters-in-law take care of." *totso* called in | they
two went. Then *totsone* they bred very many now *totsone* they are called.
Then they went on. | trees on. (?) Abalone cane he stuck in twisted
water much salt came up. They drank it. | "Yes, this is the one. Moun-
tain brushy called we came?" he said they say. South | toward we don't
go he said they say. "*ba'ni'* no, this not here looks so. This | we went
by looks like mountain projects horizontally she told us," he said they
say. *bailnikǫsi* there white shell | cane put in they say. Turquoise
cane put in they say. Two water flowed up they say. "Opposite each
other springs it will be called," | he said they say. They ate they say.
Here they turned back they say. Toward the north they say. | Ground
hard they went up. Here yonder they had come up from over there the
sharp pointed there | one they unloaded. "This *kinnicbiji* it will be called
the peaks. That one *basla* is called | cane up it is."

Cottonwood large stands it is called below water spreads out they say.
They planted corn they say. Red silk appeared they say.|"Over there where
they started from," she told them they say. "Those small one slow on the
stalk called when they are husked water | when you put in this way do.
That way let there be frequent rains you say that.Then small one pot |

donił daka dadoonłłeda hwodini djın. xatco' yołgaiɛsdzą. ako ałtcinnɛ
ɛkai djın. t'adanɛz djın. yajɛ degijdɛ. to bɛdjısdjollɛ. kodɛya cɛnahołtin
tcini djın. nabiskannɛ ła' bınnadassons. dįgo ɛka djın. ɛtt'ekɛ naki djın
cikɛ naki. atdadin djın. k'at iłnɛ'ago t'a naki nat'aj djınnɛ. ałts'an
dadɛtindɛ naizdilt'ɛ. dohwɛhwozinda nigo nat'aj djın. ado hwedɛlką'ndɛ'
sailigi' axadahakɛ t'ado tcɛhakɛdjında nigo. nat'ajn djınnɛ. ła at'ɛgo
łacki e djitdi. ako ilde djın. t'anilla djın. t'ado axadzila djın. ado djɛk'ɛ-
gidala djın hatɛgila sizlįla. hatcobągo datsi' hwodontni djın. dį
yıską djın.


F    ayac ła' bınanasons tsınłgo ndot'ac bitcınni djın. hałtcinnɛ do kwɛ
bɛnaxaicacį cittcai cidicni. axɛnołtcandɛ. t'ado hwɛdinai nakinɛltcą
dohwɛxozinnɛ ndjıtt'ajla. nlahi dak'ɛgi dziskɛ ni djın. ndot'ac nixijdinit'
ni djın nihitcobago nacit'aj ni djın. xa'adɛgo tsınisdazɛ cada'adɛgo
ł'ohozihi ɛ'adɛ γat nahokǫsɛ dɛstsin kot'ɛgo ndazdołdja. daikɛdɛ sai
ndazidołsos. ndotsigo bakaγɛ inda bɛnagi tc'il. ndazdołtcil dįdi axɛdaz-
dołtcil. e citcɛgo bikaγɛ tanixidit'ogis nihiłnɛ' nixitco' nigo sikɛ djın.
akolya djın. adɛ' k'at hwodonnigo adɛ' dɛj'on. tanasgiz djın. acki
yɛnɛ aladji sida djın. at'ɛdɛ akɛdɛ sitda djın. t'abidisgiz djın. ackiyɛn
nadągai ak'an bɛ naltsai djın. at'ɛdɛ nadąłtsoi ak'an bɛ nalts'ai djın.
ado ahwonilnɛ' djın. ałts'ą dadit'indɛ kodɛ nakizdalt'ɛ sizzį'. xactc'ɛłti
xactc'ɛoγan e djit'ila djın. nixitco' hago nihiłnɛ yołgaiasdza. kodɛ
łakgaigo axikat silį'. adabakoindzį' tc'ocgai bilatadji' nixiłdai'isdɛl, tsį
bɛl'ąi wolgeli' bilatadji nixiłdananazdɛl. e k'at tanixissogiz gɛ gɛ't'ɛgo
taxitdisgiz. bacini dzil bilatadji' nixiłdaihisdɛl nixitco bitcɛdagi nixiłnin-
xindɛl. yahit'aj nt'ɛ nihitco ąnɛ ąkǫ annɛ kadinnɛ' sa bınniłxigo yisdjol.
ado ndina. yołgai gicɛ yɛ gicidotsigo. xa'adjigo iya tsınnadza abikal-
niłtsilgo tsınnadza.    cada'ądjigo doł'iji gicɛ yɛ gicɛ yidotsigo ndɛ'
adɛt'oniyagɛ nligo tcınnatdza djın. e'adjigo ananadza djın bigis(k'ij)-
dagɛtiya¹ djın. agisi ɑnnit' nagago tsınnadza djın. nahokǫsjigo nanadza

---

¹For *dagɛt' diya*, without she walked.

put in do not fail to do it," she said they say their grandmother White Shell Woman. Then children | went they say. Growing children they say. They brought small ears. Water they put in. "Here let there be rains," | he said they say. The next day more they go to break off. Four went they say. Girls two they say | boys two. They were missing they say. Then moon just two returned they say. From each other | they were hiding two of them (in pairs). They did not find them saying two came back they say. Then they tracked them | where said was on either side their tracks not they found saying, "The two returned," they say. One girl | one boy those were missing. There they went they say. It was true, they say, not ? they say. Then (?) | what happened. To their grandmother's place maybe he said they say. Four | days passed they say.

"Small ears some go get, quickly you two return," he said to them they say. "His children not there (?) | My grandchildren, I say." They went. They came back before long. | "The lost ones they have come back. Over there in the garden they two sit," he said they say. "Go back he told us," | he said they say. "Our grandmother's place we two went," he said they say. East, mountain mahogany; south, | Mormon tea; west, cedar; north, piñon this way lay then. "From the garden sand | you get. When you have spread it on it then around it grass put. Four times put it in concentric circles. | That when it lies on it take a bath she told us our grandmother," saying they two sit they say. | They did that they say. There now saying there they come. They washed they say. Boy | that front sat they say. Girl behind sat they say. They washed they say. The boy | white cornmeal with he dried they say. Girl yellow cornmeal with she dried they say. | Then they told the story they say. From each other we were hiding here two stood. *xactc'ɛlti* | *xatc'ɛoɣan* those they were they say. "Your grandmother, 'Come,' she tells you White Shell woman." Here | something white spread became. We felt nothing *tc'ocgai* its top they alighted with us. Trees | many called its top they lighted with us. That now washed us the way | you wash us that way they washed (us). Jet mountain its top they lighted with us our grandmother in front of door they landed with us. | We went in then our grandmother here lay (?). Nearly old age was killing her she lay in a ball. | Then she got up. White shell cane with she walked. East in she went a little stronger | she came back. South turquoise cane she walked with then | walking by herself being she came back they say. West she went again, they say her cane. | without she walked they say. Very young walking she came back they say. North she went again |

djin. at'ednlįgo ts'innadza djin. nijonyedja' to baiyasn. kodo t'acinał no'kaigo. at'e sittsoke hałni djin. sin daget' dado'kai hałni djin. ado xadadest'a djin. xadotalgo xandest'a djin. sine ałtso bodjit'a djin. sin dobehasinda kodo nadedest'a djin. di· lį· biɣin aide behasin akocą' dį hwiskago at'eladjin. di kwe doła' niłtcidej'ałda. di nladji sittsoke naxaztane e nixitcido'ał. e dakodo bił tcine'ane. e denixidonni't'. badaiyo'nelego sinnenę' bihesołya' bidjiyę naxonti' łainde' dona'ada bidjindji' nixidinnit' nixitco'. dinne nakidzada nakai ade djine'aj ado lį biɣin xanadedestą ai biną 'hwil'a·. ado bacinne dzil bilatadji ni' nixenit'aj tsįbel'ai bilatadji' tc'ocgai bilatadji ado dak'edji k'at di ł'e dodaidilɣocda. dide tc'il bika tahitdisgise aide nalɣe att'ele. ehidjoltcoli et'eli nixidinit' nixitco'. aiked hazlį' djin. kiya'a binacidji' ndadjicdjit akwi kehadjitt'i djin. nt'e xe' ła' xazniya djin. dził łitcidji' t'i hindinidjaini djinne. adji dinnekaige bitcoiyade cac biligo vił yikaige' ailaha at'ela datc'innigo ade diya. dziłłitcidji' tixidinnidja·. cac naxadołteł e bił dadibą' datc'innigo ade diya ni djin deneli'. lą'ą hwodjini djin. bebolnihi djin ba'nį' lą'ą. acdlai yiskago cile ni djin ba'nį'. ado acdlai yiskago da'adilde. dinne dadesba. hiłidjingo ninna· djin. cada'adjigo nezda djin. cac tc'oyace haiyidzinz. ałna ninlai yikage nesda djin. xojon hiłidjingo t'annide sin dists'ą. ba'nį' adjinni djin. cac abidjinni djin. cilį' dziłłitci holgedji dinne tihindindja. k'at akǫ debą. cacyenę ndi'tna djin. adeska djin. ede kittcil danaisdjage batinnezdedjala e naxałtse't' la djin.


nilą'ą· catsinkez nayé'nezɣan cinicłigo becdiłxił cikego cantsinkes nelą' ą· becdiłxił sisł'ego cantsinkes becdiłxił cajkij dįngo ndok'e· becdiłxił citc'ago becdiłxił attsinniłł'ic bił dįgo sitts'an nahatdił. nna'hadiłge yadontcoñge deyui yałti benizit bidzela' yuwodji' yainnił sa'anaɣai cinicłį. binoxotdzi't cinicłigo. neląą catsinkes hinyihi hos'igo

they say. Girl being she returned they say. She was (so) handsome
we were ashamed. "Here just before my eyes | you came. It was
my grandchildren," she said, they say. "Songs without you went," she
said they say. Then | she began to sing, they say. Singing songs she
taught them they say. Songs all they learned they say. Songs | I do
not know. So they began to sing they say. These horses their songs
these I know there | four days were they found it was. " 'This here some
I do not teach you. These over there, my grandchildren, | those who live
there will teach you.' Those with she taught. 'Those,' she said. | 'do
not forget. Those songs you forget its day last more will not be (?) | its
day,' she told us our grandmother. People twelve live then two went.
Then horse | their songs they began to sing those we were taught. Then
Jet mountain its top ground we two came back | *tsibel'ai* its top *tc'ocgai*
its top then garden now this night we did not sleep. | This grass on it we
wash that good property will be. 'The people will increase will be,' she
told us | our grandmother." Fall it became, they say. *kiya'a* across
from they unloaded there they lived they say. Then some one came up |
they say. Mountain red just they were defeated in battle constantly
they say. There | those people who came from their grandmother bear
being their pet with those who traveled, "Loan is it (?) they were saying |
that for I came. At red mountain we get beat all the time. Bear loan
us that with we go to war they saying | here I came," he said they say the
strange man. "Very well," he said they say. The caretaker boss of
bear said it, they say *ba'ni'* | "Very well. Five days will be," he said they
say *ba'ni'*. Then five when days were they started. People | started to
war. When it was dark they camped they say. South he sat down, they
say. Bear young spruce | he pulled up. Across each other he laid them.
Over them he sat they say. Very good when it was dark then songs | they
heard. *ba'ni'* spoke they say. Bear he addressed they say. "My pet,
red mountain where it is called | people get beaten all the time. Now
there we go to war." That bear he got up they say. He stretched him-
self they say. | There *kittcil* where they live those who get killed all the
time those killed many they say.

You think of me *nayenezyani* I am black obsidian my shoes
being. You think of me | black obsidian my leggings my sides
four places hang down black obsidian | my hat headdress black
obsidian lightning with four times from me they shoot out. Where
it goes old | no good talk something kill you what is shot that
direction they put their hands down (get killed.) | Old age I am one
to be afraid of I am. Think of me when it was light |

dibitc'į' dadɛsbąi. e yɛgo hadaidɛlį nadaltc'i kalgai djịn ndɛ sin dists'ą djịn.

> dibɛ halgai tsɛtna' adɛsde djịn sin ci yi.
> xoxonnigɛ k'at naisdlɛl.
> ha'a biyadji' xadanigɛ dilxil nandɛldja naicdlel.
> tsa'anaɣai kabịnnihodzit nąnadildja naisdlel.
> yinyihi

(Eight songs like this.)

nɛstin bɛ tcaxolxɛl ado hwolsannigo tsɛna nildɛ. i'ągo nịnna' hojo' xilnanedjịñgo ahwot'ɛgo nanesda djịn. tc'oyaj alna nainịldɛl nahwodjịngo sịn nadists'ą djịn. cac nni djịn.

> aya'iyɛ
> cactsodilxil k'at bɛcdilxil cikɛ
> hiyai bɛcdilxil sịsł'ɛgo
> hiyai bɛcdilxil adicciej
> hiyai lick'ałaba sɛgozt'i
> hiyai bɛcdilxil k'at dɛchidja
> hiyai sitsita do lick'ałaba
> lictsodilxil bilhanaihadil
> hiyai cikɛlatado attsịnnil
> l'ic xanai idil bɛaidis'is
> cigotado atsịnnill'ic hanaiyidil bɛditdisis
> hiyai cilalatado atsịnnill'ic hanaiyidil
> bɛdididicnɛ
> hiyai sizalatado atsịnnill'ic hanaiyidil bɛyadicti'
> hiyai k'a sitsitado taditdin hadolkọn axɛyaai
> lickałaba lictsodilxil kadęya hiyaii
> bɛcdilxil atsịnnill'ic dịngo sɛts'a naxadil
> ni'naxadilgɛ yadantcọngɛ deyoiyalti bɛ'inizi'
> bidɛzla atcɛilɛcgo ka'ịl'it'

ts'a'anaɣa binoxatdzit acịnneli' k'at acịnneli' haiyihi xosidjịn ndjiɛdje' kodo cacyɛnɛ' nihiniya hadị'a djịn. k'at tciditdja ho ciyi' yicalgɛ' hogɛ'.

> nayɛ'nezɣani ciciclịgo ciyicalgo'hogɛ'
> bɛc dilxil cikɛgo bɛ dicalgi'hwogɛ'
> bɛcdilxil sịsł'ɛ bɛdicalgi'hogɛ'
> bɛcdilxil ci'ɛ'go bɛdicalgi'hwogɛ'
> bɛcdilxil citc'ago bɛ dicalgi'hwogɛ'
> bɛcdilxil ats'ịnnill'ic bịl dịgo sits'a naxadil

toward them they go to war.   Those (?) who watch they help prairie.
Then songs were heard | they say.

    This with prairie across they go they say songs I am.

Heat mirage now I become.

East toward under mirage black pointed stand up I become.

Old age one to be afraid of sticking up I become.

*yinyihi*

(There were eight songs like this).

    Heat mirage with darkness then not being seen across they went.
Sundown they camped. | Good when it was dark this way same way he
sat they say.   Young spruce across each other he put | when it was dark
again songs were heard again they say.   Bear made the noise they say.

    aya'iyɛ

Big black bear now black obsidian my moccasins

Black obsidian my leggings

Black obsidian my shirt

Gray arrow snake tied around me

Black obsidian I wear for a hat

Crown of my head gray arrow snake.

Black snake goes up from my head

Before my feet zigzag lightning darts

Snake ? with I step

My knees too zigzag lightning streams out with I step

(?) ends of my fingers zigzag lightning streams out with I work my
    hands

Point of my tongue zigzag lightning streams out with I talk

Crown of my head pollen rests as in a container

Gray arrow snake black rattlesnake they eat

Black obsidian zigzag lightning four ways from me streams out

Earth where it strikes bad things bad talk does not like you,

Missiles they spread out it causes

Old age afraid of me I am now I am *haiyihi*

    Morning it was they got up so far the bear walked he sang they
say.   "Now we are getting ready to fight me where I walk danger.

*nayɛnɛzɣani* I am where I walk

Black obsidian my feet moccasins with I walk dangerously

Black obsidian my leggings with I walk causing danger

Black obsidian my shirt with I walk causing danger

Black obsidian my headdress with I walk causing danger

Black obsidian zigzag lightning with four ways from me spreads out

niṇṇahadiłgε yadcntcoñgε diyayałti' tcałdindε
sa'annaγai binoxcłdzit niclịngo yicał
ci yidicałłεgi hogεla hiyaε' hiñyihi
kwe naki sila ndε. e doda noinłnεz. halγot' cac dịdε ałgilγotgo
xatdje xaxasł'itgo hats'ą. dadaltcigo. axεhola 'akọ tsiziz hadatsiznil
djin. dasai αltso nestsed. nheldε. hilkit hạ'a oldε hadondittsą djin
dzitdilgεsi tc'εji bił nicnajε bεsistogi bakại łitcii nicładji ł'onastasi toikał
bεstoggi baadε łitcii' dịdi yił iłna dolni. dịgo yisłago ninla·. naγε'nazγani
yidiłnigo dịgo yisł'ago ninla. tobadjictcini yidiłnigo aγεhεston ninla.
naγε'nεzγani diłnigo dịgo yisł'ago nainla. tobadjictcini diłnigo nainla.
kodjiεnnε' dịdε yił ałna' dolni tc'ilεnε iyi'itts'i bεsistogε yεdo'. nicnadjε
daiyołdjołε nicł'adji yi'itts'i tcilε bεsistogε yεdo' batis adεste djin. ho-
tsoilą nε cac αnni djin. hadi'a djin.

tsεnassila. yεnadεtdza.
naγεnεzγanε ciniciigo yεnadεtdza.
bεc diłxił cikεgo yεnaditdza
bεcdiłxił sisł'εgo yεnaditdza
bεcdiłxił ci'εgo yεnaditdza.
bεcdiłxił dịgo cacgij ndokε
bεcdiłxił citc'a
bεcdiłxił ats'inniłł'ic bił dịgo sits'a naxadił
nadiłgε yadantcoñgε bidεzla' co'odotc'i'
tsinnasila yεεnaditdza heyihi
xastą citdja ndi bini' ałalε ła' ilgit ha'anoldε da'ai αlyagεt'εgo.
hodzo' αnnedla djin. sin xastą nanasdja. bitis nadεsdε'. k'asidą' tąkεłdε
to'ixinniłt'adji hat'i.
tsinasiyañaihihi yε k'innadzittsago
naγε'nεzyan ci ciciiyigo
bεcdiłxił cikεgoyε
bεcdiłxił sisł'εyεgo
bεcdiłxił ci'εyεgo
bεcdiłxił dịgo cocgiz ndokε hiyigo
bεcdiłxił citc'a yigo
bεcdiłxił ats'inniłł'ic dịgo cits'a naxadił
naxadiłgε dεyoyałti
bidεzla' co'ohasał
ts'a'annaγa binoxatdzit k'a cinniciigo heyigo
tsinnasiyayε hihiyε kanaditdza hiyihi

Where it goes dangerous talk with it I walk
Old age causing fear I being I walk
With it causing danger I walk

Then two songs long. Then those not long ones. He ran up bear
four times when he ran around. | Their hearts he took out from them.
They were red. They lie by each other their scalps they take | they say.
He himself all he killed. They started home. Hill stands up they passed.
He stood upright they say | (a bush) (a bush) with right hand arrow point
male red, left (herb) (herb) | arrow point female red four places with across
he moved his hands. Four times curves he made. *nayɛnɛzɣani* | speaking
like four times curves he made. *tobactcictcini* talking like straight marks
he made. | *nayɛ'nɛzɣani* talking like four curves he made again. *tobactcic-
tcini* talking like he made. | This way four places with across he moved his
hands the branches he sticks | in arrow points that too. Left side he had in
his left hand he sticks up *tcilɛ* arrow point that too over it he moves (?)
they say. | (Brush) bear speaks they say. He began to sing they say.

I make a mark they won't cross it.
*nayɛnɛzɣani* I am, they won't cross it
Black obsidian my moccasins they won't cross it.
Black obsidian my leggings they won't cross it
Black obsidian my shirt they won't cross it
Black obsidian four times my sides hang down
Black obsidian my headdress,
Black obsidian zigzag lightning darts four times from me stream out
Where it goes dangerous missiles will be scattered
I make a mark they won't cross

Six songs lay his mind one hill sticks up. They pass over just that
the way he did. | Lines he made again they say. Songs six lay again.
Over they went again. Nearly (?) he sang it was:—

*tsinasiyañaihi* with they stand
*nayɛnɛzɣani* I am
Black obsidian my moccasins being,
Black obsidian my leggings
Black obsidian my shirt
Black obsidian four times my staffs hanging
Black obsidian my headdress
Black obsidian zigzag lightning four times from me they shoot out
Where it goes bad talk
What is shot it flies away
Old age one to be afraid of I am
*tsinasiyañaihi* one to be afraid of I am

hastan nadetą ąltso. bitsɨddji nilde. ąltso bitsi nildɛ. sʼin' nadistsʼą.

didisisgɛhwogɛ nazonłdisɛ cinicli.
didisishogɛ cacłaba' cinicli didisisgo.
dɛdisisgɛ' bitsʼa digic.
dedisisgɛ' binohodzit dɛdisisgɛholgɛ.
tsʼaʼanaγai binohɨtdzit cinicligo dɛdisisgɛholgɛ hiyɛhi
nɨłtcʼi biłxolnɛʼgo heyɛatʼit djɨnnɛ. tsɛbi' cidjandi' dałailɛ adaditdlą
xoγan bitcʼį' haistʼįdɛ haʼasdɛ. hanadotʼa djɨn.

cił nahodił nadzillit biką'
dɨłxɨł cił nahodił
sʼaʼannaγai binohodziʼt cinicli cił nahodił hɛyihi
kwina sila bɛni cił naitʼac. naki nanasdlą. dałaigo naididji cił
dɑnnatʼaj naki nanasdlą cił nɑnnɛskɛ. naki nanasdlą naildɛ' yołkałgo
dokos tsini do' hogɛ'. ndaditdaγɛ binɛ' botcillolɛ binigɛ' annila djɨnnɛ.
cac bɨł naildɛ go badinnotcįt djɨnnɛ. danɛtɛtcinnɛ wonnasi' daxałʼǫ'
djɨnnɛ. dosiʼdoniłdɑlla cilįʼ ni djɨn. baʼnį' dogakɛhi nilka djɨnnɛ. bika do
nda cilįʼ. yołgai baʼγa hodzanɛ acdlago łʼobadahisnil. nicnadjiʼ bilatsʼi
nɑstiʼ. kodji do' nɨsłʼadji acdlaʼ badɑssinnɛlgo bilatsʼi nɑstʼi. bikɛ do'
asdlaʼ badɑssinnɛlgo bikɛtsin nɑstiʼ. nɨsłʼadji do' bikɛ ɑsdlaʼ bikɛtsin
nɑstiʼ ɑsdlaʼ badassinnɛlgo' biγąγa hastiʼ. bidjagic dɛstci taditdin dołʼij
taditdin tsʼɨnbittadɨtdɨn tɛł bitadɨtdɨn dahisdja. dołʼijɛ bizatʼąʼ hanaʼa.
nijɛdɛanlɛgo hadanastsʼɛgo baγa hahacnij. taditdin atʼɛ bigiszas. adɛniłdɛ
adɛsγat taditdinnɛ nałdaz. cac bananoγat holgedo. di cac biza nastąʼ
holgedo. yołkałgo binɛ' honłclido bɛ sitdza honigɛʼdoyɛ nda hoditdago
bɛsoditzindo cilįʼ. dzɨł tcaxałγɛl holgɛgɛ' nɑndiłti. kodji dzɨł lijin holgɛ
nikʼe holo'. adji dɑndiditał. taditdinɛnnɛ' bizatdja ła bitagi dahisdja.
bitsɨddji disnil. ła bikɛdi dɛznil xanadota deyanahi.

Six he sang all. Ahead of him they went. All ahead of him passed.
Songs they heard again.

When I move my feet danger whirlwind I am.

When I move my feet with danger gray bear I am when I walk.

Where I walk from me lightning issues where I walk

It to be feared where I walk is called.

Old age where I walk is called

Wind telling him he did that they say. Eight lay this one I get
tired | house toward from where he had seen they come up. He began
to sing again they say.

With me it moved rainbow male,

Black with me it moved

Old age that is to be feared I am with me it moved

These two lie with me we two go. Two become again just one way
the words with me | they get home. Two lie again with me they two sit.
Two lie again they get home. | After this cough fever too danger when go
one said (?) live behind (?). That is why he said it they say. | Bear with
him they returned when he was mad they say. He ran off after him he
tied (?) | they say. "You were going to do bad thing my pet," he said
they say. *ba'ni'*. Sacred buckskin he spread they say. "On it | sit
my pet." White Shell holes five on a string lie on. Right his wrist |
encircle. Here too left five on a string his wrist encircle. His feet too |
five on a string his ankle encircle. Left too his foot five his ankle |
encircle five on a string across his breast lie. Between his ears
specular iron powder, turquoise | powder, trees their pollen, cattails
their pollen he put on. Turquoise his mouth he took out. | Your spit
being on it where it is twisted his hair he pulled out. Pollen it was he
put on it. | He shook himself pollen falls off. Bear it comes off it
will be called. This bear his mouth was put in | it will be called.
Hereafter ? I will live with from will be danger bad things stay
away with it | they will wash my pet. Mountains darkness where it is
called I found you. This side mountain black is called | your clan is.
There you walk. That pollen was in his mouth some on his head he puts. |
Before him he put it. Some behind him he put. He began to sing again
he walked.

k'at sasołdił dziłdiłxił bɛdaxonakadji deyanahi
tc'odiłxił dadinladji deyanahi.
taditdin k'ɛhɛ'ɛtindji dɛyanahi
taditdin bɛkɛkixastcin bikɛdji dɛyanahi.
taditdin biisda'k'ɛ hastcin bikadji' bɛyanahi.
bits'iddji xojongo dɛyanahi
bikɛdi hojongo dɛyanahi
biyagi hojongo dɛyanahi
bik'igi hojongo dɛyanahi
bina'ałtso hojongo dɛyanahi
bizat hojongo dɛyanahiyɛ hojon djiat'ɛ djin.

kodji nt'i cac iyą dził łijin holgedji'. e ba cac dodildaca ciłni citcai
baiłnikǫnsi nɛsdoitso t'a'ai bɛhikɛgo hanadilya djinnɛ. dził łitsoi holgɛgi
nandiłti cilį'. adji tsɛłłitso holge adji dandaditał e bą aidji nɛsdoitso
t'ohaiyoi djinnɛ. k'adi. kodji nt'i.

Now big bear mountain black (?) he steps
Spruce black his door post he walks.
Pollen in his trail he walks
Pollen his foot its image on it he walks.
Pollen where he sat its image on it he walks.
Before him fortunately he walks
Behind him happily he walks,
Below him happily he walks,
Above him happily he walks,
All around him happily he walks
His tongue happily he walks they say.

Bear went mountain black where it called. That because bear are mean there (?). He told me my maternal grandfather | *baiɫnikǫnsi*. Panther same way they decorated they say. Mountain yellow where is called | I will find you my pet. There yellow stone called there you walk that because there panthers | many they say. Enough. Here its end.

# FREE TRANSLATIONS
## THE EMERGENCE

It was named "water everywhere," "black world," "one word," and "trees standing." It was also called "white-shell waves moving," "turquoise waves moving," "white shell stands vertical," and "turquoise stands vertical."

Here where the sun would rise in the future, blackness rose up and whiteness rose up. There where blackness and whiteness rose together First Man came into being. With him was a white ear of corn of white shell which was kerneled completely over its end.

Here (in the west) blueness and yellowness rose up. Where they rose up together, First Woman came into being. A yellow ear of corn of abalone shell, completely covered at the end with kernels, came into being with her.

The man started walking. When blackness rose up, he saw a fire in the distance, but when whiteness came up he couldn't find it. When this had happened three times, he put up a stick so that it pointed to the fire. When blackness went away and whiteness came again he sighted along the stick and located smoke near a hill. He walked around the hill saying to himself, "Whose house is this that I have come to in vain? Who lives here? Why doesn't the person come to me?" The fire was rock crystal. He went back.

When blackness came up she discovered a fire. When whiteness came up again she started to travel. She came to a gap in a ridge and set up a stick pointing toward the fire. When she sighted along this she found the fire she had seen was by the side of a hill where there was smoke. The fire was of turquoise. "Someone is living in a house I cannot see," she said to herself.

"Are you walking about? Did you come here?" the man asked. "Why should it be thus? Your fire is rock crystal; mine is turquoise. Why should we be separated. Let us live here together." "All right, let it be my house," the woman said. Then they lived together.

Someone came there. It was "Water Coyote" who runs on the water and knows everything about the water. From this direction came Coyote wearing a coyote skin blanket. He knows everything on the land. Others came there, whose bodies were short and their legs so long. They were yellow-jackets who have stings with which they witch people.

Four others came there, who were short bodied and wore black shirts. They were tarantulas. Four more came, black ones, black ants that had stings with which they witched people. Three others came there, they were also black, but they had nothing with which to sting. They were named *xolɛdjinnɛ*. They wanted to live there but they were not wanted. These began stinging and killing each other by witchcraft. "There is no use trying to live with them," First Man said, and went up through the sky to the world above. The others moved up after him.

That was the blue world which was lying there and all those living on it were blue. They were birds, blue birds, jays, small jays, chapparal jays, and blue jays. The world was small and became crowded. They did the same way again; they began to witch each other. Then First Man, First Woman, Water Coyote, and Coyote, went up again to another world which was yellow. They found it was like this. To the east stood a mountain called *sisnadjinnɛ* (Pelado Peak), to the south was *tsodzil* (Mount Taylor), to the west was *dogostil* (San Francisco Peaks) and to the north was *debentsa* (La Plata Mountains). In the center was *dzilna'odilɛ* and on the east side of it *tc'olį*.

There were living there yellow ant people, red ant people, and black ants with red heads. On the east side of Pelado Peak Turquoise-boy lived with twelve male companions. They had large male reeds. Mirage people lived with him. Toward the west where the sun will set in the future lived White-shell Woman with twelve female companions. They had large female reeds. Female shimmering heat people lived with her. Here at a place called, brown mountain, turkey lived. He had brown corn.

Now it was becoming crowded. First Man spoke. "Let them live as married people," he said. They made five chiefs; large snake, bear, wolf, panther, and otter. These five held a council and established clans. "If you marry one of your own clan you will go crazy and go into the fire." That is why they are afraid to marry into their own clans. "Now go home and let those who like each other get married. There will be hermaphrodites who will know women's work and who will live like women. They will know the ways of both men and women," First Man said.

First Man planted the white corn which was created with him, and First Woman her yellow corn, and Turquoise-boy his blue corn. "Now you who live at Brown Mountain, it is your turn," First Man said. Then Turkey danced four times back and forth saying "da da da da." First he dropped brown corn, then watermelon seeds, musk melon seeds, and last spotted beans. Much got ripe and they harvested the corn.

The wife of First Man was untrue to him. Mirage Man went to First Man and talked to him until blackness arose. They continued while blackness arose four times. The people didn't hear any one. They listened in vain for the second chief. After that blackness came up again. The next chief talked but they didn't hear him. The next talked and they didn't hear him. Finally, Otter spoke. "What is the matter that we do not hear? You who are the leader, tell us why you do not talk." "Very well," said First Man, "tell yonder hermaphrodite to come here." When he arrived, First Man asked who made the pot for him. "I made it for myself," he replied. "Who made the little gourd cup?" "I planted it," he said. "Who made the metate for you?" "I did," he replied. "Who made the hairbrush?" "I made it," he said. "Who made the stirring sticks?" "I made them," he replied. "Who made the water-basket?" "I made it," he said.

First Man had not eaten or drunk for four days. "Get some water for me. I want to eat. Prepare some food. I am hungry. She scolded me badly. I am like this because she was false to me," he said.

"Make a raft," he said. "We will find out who is the stronger. All of us men and boys will go across on the raft which they are making." They made a raft so large and all the men arrived on the other side of the river on it. The women lived on one side and the men on the other, and a large stream ran between them. The men made new farms. The women went about singing, while they planted the old farms to their full extent. They raised a crop of corn. The next year the men planted more land to corn, but the women did not plant all of the farmland. The next year the men planted still more and the women again fell short of the year preceding. The fourth year, the men extended their fields still further, but the woman's fields had all reverted and were gone. The men had plenty, but the women had no crops and famine was killing them. They were especially hungry for meat.

"Bring the raft across," they called, but the men did not hear. One woman called and ran into the water and drowned. Another did the same, and a third and fourth. The second chief came across with the raft. When he had returned to the men, he reported the women to be poor and starving. "What is to happen?" he asked. "There can be no increase living this way." In the same manner the third and fourth chiefs spoke. "They have learned their lesson by now. Are they not punished enough?" asked the last chief. "All right," replied First Man. "They are poor. Tell them never as long as they live to do such things again. Bring them across."

They brought them across. First Man told all the men to bathe and dry themselves with white cornmeal and then to apply pollen to their bodies from head to foot. The women were also told to bathe and to dry themselves with the yellow cornmeal and to apply the pollen in the same manner. They were requested to refrain from intercourse for four days, after which they were allowed to come together.

To the leadership of First Man they attributed the misfortune of the women, the deaths from famine and drowning.

When there was blackness, Coyote came wearing his blanket. First Woman instructed and provided him with a rainbow. The two children of *toholtsodi* were swimming where the water flows out in four directions. Coyote caught them with the rainbow and drew them out. Whiteness arose here and here. The weather became cold. From the east white ones flew, from the south blue ones flew, from the west yellow ones flew, and from the north black ones flew. First Man sent black hawk toward the east to investigate. When he returned he reported that it was water. He sent hummingbird toward the south. He returned, bringing the same report that it was water. This way he sent the chief of the water, egret, who can walk on it who confirmed the report. "What shall we do about it?" he asked. "My children," said First Man, "we will go to the top of Pelado Peak." They all moved there and everyone living on the earth joined them. The First Man took up some of the soil in turn from Pelado Peak, Mount Taylor, San Francisco Peaks, La Plata Mountain, *dziłna'odiłi* and *tc'ol'į.* The people came after him, Turquoise Boy with black bow wood and the large male reeds. After him came the twelve men who lived with him and after them the male Mirage people. Here from the west of Pelado Peak came White-shell girl and the female large reeds with mulberry bows. After her came the twelve women and the Quivering Heat people. "Why didn't you tell me," said Turkey who came from Brown Mountain.

The water had reached the middle of Pelado Peak when First Man said, "Where is my medicine? I shall have to die some time. I am going back for it." "No, I will go back after it for you," said Blue Heron. He flew up and then went down hard to the bottom of the water. He came out with the medicine, but his legs were long. That is the way he got his name.

The water came to the top of Pelado Peak. He erected a large reed and blew against it so that it grew up until it reached the sky. Nodes were formed inside the reed. All of them entered the reed and started to climb up, but as Turkey was last his tail protruded into the water so that the ends of the feathers were washed white. When they reached the sky, Turkey said, "Let the water stop here." They couldn't break through the sky. "Well, sir, try it," First Man said. Then Woodpecker started pecking. The place became thin and finally gave way. The people moved up until they came to the sky hole, then *toholtsodi* appeared with his horns, the ends of which are blue, and asked for his children.

Coyote had his blanket girded around him. "Look in that," someone suggested. Then they filled an abalone shell basket with hard jewels, water mineral powder, blue pollen, and cattail pollen. They put the filled basket between *tohotltsodi's* horns.

Then Coyote spoke. "No, I will give you only one of the children. With the white fabric of the other I will cause male and female rains and make the black clouds. I will cause flowers to grow on the mountain tops and vegetation to spring up. With the moisture we will be able to live." To this *tohotltsodi* gave his assent. The girl was returned to him and the water stopped rising.

Cicada made himself a headband and fastened two feathered arrows crossing each other in front and two arrows feathered with yellow tail feathers behind. Where the hole had been drilled through to the upper world water was lying they say. Cicada made a pile of mud on which to stand.

Then a grebe came to him from the east plowing out the water, so that Cicada was splashed with it. The grebe had crossed feathered arrows in his headband in front. He stared at Cicada and then took off a pair of arrows and passed them through his alimentary canal from above and below so that they passed each other and were drawn out in opposite directions again. "Do this if you want to live here," he said to the Cicada. "Oh, that has already been done to me," said Cicada, who then took off a pair of his arrows and thrust them through his chest from side to side drawing them out so that they passed each other. "Do this if you want to live here," he said to the grebe who, without speaking, went away again, plowing up the water which flowed away after him toward the east.

Then a blue grebe came from the south, stared at Cicada, and splashed water on him. He too took yellow feathered arrows from his headband and passed them through his alimentary canal. "Do this if you wish to live here," he said to Cicada. "It is already done, but you do this," Cicada replied and passed two arrows through his chest. The blue grebe without a word turned and plowed through the water toward the south, taking the water with him.

Next came a yellow grebe from the west, throwing water on the Cicada, and staring at him. "People do not live here," he said and proceeded to pass the arrows through his digestive tracts. "Do that," he said, "if you would live here." "Oh, that has already been done, but you do this," Cicada replied, and taking a pair of arrows passed them through his chest. The yellow grebe, without speaking, turned back toward the west, plowing out the water which followed him.

Last of all, came a black grebe from the north, plowing out the water and staring at the Cicada. He, too, took a pair of arrows from his forehead and passed them through his alimentary canal in opposite directions. "Do that and you may live here," he said. "Well, that has already been done, but try this," Cicada replied, and passed a pair of arrows through his chest in opposite directions. The black grebe said nothing, but went back toward the north, plowing the water and taking it with him.

Now all the water which had been there was gone; it had flowed together to form the ocean. Cicada returned and reported that there had been water above, but that by a hard series of contests with four grebes he had secured its removal and that now there was nothing but mud.

Then they secured turquoise, white-shell, abalone, red shell, jet, and powdered iron ore; also powdered blue flowers, pollen, and tree pollen. These hard substances and pollen they sent by Small Wind as a fee for those living above, that they should dry up the mud. Then the winds blew for four days and four nights and the earth was dried up.

Badger was sent up to investigate conditions. When he returned, his legs so high up were black from the mud. "It is dried up a little," he reported. "Go up," he told them. "Wait," said First Man. Then they decorated panther and wolf. They adorned wolf with eagle tails and panther with variegated corn.

The first to come up was "Water Coyote," then First Man, and next First Woman, and finally First Warrior. After them came the people generally. They had now arrived on the white earth.

They heard singing below and Panther with Wolf was climbing up. "Pull Panther out!" First Man told them. One side (Navajo) trotted there, but they missed him, pulling up Wolf instead of Panther. "This one will be ours," they said. The ancient Pueblo people who built the straight walled houses pulled up Panther. The Pueblo people have houses and they like corn the same as we. From the black earth, from the blue earth, from the yellow earth, from the white earth; some of the people are from the black earth, some from the blue earth, some from the yellow earth, some from the white earth.

"Now that all have moved up, there will be a hogan," First Man said. On the east side he put up a male reed, and on the west, opposite it, a female reed. On the south side he leaned an oak timber, and opposite, on the north, a mulberry log. "I will put cornmeal on these four timbers," he said.

Over there, the ancient Pueblo peoples had built straight-walled houses with clay. "We have built a round house. We are tired from our travels," said First Man, "let us rest, my children." "You make a sweathouse," he told Beaver. "Bring up some stones." He brought them up and they found Beaver had made a good round sweathouse which he had plastered with mud. He had also made a fire and had put the four stones in it where they became white hot. He made a good door and on the north side a place to crawl out. He put the four stones inside. Then he hung a white coyote blanket over the door and above that a white blanket, over that a black fabric, and over that figured calico. When the four were hung he shouted out, "Ooohwu, come into the sweathouse." Many came in. "It is crowded," said First Man to Beaver. "Phu, phu, phu, phu," he said as he blew and the sweathouse became larger and the others came in. "Weh, old man," he said and Beaver began to sing.

> "Those who came on top built it.
> Sticks women with he built it.
> Black stones with he built it.
> Earth with he built it.
> Living old age in safety with he built it."

Those who had been tired had now sweated and were rested. The Pueblo people who have houses do not have sweathouses. Those led by First Man, who have the round hogans, are accustomed to go into sweathouses.

First Man, First Woman, First Boy, and First Girl went into the hogan which had been made. First Man lay this way and First Woman nearer the door with First Man's medicine between them. Lying thus (with their heads pillowed on their arms) they began to talk, speaking softly. First Boy and First Girl, lying on the other side of the fire, were unable to hear and listened in vain until morning. Dawn came without their having slept. During the following day it was the same; the talk went on so softly the children could not distinguish the words. If they approached nearer, so they might hear, the talking stopped entirely. The next night was also spent by the elders in talking so softly that the children could not hear what was said, although they stayed awake all night listening. Day dawned but the talking continued. First Boy stood listening until night. The parents lay huddled up that night also talking until morning.

Four nights and four days had passed without their sleeping making eight altogether. Then First Boy addressed them. "Why don't you talk before us? We cannot sleep and we are suffering from sleepiness." When he spoke thus language was originated.

First Man replied that they were discussing what should be in the world. They wanted to know how to live until old age. They had also discussed the sun, the mountains, the months, the trees, and what should be upon the earth.

He stationed guards in a circle around the hogan before he began his plans, but Coyote stepped in without being seen. "What are you doing?" he inquired. First Man covered the diagram drawn on the floor and replied that nothing was being discussed. Coyote went back.

The next day, guards were stationed in two circles around the hogan and the work resumed. When the plan was drawn Coyote again stepped in without being seen by the guards. First Man spread something over his drawing. "What are you talking about?" Coyote inquired. "We are not discussing anything," First Man replied. "So you are not planning anything," Coyote said, and returned. It was morning again and he placed guards in three circles around the hogan before resuming his work. Just as he was finishing his plan Coyote appeared, having again passed the guards without being detected. First Man covered his work again. "Cousin, what are you planning?" Coyote asked. "We are not talking about anything," First Man replied, and Coyote went away again.

It was day for the fourth time. Guards were placed in four circles around the hogan. "Go to *tsedadin* and invite the venerable Black God who resides there. We want his fire to make the sun hot." They made the sun glowing hot with it. The moon they made just a little warm with rock crystal. That is why it does not give out heat. "It will give a little light," he said.

Then with a diagram on the ground he named the months.

This month will be called *natac*, "spider." The traveling of animals will be its soft feather. In this month the mountain-sheep will run together. The heart of the month was made of shimmering heat.

This month will be called *niltc'its'osi*, "slender wind." *hastin ak'ai*, "old man standing with his feet apart," will be its soft feather. In this month antelope will mate. Its heart is made of slender heat.

This will be named *niltc'itso*, "large wind," *tse'etso*, "first large," will be its soft feather. Its heart is made of cold. In this month deer will run with each other.

This will be called *zasnilt'es*, "snow cooked." Its heart will be *tin*, "ice." Its soft feather will be *ik'aisadai*, "morningstar."

This one will be called *atsabiyaj*, "young eagles." The eagles will warm their nests. Its soft feather will be *gaxal'ε*, "rabbit track." Its heart is made of round hail. During this month rabbits will mate.

This will be called *xoztcint*, "horns lost." Its soft feather will be *dibεni*, "Say's phoebe." Its heart is made of small hail. At the end of this month mountain-sheep will give birth to their lambs.

Now winter has passed and summer begins.

This will be called *hil'atcil*, "little vegetation." Its soft feather is *dεl*, "crane." Cranes will migrate in that month. Its heart is made of *tc'il*, "vegetation."

This one will be called *at'ạtso*, "leaves large." Its soft feathers are made of *natta'*, "rain" and its heart of *niyol* "wind." In this month the antelope have their young.

This month will be called *ya'icdjactcillε*. Its soft feathers will be *djadεyac*, "Young antelope." Vegetation will begin to ripen its fruit. Its heart will be *xadots'osi*, "slim heat."

This one will be called *ya'icdjatso*, "seeds large." Its soft feather is made of *ndjijoc*, "little strings of rain" and its heart of *xado'* "heat." In this month deer have their fawns. The Pleiades come up in this month and they will lie on the backs of the fawns.

This month will be called *nt'ạ ts'osi*, "slender ripe." Its soft feather will be *nittsạ' bikại*, "male rain." Its heart is made of *nd'ats'osi*, "slender ripe."

This will be called *nt'atso*, "large ripe." At the end of it all vegetation will be mature. That will be its heart. Its soft feather will be *nitts'a ba'at*, "rain female."

He had now placed all six (of the summer months).

Then he asked Turquoise Boy who was to step inside (the sun), where he was from. "I am from the east side of Pelado Peak," replied Turquoise Boy. "Step inside," he told him. "Put the flute made of large reed with twelve holes under your shirt. Let the Mirage People step in with you. By means of them you will pass by unseen." "All right," he replied. "but whenever I pass by I shall be paid by a person's death. Not only your people here, but wherever they move they must pay it. I have 102 roads and that number of people will die."

Then he asked White-shell Boy where he was from. "I belong on the west side of Pelado Peak. I am White-shell Boy," he replied. "You step into the moon," he told him. "Hereafter if something happens you two will trade places."

Although there were four lines of guards, Coyote came without being seen. First Man covered up the drawing from Coyote. Small Wind warned him that Coyote was about to say something unfortunate. He had gone to see Black God where he had fire, "Why didn't they tell us about it?" he said. Over there he had made a picture of the sun, but what kind is not known. He handed it to Black God who got angry, said "gaaa," and tore it up. Coyote ran off because Black God was the one person he feared.

He had made a drawing on a background, white above and yellow below. He had drawn lines across it with turquoise, abalone, jet, white shell, and rock crystal, five lines in all. He had this under his blanket fold.

"Why did you hide this matter from me? Tell what is on this. You wouldn't tell me because you said I would make everything crooked. It is true I did that, but not on my own initiative. With you, First Woman, as my leader, I did it. Your leadership was altogether unfortunate. You told me you wanted to win. By your direction I took the young of *tohoĺtsodi*. I did a little better than that however." Saying this, he put the stick with which he had made the drawing down in the center.

Then Young Wind told First Man that he must guess what the drawing meant or it would be established. He told him in detail what was intended by each mark. First Man began to explain the design. "You drew this with turquoise to represent the green vegetation. You mean that the vegetation has fallen off by the line drawn with abalone. The line of jet means that the leaves are all off and that there are black horizontal stripes on the mountains. The line drawn with white shell is for the mountain tops covered with snow. The rock crystal line is for ice to which all the water has turned. You have put down six on the other side. What will the names be? What more are you to do?"

"We will get all mixed. You finish it," Coyote said and went home.

He put them in the sun. When they were making the sun, they sang this way.

> His face will be blue.
> His eye marks will be black.
> His mouth mark will be black.
> A horizontal yellow mark will be across his cheek.
> His horns will be blue.
> He placed it in the sky with a mirage.

Saying this, First Man chewed a medicine called *adzilĺ'ijtso* and blowing it out of his mouth sprinkled the sun in four places. He then put the sun in the sky and it began to move. "I will go to this place called *dzaxadzis*, "low place," or "reservoir" and there I will eat lunch. The blue horse that I ride will eat there also. . . . ."

He traveled. By the time he went down, the people were nearly roasted. "You nearly burned them," he said. The next time he passed over higher up. This made twice he had crossed over. It was very warm and the people nearly boiled. He went over the third time and it was hot. Again he raised it up and when the sun went over the fourth time the temperature was just right.

Then they made a model of the world, so large. Pelado Peak was adorned with White-shell, Mount Taylor was decorated with turquoise, San Francisco Peaks with abalone, La Plata Mountain with jet, *dzitna-xodilɛ* with mirage. They made the heart of the earth, named *tc'ol'i*, of jewels. It was made round. "This will be called *yoditdzil* (Bule Mountain) and this *nittsadzil* (Rain Mountains). Then he made a mountain ridge and placed it north and south. *noxozili* was its skull. They covered it with *bɛc*, "iron" or "obsidian" and stuck arrowheads up around it. They became the black peaks that stand up. Way over on the west side they made its breast. Water flows out of the ground there. "Here it will be called prairie," he said. Here where water will flow are the pericardis and diaphragm. The stream at its base will be called *atnasdli* "flowing across each other."

"Let those having seed plant them on Pelado Peak," he said. Gray Pine Squirrel planted pines and Black Squirrel, spruce, Blue-jays planted piñons, and Small Squirrel, cedar. After that, all the people each planted the seed of the vegetation on which he lives. They still grow on the earth.

First Man then took the soil he brought from the third world and put down Pelado Peak, Mount Taylor, San Francisco Peaks, La Plata Mountains, four of them. He put ground-up mirage stone on *dzitnaodilɛ* and precious hard stones on *tc'ol'i*. "Who brought up the stone?" he asked. "I did," replied Cañon Wren. He took that stone, pounded it up, and sowed the pieces back and forth. They became the rocks which stand in a line.

Then the four people who stand under the earth began to sing, and, moving away from each other they stretched out the earth. The mountains grew large.

They say they have them in Mesa Verde. Now it was complete.

He put the Pleiades in place, and then *atsɛts'oz, hastin sakk'ai, atsɛtso yikaisdai, gaxat'e, naxokos bikɑ, naxokos bi'adɛ,* and here put *bɛkon.*[1] He placed Coyote's star also. Then Coyote said, "These will

---

[1] According to the Franciscan Fathers, the following stars or constellations are meant: *atsɛts'oz,* belt and sword of Orion; *xastin sakk'ai,* a square in Corvis; *atsɛtso,* the fore part of Scorpion; *yik'aisdai* (perhaps milky way); *gaxat'e,* cluster of stars under Canis Major; *naxokɔs bikɑi,* Ursa Major; *naxokɔs bi'adɛ,* Cassiopeia; *bɛkon,* "its fire" in this case is the North Star.

be my stars," as he pulled out hairs from his head and blew them up.
They appeared as red stars. Then Coyote gathered up all the other stars
and, blowing four times, sent them to the sky in unplanned clusters.
First Man was going to arrange them all, but Coyote did this. "They
look nice that way," he said, and went back home.

Over here they made a representation of the sun on a rock, and it is
there to this day. (By means of it they know the days [?])

It was day again. A person died. When she had been dead four
days they talked about it. "Where has she gone?" they asked. Two
persons went east and returned without results. Two went south. Two
went west. Then two went north. "She isn't in any of these places,"
they reported. Then the two who carry the corpse, one in front and one
behind, put on masks and went to the place where the people had come
up from the lower world. When they looked down, they saw the
woman who had died sitting below combing her hair. The two men became nervous and that is why those who see a ghost become nervous.
When they returned, they reported that the dead person was sitting
below. First Man said, "They will not die for all time. Women will
not have menstrual periods. They will not give birth to babies." He
took up a stick over which skins are draped for dressing. It was painted
black. Throwing this into the water which stood there he said, "If this
floats up people will not finally die." Coyote picked up an ax and throwing it in the water said, "If this floats up people will not die." The ax
sank, but the stick floated. Because it floated, a person's soul comes to
life again. Because the ax sank people die.

A sapsucker came there. "Menses have become," she said. "A
person's hair will not turn gray. It will remain black," he said. Soon a
western robin came there. "Children," she said, "my head has become
completely gray."

"The men shall work hard. They shall plant and bring the wood.
The women too shall work. They shall prepare the food. The women
may marry. The men may marry," he said. Coyote came there and
said, "Cousin, I am married." That is why men marry.

First Woman thought about it and resolved to be the leader in these
matters. She concluded that she would not be the only one to commit
adultery, but that women in general would do that. She planned that it
would be hard for men and women, once attached, to separate again.
She decided that both men and women should have medicine to attract
each other. Then she made a penis of turquoise. She rubbed loose
cuticle from the man's breast. This she mixed with yucca fruit. She

made a clitoris of red shell and put it inside the vagina. She rubbed loose cuticle from a woman's breast and mixed it with yucca fruit. She put that inside the turquoise penis. She combined herbs with waters of various kinds which should be for producing pregnancy. She placed the vagina on the ground and beside it the penis. Then she blew medicine from her mouth on them. That is why when people marry nowadays the woman sits on the left side.

"Now you think," she said to the penis. It did so and its mind extended across Mesa Verde. When the woman's organ thought its mind went nearly half way across and returned to her hips. That is why her longing does not extend to a great distance.

"Let them shout," she said. The penis shouted very loud, but the vagina had a weak voice. "Let them have intercourse and try shouting again," she said. When they tried again penis could not shout loud, but vagina had a good voice. The penis had lost its voice. As the organs were being put in place between the legs Coyote came. He pulled some of his beard out, blew on it, and placed it between the legs of both the man and woman. "It looks nice that way," he said.

While First Woman was doing this Great Snake, second chief, had been biting the people and killing them. Bear, who was the next chief in rank, had torn people. For these reasons both Great Snake and Bear were discharged from being chiefs. Panther and Otter didn't do anything and because of that their skins have value. To this day, if a chief does something bad he is discharged from office. "There will be chiefs," they said. "Now go wherever you like," he said. "I am studying about something else. There will be people."

It happened they were traveling in Mesa Verde with a groud dipper. They were traveling with a cat. They were bewitching the people who died as a consequence. Many people died.

There was a well behaved girl who had her hair covered with images of coyote, bluebird, and other birds made of turquoise. She had, besides, a disc of turquoise so large that a man standing could (just) put his hands on top of it. There were twelve white tails (eagles) and twelve red tails (hawk) fastened to its border.

The tribe moved away with her, going to *dzilnadjinnɛ* (Ute Mountain) and then to *kittsilbito'*, "Kittsil its spring." They were doing the same thing at both places. The people were dying and they were suspicious of each other. They moved away from the others and settled at *xats'abitoγi* (Dolores). At that place there was witching again. The people would not listen to advice and they moved to a place below *dzilic-*

*dlai.* Then the chief said they would go to *xadjinai.* They all consented to this. Finally, they came back and settled at *kintɛl* (the Aztec Ruin). Then fighting began, for the holy people wanted to kill the girl to get her treasures. Some of the people remained at Aztec and others moved to *kindol'ijɛ* (House Blue). They came there to fight also and they moved again to Mesa Verde. After that some of them went to explore Chaco Cañon. They found a good place for farms, much wild fruit, and plentiful game including deer, antelope, and mountain sheep. They decided to move there.

Then the sun had intercourse in a magical way with a woman named *naxoditdai,* "She picks up little things." This woman found herself pregnant and in nine days gave birth to a boy. Because of that the normal gestation period is nine months. Fifteen days after this boy was born he was grown up. For that reason a man matures in fifteen years. He ran a footrace around Mount Taylor. He had a bow and arrows and began killing pack-rats.

Large-fly came to him and said "Grandson, what are you doing? You should go to your father. Sun is your father. If you wish to go to him step on this," indicating a rainbow. He stepped on the rainbow and was carried to the summit of Mount Taylor and then to Pelado Peak and the sand dunes and was finally landed in front of Sun's door at a place called *i'a'itsɛ'na',* "Magpie's tail."

"No one goes around here with us. What do you come for?" the sun asked. Being instructed by small wind he replied, "I have a hard time and come to you for help."

(Omission of tests.)

"You are certainly my son," the sun assured him. When four days had passed, they two came to the middle of the sky. The sun put his hand in his blanket fold and drew forth a golden plate. He put water in this and mixed in some pollen and made mush. "Eat it with your five fingers," he bade his son. He tried, in vain, to eat all of the mush. When he couldn't do this he returned the plate with the remnants which the sun disposed of with four motions, dried the plate, and returned it to his blanket fold. The sun then gave his child a small wind which should ride on his ear and tell him what he should know. He gave him also turquoise earrings which would prevent him from losing when he gambled.

When he had returned, the people began to talk about the very valuable earrings which *naxodidai's* son was wearing. They inquired in vain where he could have gotten them, saying that there were none like them in their pueblo. They tried to trade for them, but without success. They offered him paper bread and finally the chief offered him a girl to be his wife. He refused to trade, but agreed to stake them in play. The other side wagered paper bread which filled a basket two feet high. The gambling was to be with seven wooden staves thrown as dice. It was agreed that the bet should be decided by one throw of the dice. The chief claimed the first throw, but the young man insisted that since the dice were his he should throw first. They came down white and he won the bread which he put away. Continuing to bet the turquoise he won all their goods and then their houses. He then offered to bet all his winnings against a woman. Then he won all the people.

When the gambling was done, he made slaves of the people and set them to work, feeding them with the bread which he had won. He had them build him a house, the round one that stands there, and then had them make a race track around it. The people came from the east and the west. Some of them (those from the west) lined up with him and the others were opposed.

He instituted the contest of pushing over a post set in the ground. He also made a *najǫci* pole. On this he put eagle claws and panther claws, the claws of all those which scratch. Those who knew how, put ten of these on the border of the pole. Its name was lightning or measuring worm. He made a ball, too, which should be thrown through a hole in the walls of one of the houses. If the ball went through, the other side would win the young man, but if they missed the hole they would lose.

The people of *kintel* (Aztec Ruin), *kindolij*, and *tsedɛs'a* were all talking about the gambler and what he was doing. They found he had guards watching for him in four places. When they had come, they bet their wives and the gambler won them. Then he bet the two women, all the assembled people and himself. He won a second time. Next he bet himself and his slaves against the land of the others. He won again. The visitors had only the large turquoise left. The gambler offered to bet all his winnings and himself against the turquoise. The contest was to be a footrace on the track which had been made and the contestants were required at the finish of the race to push over the posts which had been set in the ground. He had put one of the posts deep into the ground, but the one he was to push over was put down only a little way.

When they started on the race around the house the gambler let his opponent run in the lead. He then began bewitching him by shooting magical objects into his body. He shot him first in the muscles of the lower legs, then in the thighs, between the shoulders, and at the base of his head. The bewitched man staggered as he ran and the gambler passed him. Wailing went up from the partisans of the defeated man and shouts from the followers of the gambler.

The gambler pushed his post over with ease, but the other ran in slowly and worked at his post in vain. The sun came there saying he was after turquoise so large that one standing by it could just reach the top with his hands. His son replied, "Gamble me for it," and began to sing, "Come down all white." The sun, disappointed and angry, turned back, saying to himself, "I thought it was mine." *nohwilbin*, the gambler, secured the girl for his wife.

The sun had intercourse in a magical way with *estsạdilɛ̓ijɛ*. She discovered she was pregnant and in nine days she gave birth to a boy. Because of that, gestation now lasts nine months. In fifteen days the child was grown up. "Where does the man live who is father of *estsạditcijɛ́'s* son?" they were asking. Various men claimed him, saying, "He is my son."

Large-fly came to the boy calling him, grandson, and telling him his father wanted him. The boy did not know who was his father. "The sun is your father," the fly told him. White stripes appeared upon which the boy was asked to step. They were sunbeams which transported him to *ts'ɛl'a*. An old corrugated man lived there who was caterpillar or tobacco worm. "Your father is dangerous. He kills people with tobacco." The old man vomited and gave the boy what he had thrown up. He then was transported to the door of Sun's house.

"It is hard for *nohwilbin* has won everything from us. That is why I have come to you. He picked out a turquoise pipe and filled it and smoked it all. He cleaned the pipe and refilled it. The boy smoked it all, but began to feel dizzy. The sun cleaned and refilled it. The boy put in his mouth some of the vomited matter his grandfather had given him. He then smoked the pipe. Again, it was cleaned and filled and he smoked it again. Nothing happened to him.

"You are truly my son," the sun said and called to his daughter who came and washed him first in a turquoise basket, then in a white-shell one, in an abalone one, and finally in a jet one. Then the sun stretched his hair until it was like *nohwilbin's*. He put a black medicine in the water and stroked his hair with it and then his leg muscles. "The turquoise which you win in the last bet will be mine," he said.

The son agreed to that. They two went to the center of the sky where the sun prepared a smoke and blew smoke downwards four times. "Go to *hactc'ɛoɣan* and you will get the things you will use in betting with *nohwilbin*. He brushed around in a circle, saying he was looking for his pay which would be (?) abalone shell. He gave his son a small wind which would sit on his ear and keep him informed. He called him "son" and they two arrived on the earth at the top of *tsɛsgit*. *hactc'ɛoγan* already knew about it and small wind went as a messenger and summoned all the holy ones to a council. They met at the hogan called "yellow shining." There they made wooden staves to be used as dice. One side was left white and the other was blackened. They gave bat a small yellow skin as his pay and told him to go up into the roof of the house in which the gambling would take place. He was told to take these dice with him and when the other dice were thrown up in the play to make substitutions and throw them down so the young man might win. They arranged with large snake that he should go into the loop used in *najonci*. Red-shell which he was told to wear on his forehead was given him for pay. Woodpecker was asked to go into a mudball and white-shell was given him for pay. Rat was hired to go into another ball and abalone shell was given him as his pay. Measuring Worm was asked to go into the stick which when thrown would stand up as a wicket in another game and hard substances were his pay. Whirlwind was directed to screw one of the trees deep into the ground and hard substances were his pay. Wood Worm was hired to gnaw off the roots of the other tree and he was paid with jet.

In the morning they dressed the young man up and were starting off when *hactc'ɛoγan* inquired about his fee and was promised (?). "Do not go today, my grandchildren," he said. "Stay another day, there are many on watch. What are you going to do to confuse *nohwilbin's* mind?" It was morning. In the middle of the day they made his fee. He put hard substances in an abalone basket, circling around with a brush (?).

When it was dark the songs started and they continued until morning. With these songs *nohwilbin's* mind was made forked so that it would be divided. The young man then went where *nohwilbin's* wife was getting water. He asked her for a drink and what was left in the cup he put on his head. He then went over where she was and played with her. When he had finished, he returned to his party and reported that he had played with his opponent's wife.

The woman returned and was greeted by her husband with the remark, "Are you back so soon? You played with someone who resembled me." "Oh, I have been false to my husband," she said to herself; and to her husband she replied that it was someone who, walking in the distance, looked like him. "Well, we shall find out during the day," he replied. When it was fully light, white-shell, abalone shell, jet, and hard substances, five altogether, were given whirlwind that he should raise a sandstorm, making it dark and blowing dust in the eyes of the guards. He asked the small wind on his ear to make *nohwilbin's* mind dwell on the fact that his wife had been tampered with. When he approached, the woman who sat with her face turned nearly away, laughed and turned around. "That one was my husband," she thought the wind told him.

"Well, my friend, I have come for something," he said. "Gamble with me," he said and took up the dice and began to swing them back and forth, singing a gambling song. "We will bet our wives. Just as many on each side and wager them on one throw of the dice." He consented to this, but told his opponent if he hoped to win he must not look up and must throw the dice against the roof beams. *nohwilbin* began making motions and singing, "White, white, white, white." He threw the dice and put the basket on the ground. Bat, sitting on the timbers, caught the dice with his wings and threw down the others in place of them. *nohwilbin* jumped toward the basket saying, "You lost." "No," said the young man, "you lost, it is my play." *nohwilbin* swore, for he was still thinking about what had happened to his wife. "Now I will skin you," the young man said and threw the dice. Bat caught them and substituted those of *nohwilbin* which he had caught in the play before. "I win from you," the young man said to *nohwilbin* who jumped toward the dice and threw them to one side, swearing.

"Well, outside this time. You bet all those you won and your own wife. I will bet as many and my wife," *nohwilbin* proposed. They went outside to play *najonc.* "I will roll my hoop," *nohwilbin* said. "No, I have my own hoop, I won." Large snake made himself into a hoop saying, "Throw your pole and when it falls near me I will get up and lie on it. When he throws his pole he will slam it down hard on me and bust my belly." He rolled his hoop and threw his pole with it. It had "claws" tied under it. It fell close to the hoop which rolled to it and fell over on it. *nohwilbin* ran to it and pulled the "claws" to one side. "What are you doing to my hoop? I win from you."

"Well, inside next. We will play measuring worm. If this arched stick falls curved you win from me. You bet all you have won against an equal number." The young man consented to this. When *nohwilbin* was picking up an arched stick the young man objected, saying he had one of his own. "Now I will beat you. You will cry. The young man threw it and it stood up nicely arched. It was a real measuring worm. *nohwilbin* tried to throw it down, but the young man stopped him, saying he had won.

"Well," he said, "You have won all you bet. We will play football outside. If it drops this side I will win these from you, but if it falls on the other side you win from me." "All right," he said. They began kicking. He kicked it about so far (two feet) and Woodpecker flew beside it so that it fell on the other side. "I win," the young man said. "Yes," *nohwilbin* said, "we will bet ? at one time." The young man consented. They were to guess what was in a row of water baskets. Small wind assisted him. "What is that?" he was asked. "A water basket with a black cloud inside." "What is the one beside the white one?" was the next question. "A water basket containing female rain," was the reply. "What is that which stands by the image of a boy?" he was asked next. "It is an image of a girl and beside it a bird comes up singing." He had poison and was witching people. I have won from you," the young man said. "All right," *nohwilbin* replied.

"Now you bet all you have won and your wife too on one play." He agreed to this and they went outside where stood the house with a hole through the wall. "You kick four times and if you miss putting the ball through you lose, but if it goes through you win." There was a rat inside the ball. He pretended to hit it and the rat ran with the ball. They ran after the ball which went through the hole. "I won from you," the young man said. "Well, I will bet you male rain, female rain, all the houses and farms and myself, too. If you win you may kill me," *nohwilbin* proposed. The young man consented. "We will run a footrace around this track." They started running side by side, but the young man, taunting *nohwilbin*, ran ahead of him. After they had passed each other several times and the young man was in the lead, Wind told him that *nohwilbin* was about to shoot him with witchcraft in his leg muscle and that he must dodge the shot by jumping up. When *nohwilbin* shot him the young man jumped up and caught up the missile. Next, he was warned the shot would be at his hip and that he must throw himself to one side. He did this and again caught the missile. The warning the next time was that he would be shot between the shoulders and that he should dodge downward. This he did and again caught the missile. The last time the shot was at the base of his neck, which he escaped in the same way, again securing the missile.

Then *nohwilbin* ran along beside him taunting him. "I will skin you. Poor fellow take your time." When *nohwilbin* was ahead of him, the young man, using the missiles he had picked up, shot him in the leg muscles, in the thigh, between his shoulders, and at the base of his head. Then he overtook him. "Let him run a long distance behind you,"

Wind advised the young man. Then as the young man ran by, he said, "Now I will run away from you, *nohwilbin*. Poor man. Take it easy." The young man ran on *nohwilbin's* side of the trail and the onlookers were deceived. *nohwilbin's* partisans were shouting with joy and the young man's friends were crying. Then when he came over the hill the matter was reversed. The friends of the young man began to shout and *nohwilbin's* friends cried.

When the young man came to his tree he grabbed it and ran along with it. *nohwilbin* came in slowly and tried in vain to pull his tree out. He trod the ground down as he fought with it. The young man came up to him, said, "You take too long at it," and pulled the tree up. Then *nohwilbin* said he was out of breath and, passing him an ax, asked to be killed with it. Wind warned the young man, however, that with this ax, the one who wielded it killed himself. "No," the young man said, "shut your eyes." He was going to strike him with his own ax when the sun came and said, "Wait, my son, he is not boss of anything. Let him be boss of something. You shoot him up with your black bow." They two went there and the young man said, "Step on this," indicating his bow. He shot him up into the sky. He stopped halfway up. "For a long time my thoughts have been at the earth's heart," he said. Again he stopped. "Always my thoughts will come back to the center of the earth," he said again. He stopped the third time and said, "My thought will come back to the center of the world, it may be for good, it may be for evil." When he stopped the fourth time he said, "Adios."

When this had happened those who had been with *nohwilbin* began to cry. "Why do you cry, slaves of *nohwilbin*, I shall not treat you that way. Go wherever you please and take back your houses and farms," the young man told them. "Thanks," they all said and embraced each other. That is the way it is told. The people went off in various directions. "It will be so always, my son," the sun said. He breathed out four times. "The one who stays inside will be mine you are thinking," he said.

The people scattered out, some staying there at Pueblo Bonito and others investigated about Jemez where they found wide fields. "This will be our country," they said. "All right," the others replied.

Some of the people returned to *tsedɛs'a* and from there to Salt Cañon. I do not know how many years they lived there. Then they moved to *tsedɛgonɛnɛgɛ'* where they lived five years.

Then First Man and First Woman went to the top of *dziłnaodiłɛ* where the Navajo people were to be made. There they studied about it and decided that Navajo would be made where the round heart of the earth is at *tc'oli'*. They made an image of a man of the ear of white shell corn, rounded at the end, with which First Man came into existence. Then they made an image of a woman of the yellow ear of corn made of abalone shell, rounded at the end, with which First Woman came into existence. Then there, Turquoise Boy, and on this he made more so that they would have beads which covered them up and he who lives in Pelado Peak stepped over them. He who was made in Mount Taylor arrived and stepped over them. He who was made in San Francisco Peaks arrived there and stepped over them. He who was made in La Plata Mountains arrived there and stepped over them. Then he began to sing and in the morning they began to move and breathe. The newly created pair couldn't get up, however. They invited the holy ones in vain. Finally, they sent messengers to the sky with hard substances as a fee. Then smoke came and blowing through the new pair, passed each other and came out. This made the body hairs and air came out (the pores of the skin). Six women and six men, twelve all together stood up. Thus Navajo were made.

## ORIGIN OF SOME NAVAJO CUSTOMS[1]

Times were hard in the world. Everywhere there were beings who were eating people. One day a dark rain cloud was seen resting on the top of *tc'ol'i*.[2] The next day the rain was seen to be falling nearly to the middle of the mountain. The third day it reached well beyond the middle and the fourth day the rain enveloped the entire mountain and was falling at its base.

First Man, observing this from the top of *dzilna'oditi*, addressing First Woman said, "Old woman, four days ago there was a dark rain cloud on the top of *tc'ol'i* and now the entire mountain is covered with rain. Something unusual has happened. I am going to see what it is." "There are things to be feared there. The devouring ones are many. Why do you go?" First Woman replied. "Nothing untoward will happen," First Man said and started away on a run. When he had run some distance he began to sing:—

"I am approaching, close I am approaching.
I being associated with the dawn, First Man I am.
Now the mountain Tc'ol'i I am approaching.
Where it is black with rain clouds I am approaching.
Where the zigzag lightning lies above I am approaching.
Where the rainbow lies above I am approaching.
Where it is murky with the rebounding water I am approaching.
Possessed of long life and good fortune I am approaching.
With good fortune before me,
With good fortune behind me,
With good fortune under me I come to it.
With good fortune above me I come to it.
With good fortune all around me I come to it.
With good fortune proceeding from my mouth I come to it.

Having arrived at the base of the mountain with this song he climbed the mountain with a similar one, but with the refrain, "I am climbing." When he was ready to return the song had for a refrain, "I start home." On the way back he sang a similar song saying, "I am traveling home." This was followed by one with the refrain, "I have returned." The final song has for a refrain, "I sit down again."[3]

When First Man came to the top of the mountain he heard a baby crying. The lightning striking all about and murk caused by the hard rain

[1]First Man and First Woman were living on the mountain which the Navajo call *dzilna'oditi*. It has been identified with Huerfano Mountain in San Juan County, New Mexico, but verification should be made.
[2]A mountain peak about twenty miles east of *dzilna'oditi*. The relative positions were shown by a drawing on the sand.
[3]There are no doubt eight songs, the first being, "I set out." When songs of this character, that is of magical power, are given incidentally, sometimes one song is withheld preventing the transfer of the power.

made it difficult to see anything. He discovered the baby lying there with its head toward the west and its feet toward the east. Its cradle consisted of two short rainbows which lay longitudinally under it. Crosswise, at its chest and feet, lay red rays of the rising sun. Arched over its face was a rainbow. The baby was wrapped in four blankets; dark cloud, blue cloud, yellow cloud, and white cloud. Along either side was a row of loops made of lightning and through these a sunbeam was laced back and forth.

First Man, not knowing how to undo the fastenings, took up the baby, cradle and all, and started home with the songs mentioned above. When he arrived he called out. "Old woman, it is a baby, I found it there where it is black night with rain clouds."[1] "Ee," First Woman exclaimed. They heard immediately *xawu', xawu', xawu',* the call of Mirage *xactc'exti.* This was followed by *xuuuxu Xuuuxu Xuuuxu wuwuoo,* the cry of his companion Mirage *xactc'eoyan.* The two gods came in with *xactc'exti* in the lead who clapped his hand over his mouth and then struck them together, crying, "Something great has happened, my grandchildren. This is the one we have been talking about. Hereafter her mind will be the ruling power." He put the baby on the ground back of the fire, pulled the string, and the lacing came free in both directions.

"The cradle shall be like this. Thin pieces of wood shall be placed underneath. There will be a row of loops on either side made of string. The bark of the cliff rose, shredded and rubbed fine will be used under the child for a bed."[2] It was a girl.

"Ee," said First Woman, "*citc'e* (my daughter, woman speaking) she shall be." First Man said, "She will be *sitsi*" (my daughter, man speaking).

A day was the same as a year. The second day the baby sat up and when two days had passed she looked around. She was then dressed.

Well, White Shell woman gazed about.
With moccasins of white shell, their borders embroidered with black she gazed about.
Her shoe laces of white shell she gazed about.
Her leggings of white shell she gazed about.
Her legging pendants of white shell she gazed about.
Her skirt of white shell she gazed about.
Her belt of white shell she gazed about.
Her shirt of white shell she gazed about.

---

[1]Matthews recorded a version in which First Woman made the journey and found the baby, *Legends,* p. 230.
[2]It was explained that *xackc'elti* took the supernatural cradle away.

Her face of white shell she gazed about.
Her mind of white shell she gazed about.
Her soft feather[1] of white shell she gazed about.
Having on the crown of her head a bluebird with a white stripe across its mouth and a nice voice.
Having long life and good fortune she gazed about.
Good fortune ahead of her.
Good fortune behind her she gazed about.
Good fortune below her she gazed about.
Good fortune all around her she gazed about.
Good fortune proceeding from her mouth she gazed about.

When she was two days old she walked and when three days had passed she danced. Four days after she was found she ran some distance. When the fifth and sixth days had passed First Woman walked with her, calling her daughter. The seventh, eighth, and ninth days passed and on the tenth at dawn she was named *yolkai esdzạ* "White Shell Woman." Eleven days passed and on the thirteenth day, when the sun reached the exact place in the sky where it was when the girl was found, she was discovered to be menstruating.

"Mother, something is passing from me," she said. "That, my daughter, is called *tsidєsdla*.[2] A girl will reach puberty at thirteen years of age." When all had passed she washed in a white shell basket, in a turquoise basket, in an abalone shell basket, and finally in a jet basket.

Then he dressed his child.
Now First Man dressed white shell girl.
Back from the center of his house I dress her.
Her moccasins being of white shell he dressed her.
Her white shell moccasins having a black border he dressed her.
Their strings being of white shell he dressed her.
Her leggings being of white shell he dressed her.
Their pendants being of white shell he dressed her.
Her skirt being of white shell he dressed her.
Her belt being of white shell he dressed her.
Her shirt being of white shell he dressed her.
Her face being of white shell he dressed her.
Her mind being of white shell he dressed her.
Her soft feather being of white shell he dressed her.
All kinds of clothing going to her I dress them.
All kinds of quadrupeds going to her I dress them.
All kinds of plants going to her I dress them.
Male ram going to her I dress him
Female ram going to her I dress her.
Bluebirds calling in front of her I dress them

---

[1] Tied to the crown of her head.
[2] Seems to refer to the footrace which is a feature of the first menstruation.

Being a girl of long life and good fortune I dress her.
Good fortune being in front of her I dress her.
Good fortune being behind her I dress her.
Good fortune being below her I dress her.
Good fortune above her I dress her.
Good fortune being all around her I dress her.
Her speech being fortunate I dress her.

She was dressed and then a bed was spread for her with a white buckskin at the bottom, and on it a blanket of white cotton, third, an embroidered black one, and fourth, a white coyote skin blanket. The girl lay face down on this bed stretched out.[1]

"From here one runs in a sunwise circuit and then one should jump over to the place behind the fire. There you have finished running. With soft goods you finish running, my daughter. With white shell you finish running, my daughter." First Woman said. "When three days have passed." "Let all the holy ones come where we are living," said First Man. "You are appointed the leaders, Mirage *xactc'elti* and Mirage *xactc'eoɣan.*"

He drew twelve lines one after the other on *dzilna'oditi.* "There," he said, "will be house spread out, house iridescent." When the sun set they come together at the house called spread out and iridescent. First, came the Mirage *xactc'elti* who formed a line at the back and then Mirage *xactc'eoɣan* made the second line. Third were *xactc'elti* people and fourth *xactc'eoɣan;* fifth were the holy people who live in mountains; sixth were the hunchback people, seventh were *xactc'elti* people, eighth grasshopper people.

"Now it will be," he said. Then it happened; the curtain was raised and someone said, "Why were we not notified?" "Your fee will be provided," he replied. "They will make a long line," he said. White shells came in, one after the other, in pairs. Turquoise came in one after the other, in pairs. Rings of haliotis came in one after the other, in pairs. Woven beads came in one after the other, in pairs. Then red shells were, and braided beads, white coyote blankets, black fabrics, figured fabric. These formed twelve lines one behind the other.

"Now we will begin *xojondji,*" he said and drew out a sack of pollen. "Paint the house with it," he directed. Then in a sunwise circuit four timbers, one after the other, were made yellow with pollen. He called, "*weχε,*" to Mirage *xactc'elti,* being in the last row. Then their leader began to sing. He intoned as follows:—

---
[1]While she lies in this position she is kneaded and stretched into a beautiful shape.

Here hogans stand, good hogans.   At the east good hogans, the hogans of
*xactc'elti* stand.
Dawn their hogans made of stand,
White corn made of their hogans stand.
Soft goods of all kinds made of their hogans stand.
Water from all sources made of their hogans stand.
Good hogans.
At the west their hogans stand.
Good hogans.
The hogans of *xactc'eoγan* stand.
Good hogans.
Hogans made of yellow horizontal light stand.
Good hogans.
Hogans made of yellow corn.
Good hogans.
Hogans made of hard materials of all kinds stand.
Hogans made of water's child stand.
Good hogans.

When these two songs had been sung the one over whom they were
singing said: "Why do you sing thus.  Two men are lacking."  The men
in the twelve lines said they did not know who were lacking.  "There is
something you do not know about.  With what shall I live forever?  With
what shall I have good fortune?"

"Very well," he replied.  They added these two, long life and good
fortune to the others.  Then they began to sing.  They sang twelve and
then put two songs on top, making fourteen.  By that time, day was
breaking and grasshoppers began to sing.  A woman's song was heard
and when it was finished someone put a head in and said, "Why didn't
you invite us?"  "Your fee will provided," First Man replied.  They
found it was Dawn who had done this.  Then they began to sing.

They are in line.
*xactc'elti* they are in line.
All dressed in white moccasins they are in line.
All dressed in white leggings they are in line.
All dressed in white buckskins they are in line.
All dressed in white eagle feathers they are in line.
All dressed in bluebirds they are in line.
Singing with their mouth with pleasing voices they are in line.
Possessed of long life and good fortune they are in line.
With good fortune in front of them they are in line.
With good fortune behind them they are in line.

There were six songs all alike which are called dawn songs.

When four days had passed the girl said to her mother, "Something
is flowing from me again, mother."   "That is called *kindzisda'*" her

mother replied. They did the same way again. The holy people came
from both sides. "We shall never be seen after this," *xactc'ɛlti* said.
They departed in all directions. *xactc'ɛɣan* spoke: "If anyone says
'I saw *xactc'ɛɣatti* I say he shall be killed.'" Sun spoke. "They
shall not see me, because it would be bad luck if they saw me."
On account of this the assemblage was dismissed. When one
day had passed she said, "Something flows from me again." "That
is called *tcedji'na'*. It ceases after four days have passed. Because
of that the flowing of a menstruating woman will cease in four days.
She, menstruating, was lustful. She went to the top of a hill
called *tondilkons*[1] and spread her thighs toward the rising sun
so that the rays might enter her. Later in the day when the Sun reached
the center of the sky where he feeds his horse at noon she went where the
dripping water falls, and again, spread her thighs to let the water drop
into her crotch. She did this repeatedly. Afterward she and her mother
went down the mountain toward the south to a place where a grass
(*Sporobolus cryptandrus*) was growing. Before they had finished preparing the seed they started back, leaving some still in a heap. It was
nearly noon when they hastily returned.

"I will run back for that remaining in the pile," the girl said. "No,
do not do that, my daughter." First Woman replied. "I will run and be
back quickly," the girl said. "There are dangers there, many of those
who eat people run about," her mother warned her. "No, mother, I
will come back quickly with the threshed seeds. I also am not entirely
ignorant.[2] I will be wary," the girl said. "All right then, go on,
daughter," her mother replied.

The girl went for the seed and when she had threshed it all and was
arranging her load she was surprised to find a white horse standing there.
The bridle of the horse was white. The moccasins of the rider and all his
clothing were white. The horse was standing on the air some two feet
above the ground. The rider addressed her saying, "You will not accomplish it. Over there, when I rise spread out your thighs toward me.
When I come up to the summit of the sky and arrive at (?) spread your
legs at *tondilkons* that the water may drop into your crotch. You will
accomplish nothing by those means. Let your father make a brush house
toward the east and see what will happen." She was surprised to find it
was Sun who had done this. While her head was turned he vanished.

---

[1] This is a place so named on the east side of *dzılna'odıli*.
[2] Meaning of magical protection.

She walked back and when she had returned she said, "Mother, I saw something. He was entirely white and his horse was all white. 'You will accomplish nothing that way. You have been spreading your thighs toward me there where I rise. When I have reached the middle of the sky where I lunch you spread your legs under the dripping water,' he said to me," she said. "Have you really been doing that?" First Woman asked. "I really did that," she replied.

First Man came home. "It seems your daughter saw someone," First Woman said to him. "The one she saw was dressed entirely in white, sitting a horse standing right up here, not on the ground, so your daughter said. 'You will accomplish nothing the way you are doing. You have been spreading your thighs toward me here where I come up. When I come to the middle of the sky you spread your thighs under the dripping water,' he said to her. 'I really do that,' your daughter says. 'Let your father build a brush shelter to the east before the door of the hogan. Let him rake up the ground. Let him put the chips in a pile. Put some boiled rush grass seeds in a vessel.' This is what your daughter says." "The holy ones have all gone away. They said no one would see them again," he replied. "Oh you are saying that for some reason," she retorted. "Build a brush shelter there, Old Man."

He built a brush shelter and swept the ground in front of the hogan door. He also made a pile of the bits of wood which were lying about. The sun set and it grew dark. He spread down a white blanket and put down a vessel of boiled food on one side of it. The girl sat on the right side and First Man on the left. The cooked food stood there in a vessel. When it was quite dark[1] First Man went away, but *yolgaiałed* passed the night there. When it was daylight footprints were seen from the doorway on the right side. One (vessel) of the cooked food was gone. First Man returned saying, "How is it, my daughter?" "Father, there is one footprint on the right side in the doorway. The one vessel of the cooked food is gone too." When it was getting dark toward the east they two sat there again until it was quite dark. First Man came back saying, "How is it, my daughter? Nobody came. I said you were lying." "Just as it was light I perceived someone touched me. There are two footprints by the doorway and one dish of the cooked food is gone."

It was dark the second time and the two of them sat there again. When it was daylight First Man came back again. "How is it, my daughter?" he said. "I told you no one would come. I said you were lying. Why should the holy ones come when we live so poorly." "Oh,

---

[1]Ten o'clock was mentioned as the time.

do not say that," she said. "Now let us look," First Woman said. The
food was gone from a dish on the east side. There were footprints. "Go
look, father," she said. "I felt him go away on this side at daybreak."

When it was night again they two sat there. At midnight First
Man went away. He came back in the morning. The food was gone from
the north side and there were four footprints. At dawn someone left
me, I didn't see him but I woke up my crotch being wet."

On account of this the Navajo do not touch a woman for four
nights after they are married. On the fourth night they have intercourse.

Four days passed. "Mother, at dawn something here was pulsat-
ing," she said. "Oh, daughter, you are pregnant. It is the moving of
a baby you mean. That is the result of your having intercourse," her
mother said to her. It was at dawn on the fourth day that the baby
moved. The days were equivalent to months and because of that the baby
moves after four months. Nine days after they had had intercourse the
children (twins) were born. Just one day after their birth they two
sat up. For other children it will be a year. After two days the two
walked about. It will be two years for ordinary children. Ten days
after they were born First Man made arrows for them and they hunted
birds. Fifteen days after they were born they went to the summit of
*dzɪlna'odɪli*. When they were strolling about Large-fly came to them
and said, "My son's sons, why are you walking here? You were not born
for anything connected with this place." He knows everything about
this wide world of ours and he told them about it. "You two should go
to your father. That one, the sun who moves there, is your father. Ask
your mother four times who your father is and then tell her you are going
to see your father. Speak to her once."

They ran back and asked, "Who is our father?" "Oh you are everybody's kin," she replied. After a while they said again, "Who is our
father?" "Barrel-cactus was your father.[1] That is why your heads are
bushy." When some time had again passed they asked the same question again. "Sitting-cactus was your father." When some time had
passed again they said, "What were you saying? You are everybody's
kin. You had no father. Barrel-cactus was your father. He had no
father. Sitting-cactus was your father. He had no father. Now we will
start away to visit our father. Sun is our father. Mother, grandmother,
grandfather, we will come back to you in four days." They started away.
When they were a short distance in front of the door they discovered a

---

[1]Past tense is indicated by a suffix on the subject indicating he (Barrel-cactus) was dead.

white rainbow. They stepped on that and traveled with it. When they arrived their bodies were moulded, their faces made white. "Now they will be given names," he said. They invited Mirage *xactc'elti*, Mirage *xactc'eoyan*, *xactc'elti*, *xactc''eoyan*, and, from the place called black hole in the rock, they invited *xactc'ecjinne*. Sun came down. The two who were to be named stood in front. The elder he addressed as *naiye'-nezyani* and the younger as *tobadj'ictcini*. "Now make names for them," he said to them.

"Now you give a name," he said to *xactc'ecjinne*. "What you do he doesn't know (?)," he said. "He killed all the monsters. The elder will be named *naiye'nezyani*, the second because of what his mother did will be named *tobadj'ictcini*. Where will you two go?" he asked them. With a coal of the dark sky he made him black. With white clay he drew signs of a bow on him. This will ward off danger. He made *tobadj'-ictcini* red with red earth and put on wide hair frame signs with white clay. By means of these they will be protected. "They will go where the rivers join," Sun said. "They will live at the center of the earth where there is a meadow. First Man and First Woman will live here where I rise, beyond where it is called 'narrow water'. *yolgaiesdzan* will go over here where I sit. She will live there." Sun said this and added, "She will take everything with her and be accompanied by all the people. She will give her attention to her children and to providing their food. It will be that way. Everywhere I go over the earth she will have charge of female rain. I myself will control the male rain. She will be in control of vegetation everywhere for the benefit of the people of the earth."

Water Coyote ran about over there on the other side. He stepped out first. After him came First Man and then First Woman. After came First Warrior.[1] They started toward the east and First Woman began to speak, saying bad things. When I think of anything, something bad will happen. There will be coughs when I think of something. I will cause different things by thinking badly. Coyote will know about it." She always was saying bad things.

"First Woman, you shall not talk. You shall not live. We have decided upon that," said Mirage *xactc'elti* and Mirage *xactc'eoyan*. "You must not talk for we will know about it," *xactc'elti* said.

"Now get ready *yolgaiesdzan*." They decorated her and she started away, accompanied by her twelve attendants. In front, went the males and behind them the females. Ahead of her was male rain and

---

[1]Coyote.

behind her female rain; in front dark cloud and behind dark mist; before her yellow cloud and behind her yellow mist; before her white cloud and behind her white mist.

She was decorated with all kinds of herbage and flowers wherever they grow. She went away with a white shell basket, a turquoise basket, an abalone basket, and jet basket. She rose up with everything. She went with them to the place called black water and is living there now.

When she had arrived she thought horses should exist for people.

I am *yotgaiesdzan.* I am thinking of clothing spread out on there. A white shell horse lies in a white shell basket. I am thinking about. They lie in the pollen of flowers. Those who come to me will increase. Those that will not die lie in it.

## POT WOMAN TEACHES WITCHCRAFT

They went to a place called Mountain of Mud. They made clay pots in which *banatinle* hid beads. He hid also a white shell cane, a turquoise cane, an abalone and a jet cane. A large woman of *ki'ya'ani* clan had a hogan there on a rock. At that place they killed a deer. At first the woman said nothing. Then with her hand on her side she spoke. Then the *ki'ya'ani* from *ki'ya'a* moved back, taking the snake which was their pet. It was at the place where the streams unite at the south where the cañons come up near where the Ute live.

The Ute made war on the Navajo. "In some days we will come back to fight," they said. At the place where the rock stands high on top they placed stones in a circle and killed them. One was called *tsєkє*. The Mexican captives became the clan now called Mexican (*nakaidinє*).

There were twelve men who were offended because their enemies had seduced their wives. The four offenders who were Mexican were killed by the Ute. Again they came to fight. Each time Mexicans were killed. Eleven were killed. Only one was left. He was called *latc'obai*. He had only one sister. She became ill. In vain he made medicine for her. She died. Her husband married again very soon. Then *latc'obai* came to gamble with his brother-in-law. He had his bow in his hand and as he walked toward the sun he made motions as if shooting as he pronounced magic words. He shot him between the shoulders. Then the people ran after him. As he ran with his bow he shot all his arrows. He had four arrows in his quiver which was hanging from his belt and he shot all of them. Just as they overtook him, he took down another quiver containing four arrows and shot them. This he did four times. When they were all gone he sang, "Now I shall die," as he ran toward the big peaks.

After four years he was seen again. "Come back to us and be our chief. What is the use of running away?" they said to him. He went toward them, but not very close. He heard there was a sing. He came up to an old woman pot who was living alone. "Why did they kill all my people, grandmother?" he said. The woman said, "Something will happen, grandson; witchcraft this way, witchcraft that way. That man knows how to turn a bear track into a coyote who knows how to talk. They killed his brother's wife." "What is its medicine?" "I have medicine for it. Let a girl cut open the gall bladder of a live blue lizard and take out the gall. When the lizard dies the girl will die also. Let a man cut the belly of a long lizard and take out its gall. Let him too die quickly. Then take the gall of a hawk and that of a quadruped, break with them the flower of the mistletoe and when it is frozen ask the two to let you help them plant corn. Let all bring cooking vessels. They will have a hard time." "All right, grandmother, I will do as you say."

He ground corn for her and fed her. She ate. He took off her beads and put earrings in her ears. "Now you will be dressed the way I am dressed when you go. Now I will hit you." "All right, my grandson."

Then he hit her behind the head and started away. The singers came home. He tried to kill them. They chased him. He ran, they knew not where. Then, for many years, he prepared what the old woman had taught him. He captured a Pueblo girl and a Pueblo boy. He caught a blue lizard and instructed the girl to cut its belly. He caught a long lizard for the boy and it died. He did all old Pot Woman had told him. He dressed himself. A man spoke. "Why do you do all those things. We are sorry for you. Come back to us. Be our chief." "All right, I will. I ask something great of you. Carry all your little pot children along with you."

Then they did that. The pots were placed in a line. He took up a six-foot stick. He put it into the vessels as he went about dancing. Then he made a speech to the people. "You said I should be your chief. Now you eat."

They ate. Then soon they began to itch. One fell backward. Then they ran back to their homes. They were bad warlike people. He killed them all. Again they lost him. They tracked him to the junction of the Las Animas and San Juan rivers. Then they walked to where Mancos Creek flows into the San Juan and tracked him again. It had rained on the tracks some days before. Then they slept. While they were watching the sun rose. Just at midday he climbed down beyond where a rock stands up. He went down Mancos Creek. They ran so far and lay down and watched. He came up. On the hill he turned around. They did not recognize him. His hair was cut on top. They could not tell where his face was. He had painted his face red and the back of his head looked the same. He started back. They thought he had gone in and they lay down to watch again. He came back again. Then he went downstream, digging for beaver. The soles of his feet were brown. They seized him by his feet. Two others held him at the head. "*xa xaaₗ*," he said, "Today I must die. I will come up by myself." "Then let him do it. Never mind him," they said.

So they tied half of him with a rope. Four of them held him on each side by the arms. Six held him. They cut him in two by splitting. They cut off his head. His head fell off. Tears ran down his face. Then he fell over. Then they started off having left pounded soapweed where he had climbed.

## WIZARD STORY

Yellow was thinking about something. White was with him. He killed people there. There was a hard time. At *hojoñ* he shot arrows in four directions. When he shot the first time there was white corn, the second time, blue corn, the third, yellow, and the fourth, brown spotted corn of all kinds. They came to a place for a garden. They planted. They planted the blue corn that had been shot. It grew. Yellow had not put the yellow corn there, so there was no yellow corn. Yellow was sad about it. They planted the brown corn there. Silently Yellow walked around, thinking sadly, "They say very bad things of me. They even say I am dead. I am grieving to death. Who will possess my property after I am gone?"

He thought, "I will say, 'I will divide all my property among you. Let all the people who live here come together. Maybe I will give you my things. What do you say?' " "Yes, yes," they said. He led them off and lined them up. He selected some of the people. He walked a little way and took a curved oak stick. He pried deep under a rock. He took out a yucca rope and tied it on the rock. He laid hoops of oak on the rock and drew a line with the yucca about five inches long in the center. "Now go over there," he ordered. The stones lay in a circle. Then he threw the rope which had been fastened to the ledge rock down to a very great depth. When it reached the ground he said a prayer. He turned back. He stepped in the circles and arrived at the bottom of the curved rock where the stones lay in a circle. Then the people heard him pray. He put on a large mask of Talking God. He took an ear of perfectly kerneled white corn and one of yellow. "You think I am going to give you these goods," he said to them. He told them he would do something wonderful. He had put on the mask so as to do something terrible. His companion, who was called "White" lined up the people so that Yellow stood in the middle. He held ears of corn up toward him. The people stood there. "Once more look. There will be eight. I guess it is twelve," he said as he ran down from above wearing the mask.[1] Every time he said eight he meant eight years and when he said twelve he meant twelve years. The people planted, but just before the corn was ripe, it froze. A second time the crop was burned. A third time it did not sprout. They planted four times in vain. There was no rain, no vegetation, no food. Eight years from that time they stole children from each other and ate them. But in twelve years it became a little better. Then it rained again and vegetation and corn grew. Thus the man named Yellow had revenged himself.

---

[1] The man died because he spoke while he was wearing the mask, but whatever he said would come true.

GAME STORY

There was a man who, while playing the hoop game and the game of seven wooden dice, lost all his property, including a very good house. He also lost the beads that belonged to his niece. Because of this his brothers resolved to kill him. A necklace of mixed beads was hanging in the center of the house. The niece told her uncle he might wager that also. "All right, niece," he replied, and took the white shell, the turquoise, the abalone, the coral, the jet; he took five of them off one by one. He also provided himself with specular iron ore, pollen of larkspur and of cat-tails. With these he walked away to the corn pits which were full. From these he took one ear each of the five colors. He patted these together until they were small. "Well, little mother," he said to his niece, "they speak of killing me. It may be you and I will see each other again. Goodbye."

Then he put a tree into the water with himself (inside of it). He floated in the tree down where the stream enters the Colorado River. He got out of the tree there and walked along the shore. He felt lonesome there. He planted the corn he had brought with him in the form of a cross, putting the seed in one by one. Each stalk had two ears projecting opposite each other. There were twelve stalks with two ears each.

I hear there were twelve stalks with ears opposite each other. I hear on Black Mountain there were ears projecting on either side. I hear the male deer I kill will like me.

He stayed there four years and then started to return to his home. After many days he got back, arriving early in the morning at his home which was called *te'inɛisk'it*. He went to the corn storage pits, but they were entirely empty. He put four ears in them and blew on them four times. After that he went where his niece was sitting. They were having a famine. "Prepare food for me, my little mother," he said to her. "There is none," she replied. "Four days after you left the corn was all gone. I do not know how it happened." She sat there crying. "I cannot cook food for you, my uncle." "Go and get something," he said again. "Do not say that, uncle, there is none, none." When they had spoken to each other four times she went to the pits.

When she got there the pits were full. "Thanks, uncle," she called as she ran back with the corn. The girl then ran to the men and told them her uncle had come and that the corn pits were full again.

"Welcome," they said, when they came in and they they embraced him. "You are the only one, younger brother. In the future we will not speak evil of you.   Something has happened to the game animals.   We hunt in vain."

Wondering what had happened the returned brother hunted for days in vain.   One day when he was hunting he went to the top of *te'in∊sgit.* Below a cliff he saw a deer standing.   He ran around and crept up where the deer had been, but it had vanished.   He examined the ground, but the soil had not been disturbed.   The next day he climbed the mountain again and there the deer stood again.   This time he walked directly toward it trying to keep it in sight; but where it had been standing there was nothing but some deer dung.   A little distance from where he stood there had been a spruce tree, but when he turned his head away and then looked in that direction again *xactc'eyaɫti* stood there.   "What is it, grandchild?" he asked.   "A deer which was standing right there has vanished," he replied.   "Have you white shell, grandson?"   "I have them all, grandfather."   "My grandson has everything.   We will do it," *xactc'eyaɫti* said.

He found the door fronts were darkness, daylight, the moon, and the sun.   Inside *xactc'eyaɫti* and *xactc'ejinne* were sitting on either side, facing each other.   "Well, go on, my grandson," *xactc'eyaɫti* said. He took steps on the right side of the house four times, blowing as he did so, and four footprints appeared.   He discovered that *xactc'eyaɫti* had pets which he kept far in the interior.   He heard from inside someone say, "Ho, I smell earth people.   The polite master has brought in a human being."   "Do not say that; he has everything," *xactc'eyaɫti* said.   Back of the fire a male deer was lying.   On him lay a feathered arrow with a red shaft.   It had just been pulled out.

The man took a seat in the center.   He put down one each of white shell, turquoise, coral, abalone, jet, specular iron ore, blue pollen, cat-tail pollen, and then covered them with a blanket.   He stepped over these four times and they became a great heap.

*xactc'eyaɫti* was sorrowful and said, "I do not think we can give you a fair equivalent."   He found out afterward that he stayed there in the house of the game animals four days.   *xactc'eyaɫti* and *xactc'ejinne* distributed the precious objects.   They gave each of those present fifteen pieces, then thirteen, then nine, then seven, then five, then three, and all had been given out.

This is the way deer should be skinned.   Break the legs here at the wrist joint, but let them hang by the tendons.   Leave the skin on the nose and lips.   Draw the skin carefully from under the eyes.   Do not cut through the bladder.   Turn the hide back to the hips.   If you do this way you will always kill game. "Put the head toward the center, but do not let the eyes burn or the teeth. You must not cook it by burying it in the ashes. Game animals must not be thrown away. Sickness will result if you do not observe these things. If the teeth are burned the hunter's teeth will hurt. You earth people will have a cure for it, grandson," he told him.

He had everything prepared. "What did you come for, grandson?" Small whirlwind told him that on that side were images of the game animals standing side by side. On the east side was the paunch of an animal in which were deer songs. The man pointed to these. *xactc'eyalti* looked down and said, "All right, grandson. It was for these you came."

> Being *xactc'eyalti* I came up.
> To the abode of the deer I came up.
> To the door post of darkness I came up.
> To the door post of daylight I came up.
> To the door post of moon I came up.
> To the door post of sun I came up.
> To the place where *xactc'eyalti* with *xactc'ejin* sat facing each other, I came up.
> To where the black bow and the feathered arrows with red shaft lie across each other, I came up.
> Over there they lie across each other, red with the mouth blood of a male deer.
> Over there the deer I killed likes me.

He sang only one deer song.

They were here when I was hunting them in vain he thought to himself. "Shoot them in the brush," he told him. This is where they are.

> I being *xactc'eyalti*.
> On the trail to the top of Black Mountain,
> On the trail among the flowers,
> Male deer are there,
> The pollen of herbs I will put in its mouth,
> The male deer steps along in the dew of the vegetation.
> I kill him but he likes me.

One was there. He shot into the brush and a deer rolled over with the arrow in him. He shot into another kind of brush and a fawn rolled over with the arrow in him. He shot into another kind of brush and a yearling rolled over with the arrow.

"I have done something important," he thought to himself as he ran back. They found he had killed them all. That is why when they get away we track them.

There are very many game songs. If one does not know them he does not hunt. We are afraid about these things because they are pets of *xactc'eyalti.*

## The Creation of the Horse

Something was spread over it. It moved and became alive. It whimpered. Woman-who-changes began to sing:—

> Changing Woman I am, I hear.
> In the center of my house behind the fire, I hear.
> Sitting on jewels spread wide, I hear.
> In a jet basket, in a jet house, there now it lies.
> Vegetation with its dew in it, it lies.
> Over there,
> It increases, not hurting the house now with it it lies,
>     inside it lies.

Its feet were made of mirage. They say that because a horse's feet have stripes. Its gait was a rainbow, its bridle of sun strings. Its heart was made of red stone. Its intestines were made of water of all kinds, its tail of black rain. Its mane was a cloud with a little rain. Distant lightning composed its ears. A big spreading twinkling star formed its eye and striped its face. Its lower legs were white. At night it gives light in front because its face was made of vegetation. Large beads formed its lips; white shell, its teeth, so they would not wear out quickly. A black flute was put into its mouth for a trumpet. Its belly was made of dawn, one side white, one side black. That is why it is called "half white."

A white-shell basket stood there. In it was the water of a mare's afterbirth. A turquoise basket stood there. It contained the water of the afterbirth. An abalone basket full of the eggs of various birds stood there. A jet basket with eggs stood there. The baskets stand for quadrupeds, the eggs for birds. Now as Changing-woman began to sing the animals came up to taste. The horse tasted twice; hence mares sometimes give birth to twins. One ran back without tasting. Four times, he ran up and back again. The last time he said, "Sh!" and did not taste. "She will not give birth. Long-ears (Mule) she will be called," said Changing-Woman. The others tasted the eggs from the different places. Hence there are many feathered people. Because they tasted the eggs in the abalone and jet baskets many are black.

## Wanderings of the Navajo

*yolgaiesdzan* asked Mirage *xactc'elti* and Mirage *xactc'eoγan* to go back toward the east and investigate. They started back and came in turn to White Shell Mountain, Turquoise Mountain, Abalone Mountain, and to Jet Mountain. When they came to the top *xactc'elti* began to sing. As they came to the top of White Shell Mountain they called greetings to the distant mountains.

*sisnadjinne* sticks up.
White Shell Mountain sticks up.
Mountain peak sticks up.
Long life sticks up.
Good fortune sticks up.
Greetings far away stick up.
Mount Taylor sticks up.
Turquoise Mountain sticks up.
Mountain peak sticks up.
Long life sticks up.
Good fortune sticks up,
Greetings far away stick up.
San Francisco Peaks stick up.
Abalone Mountain sticks up.
Mountain peak sticks up.
Long life mountain sticks up.
Good fortune sticks up.
Greetings far away stick up.
La Plata Mountain sticks up.
Jet Mountain sticks up.
Mountain peak sticks up.
Long life sticks up.
Good fortune sticks up.
Greetings far away stick up.
Huerfano Mountain sticks up.
Soft goods Mountain sticks up.
Mountain peak sticks up.
Long life mountain sticks up.
Good fortune mountain sticks up.
Greetings far away stick up.
*Tc'ol'i* sticks up.
Now round mountain sticks up.
Mountain of jewels sticks up.
Mountain peak sticks up.
Long life sticks up.
Good fortune sticks up.
Greetings far away stick up.
Before him good fortune sticks up.
Behind him good fortune sticks up.

Under him good fortune sticks up.
Above him good fortune sticks up.
All around me good fortune sticks up.
Greetings far away sticks up.

They came with a rainbow to the summit of one mountain which was lying there. Next they came to the summit of Turquoise Mountain. A beautiful mountain stood there, it projected beautifully. Now it stood up beautifully. They came to Abalone Mountain. Now its head could be seen. Behold, it is that one. Very holy it sticks up. Now being holy with you it stands up.

Here they come. Jet mountain on its top they arrived. Look we are going to that one. That is the one.

I being *xactc'ɛlti* I am going to it.
I am going to *sisnadjinne.*
I am going to White Shell Mountain.
I am going to mountain peak.
I am going to long life and good fortune,
I am going to it.
I being *xactc'ɛlti* am going to it.
I am going to Mount Taylor.
I am going to mountain peak.
I am going to long life and good fortune.
I am going to it.
I being *xactc'ɛlti* I am going to it.
I am going to San Francisco Peaks.
I am going to Abalone Mountain
I am going to mountain peak.
I am going to long life and good fortune.
I am going to it.
I being *xactc'ɛlti* I am going to it.
I am going toward La Plata Mountain.
I am going toward Jet Mountain.
I am going toward mountain peak.
I am going toward long life and good fortune.
I am going toward it.
I being *xactc'ɛlti* I am going toward it.
I go toward Huerfano Mountain.
I go toward soft goods mountain.
I go toward mountain peak.
I go toward long life and good fortune.
I go toward it.
I being *xactc'ɛlti* I am going toward it.
I am going toward *tc'ol'i.*
I am going to the mountain of jewels.
I am going to the mountain peak.
I am going to long life and good fortune.

I am going toward it.
Good fortune before me.
Good fortune behind me.
Good fortune below me.
Good fortune above me.
Good fortune all around me.
I go toward it with good fortune.
My speech being fortunate I go toward it

They passed around the bases of these four mountains and as they passed under it (he sang):—

The mountain, I who came to it, *sisnadjin.*
I arrive at its summit.
The mountain, I who came to it, Mount Taylor
I arrive at its summit.
It is well with me.
It is well with me.
I arrive at the summit of San Francisco Peaks.
Now, I who start back, I arrive.
At the summit La Plata Mountain.
Now I start back,
Now I start back,
I arrive at the summit of Huerfano.
I arrive at the summit of *tc'ol'i.*
I, the one returning, I arrive
Now I am the one who sits down on the shores of White Shell Woman.

"How is it over there?" "It is beautiful." "Now, it is beautiful, my children," *yolgaiesdzan* said. "Flowers are spread everywhere. Strong springs of water flow up out of the earth. My children shall live by use of them."

Here where the mountain lies, soft goods mountain, rain mountain, jewels mountain, pollen mountain, the one that is so named will lie. There will be many Navajo living on either side of it.

Now, this white shell mountain lies. Inside of it is spotted wind. In young eagle's mouth thunder will first sound. Vegetation will come to life. Spotted wind will move it with itself. The vegetation will be spotted toward it. Blue wind will make it move inside of Turquoise Mountain. Blue vegetation will appear.

Black wind is inside of Abalone Mountain. The vegetation will come to life. Black vegetation will appear.

Yellow wind is in the mountain of jet. It will stir with life. The flowers will wake up. Some of them will be red, some white, some blue. Flowers of all kinds will be seen. It will thunder there four times. First it will thunder as our bear will wake up. He travels with the aid of his belly. He will stretch himself. He will bring back the news that *tc'act'εzε* is springing up. "Now they are all coming," he will say. Then those that fly, blue bird, Say's phoebe, buzzard, dove, crane, all will come. She ground up white shell mixed with corn of all colors. She rubbed her breast in this manner. A piece so large (match stick) fell down. She rolled this up in a black cloud. She stepped over it four times (singing).[1]

The two got up looking just like persons. "Go toward the south, grandchildren," she said. "I have some grandchildren living there." She was referring to the twelve persons. There, by the shore of the ocean was a hogan. Children who played on the seashore came to her there. They played with the shells which the waves left. *yolgaiesdzan* sent word to the twelve persons and when they came she told them that she did not like to have the children play with these shells for they were her food. When the twelve returned they said: "Your grandmother sends word to you that she likes the white shells, that they are her food. She says you are not to pick them up. You will live over yonder by Black Mountain."

There they moved to a mountain named darkness. There according to their grandmother's plan they picked up a bear so large. It became their pet. At a mountain which will be named yellow mountain they found a panther. By the will of their grandmother the bear and panther grew up by magic. Both were males. They grew in four days, which became four years.

She summoned the twelve persons and told them that she had not made her grandchildren to live in that place. The messengers came back and said, "Your grandmother asks that the men named *ba'ni,' bailni-kǫsε, banatinĺ* and *gicdo* should come to her." They went and then she said to them, "I did not make my grandchildren to live in this country. Go to the Navajo country. The Navajo country is where rain mountain lies. You go beyond where the mountain named White Shell Mountain lies, beyond where the mountain called Turquoise Mountain lies, beyond where the mountain called Abalone Mountain lies, beyond where the mountain called Jet Mountain lies. It will take you four days to go there. Then there will be a mountain sticking up in the distance. It is called White Face Mountain. You go on past that toward the north. When you have climbed one mountain just a little can be seen of a mountain there which is called crescent. Right under it you will cross a stream. Right across that lies a mountain which is called Black. At one end of this mountain is a flat and on it stands a mountain called *balok'ai.*

---

[1] The narrator said to me. "Not this song, I live by means of it. I live with it."

You go across that. On the other side, in this direction, a mountain stands, below which you should go. Over this way will be a mountain called Brushy Mountain. You will pass on the south side of that. There some Navajo are living. You will live there by Rain Mountain." When she had said this she went back and picked up a string with four shells which she had lying in water. Then she went this way (south) into a room and came back in the same way with a string. Then she went west and brought back a string on which were four (beads). Next she went north and the same way brought back a string. She went again into a room at the east and came back with a cane of white shells. She went into a room to the south and brought out a turquoise cane. She went into the west room and brought a cane of abalone shell. She went next to the north room and came back with a cane of jet.

"When you are about to die of thirst set one of these in the ground and rotate it sunwise and water will flow out." She repeated these directions for each of the four canes, using the same words. Then she gave them the four bags in each of which was a string. "You are not to open these until after four days when you will have passed beyond the four mountains and then you may untie them," she said. (You shall not hear the songs with which they were to be opened.)

They started out and spent the night just beyond the mountain of white shell. Beyond the mountain of turquoise they slept the second night. The bags they were carrying became heavy, but they went on. They slept the third night beyond the mountain of abalone. Those beads became very heavy. They went on beyond the mountain of jet. The bags which they were carrying on their backs were very heavy. They camped there. The chief named *ba'ni'* said, "Now, you may open the bags." They opened them and the beads had increased and there were very many of them. He distributed them among the people and then the load each carried was very light.

When it was day, they did not know which way to go. They sat down on a hill and discussed the matter. "That mountain sticking up there may be White Face Mountain. We should go that way." They started away toward the north. They saw where someone had walked along. "My pet, it seems someone has been walking here," the chief said to the bear. The bear looked at the place and stretched himself. "We will see who it is, my pet," he said and they stopped where there was a cliff. The sun was setting. "What shall we drink?" *bailnikọsɛ* asked. *ba'ni'* replied, "'You shall use this when thirst overcomes you,' she told us." He took up the white shell cane and turned it sunwise. Water sprang up, they drank, and spent the night there.

*ba'ni'* the chief said, "We may see someone today. There are tracks here." As they were going down they saw there was much corn growing in the cañon bottom. The corn was in tassel. They camped there. One of the men looked about. There was no one to be seen, but a hogan stood there. Two persons went inside and then stood in the doorway. Behind them two others came, one was a man and one was a woman. The hogan was full. They discovered that Arrow People lived there and they greeted them as relatives. "Where are you from?" they asked the travelers. "We are from our grandmother's shore. We are going to the Navajo country," they replied. "Stay here and we will get acquainted with each other," the Arrow People said. "You may eat the food which has ripened here." Two of the messengers came back. "Camp here," they said to us, "and eat what has ripened." "All right," he replied. Some of them went among them and came back with corn. It grew dark and the single men and single women found partners and lay with them. The people of that place gave corn and the travelers gave beads as marriage gifts.

They remained there exchanging hospitality. They joined in rabbit hunts by surrounding them. They also hunted mountain sheep. They removed the hair from the skins which they softened and made into sacks. Others made shirts for themselves.

Their pet panther lay on the piled up loads eating like a cat. The bear sat in a low place where he was fed. "We shall soon move on, my pet," *ba'ni'* said to the bear. When it was dark *ba'ni'* made a speech, "Tomorrow you will get ready to go on. Grind the corn they have given you and prepare provisions for the journey."

The Arrow people built a fire in their sweathouse. "Come to the sweathouse, come to the sweathouse, come to the sweathouse," they called. The four chiefs, *ba'ni'*, *bailnikọsɛ*, *banatinł*, and *gicdo* went there and went into the sweathouse. The curtain was lowered. "Yes," said *ba'ni'*, "My sons-in-law and my daughters-in-law seem to like each other. We are starting off. We are going where Rain Mountain lies, as we were told to do by our grandmother. We shall go in two days. Tomorrow we shall spend preparing the corn you gave us." The Arrow People said nothing. They said to each other. "Our sons-in-law, our daughters-in-law did not become friends for just one day." The Arrow People went out of the sweathouse, put dust on themselves, dressed, and went home. The others too went home. Nothing was heard from the hogan for two days. Afterwards they found out the Arrow People had said, "They are traveling with good women and many beads. We will kill all the men and the women will be ours." Then the travelers started on leaving behind the men who had married their women and also the women who had married their men. They camped and passed the night. When it was dark the second night the bear went toward the south, pulled up young spruce trees and put them across each other. He sat down on top of them. *ba'ni'* said, "*n n n sos sos sos.* I guess my pet is giving us a message about things which are happening behind us that we do not know about. After a little while the bear began singing bear songs.

> My hogan,
> I being a whirlwind,
> My hogan,
> I being a gray bear,
> Lightning strikes from my hogan,
> There is danger from my hogan,
> All are afraid of my hogan.
> I am of long life of whom they are afraid.
> *hihinyi hi'*
> I blow my breath out.

Singing thus, his songs were made. He sang ten songs there. Just as it was becoming light a little they again heard some songs:—

> They are afraid of my black face.
> I am a whirlwind.
> They are afraid of me.
> I am a gray bear.
> They are afraid of my black face.
> It lightens from my black face.
> They are afraid of the danger issuing from my black face.
> I am long life, they are afraid.

When he had sung two songs like this he got up, putting up his hand, he threw himself over backward and ran away.

They found Arrow People had circled around them in order to kill them. The bear had run around them four times and had chased them to a hill which stood there. *ba'ni'* spoke, saying, "My pet come here." One of the Arrow People spoke, saying, "We were sorry and were coming after you." "No, no," *ba'ni'* replied. "You would have killed us if my pet had not run around you four times. If you were sorry for us why did you come at night. Why didn't you come in the daytime? You had better go back before you get torn up." "Well, some time I will come after you," the Arrow men said. "Well, come in the daytime so we will recognize you," *ba'ni'* said. It was for this reason they had taken the bear.

They started off and traveled, I do not know how many days.

After a short day's travel they camped for the night. The provisions they had been carrying were all gone. Hunger was killing them. They built a brush shelter and piled up the loads they had carried. Panther was lying on top of them. "Do something for us, my pet. There is nothing here for us to eat." Panther stepped down, stretched, gaped, curled up his tongue, and started away. He went away and soon came back and lay down again on the loads. He licked his feet and then his lips were red. "My pet has killed something," he said. They followed his tracks back and found a young antelope lying dead. He had been gashed open along his side. He brought this meat back. They ate it and were saved. They then started on. Then panther went off by himself. He soon came back and his front paw was bloody. Two men followed his tracks back and found he had killed two antelopes. They prepared food for themselves and traveled on. They camped again and the panther got up by himself. He soon returned and his jaw was bloody. A party of men followed his tracks back and found he had killed three antelope. They prepared a meal and went on again. When the sun was about here (nearly down), they stopped for the day and made camp. The panther went off and soon came back. When they followed back on his tracks they found four large antelope lying dead. The panther had eaten the intestines of each. The men came back bringing much meat. *Ba'ni'* directed them to roast the meat and make it into pemmican, so that it would not be so heavy. It was for this reason they had taken the panther. They were carrying out the intention of *Yolgaiesdzan.* When they had made the pemmican, they started off carrying it. They came to Navajo Mountain. "This is the mountain she told us not to climb, but to cross the ford at its base." When they came there they found a bank or hill and water beyond flowing here and there. "That is the place," they said and they crossed the ford.

"We will stop here and eat, my children," *ba'ni'* said. They built a fire there. They saw something black over there where they had come down. "Those married men have come after us," *ba'ni'* said. One man went down to the river bank and told them the way to cross. "We were sorry and came after you," they were saying as they embraced each other. (At that time we didn't shake hands.) Those who came they found were not the husbands who had remained behind.

"Well, if you are sorry about being separated from us we will be kinsmen from henceforth." Just as they were starting to eat there was something black over there. One man went back and shouted to them telling them where to cross. They found they had come right from the shore of *yolgaiesdzan.* "She told us to follow your tracks." They were carrying a large snake on their backs. They had it to kill animals for them. They carried pollen for its food. "Your pets are the bear and panther. Ours is the snake. We will be all one clan." "All right," the others said. "Now being all one clan we will travel in front." They came to a place called Much Wool where they stayed for a year. During the year they stayed there they lived on mountain sheep. They piled up the wool from these sheep about the hogan and in that way the place took its name.

"When it is spring and the ground is yellow she told us to go up on this mountain called Black Mountain." The bear began to work again. He went ahead of the people and dug out *tc'act'ɛzɛ* with his paws. He also dug out wild onions. These served the people as their food when they arrived. They camped there and wondered where they could get water. "You have a cane, *bailnikǫsɛ,*" they said. He stuck the turquoise cane into the ground and twisted it twice. The water flowed out and they ate their food with it. They slept there that night and when it was light, they went on, arriving at a place called Skunk Bush Spring. They went toward a place called Where-two-stars-lie, close by where they got lost, and came to the edge of Cañon de Chelly. They arrived where the rocks join and the water flows. There was much wide grass there and trees covered the top. They were following each other by this place. When someone called out "Wait," they stopped and said, "This woman has given out we will remain here. Go on." The *kiya'ani,* went on. The others remained at the place called *tsinl'oik'a.* A strange man came there. They found he was a *latcini.* The others slept at *tsɛniidji'-dɛ* and early in the morning started on again. "Wait, a woman has given out." They found she had a husband. "Go on," *ba'ni'* said. "Take care of my son-in-law and my daughter-in-law."

The pair went to the place called *totso* and the clan *totsoni* are descended from them. There are now many of the *totsoni* clan. The others went on. At a place called *tsɛbasozołłeigɛ* he stuck the abalone cane into the ground and twisted it. Abundant salt water sprang up. They drank the water and ate their meal. "Yes that mountain to which we have come is the one called Brushy Mountain. We do not go toward the South," *ba'ni'* said. "No, this place does not look like the right place. The one we went by has a mountain projecting horizontally as she told us," *ba'ni'* said. He put the white shell cane and the turquoise cane into the ground and water flowed up at both places. "'Springs-opposite-each-other' this place will be called," he said. They ate a meal there and then started back toward the south. They went up over hard ground. There was the place they had set out from. They unloaded on the other side where there was a sharp point. Those points came to be called *kinniobiji*. The one they had come up was called *basta*.

There is a place called large "Cottonwood-tree-stands" beneath which water flows much spread out. The Navajo stopped here and planted corn. Red silk appeared on the corn and they recalled the directions they had received from *yolgaiesdzan* before they left her. She had told them to gather the ears low down on the stalks, husk them, and when they put them in the water to say, "Let there be frequent rains." "Put them in a small pot to cook. Do not fail to do this," their grandmother had told them.

Growing children went for the ears of corn and when they put them in the pot they said, "Let there be showers here." The next day four children, two boys and two girls, went for more corn. They did not come back at once. At midday just two of the children came back, saying they had been playing hide-and-seek, in pairs, in the corn. They failed to find the other pair and when they followed the footprints to a place where there was sand the tracks ceased. A boy and girl were missing. Some of the people went there to investigate and came back saying that what the children had reported was true. They wondered what had happened to the vanished pair and thought it possible they had gone to their grandmother's place in the west.

Four days later he (the chief) sent two children to get some young ears telling them to come back quickly. They came back very soon, saying the lost children had returned and were sitting in the field. "They told us to come back and tell you they had been to our grandmother's place. They told us to get some mountain mahogany from the east, some Mormon tea from the south, some cedar from the west, some piñon from the north, and put them up in this manner. Then, they said, you were to get some sand from the garden and spread it down and stand up some brush on it in four concentric circles. When this is arranged they said their grandmother had told them to bathe on it. That is what the two sitting there told us. They arranged this according to the directions and then the two came there and washed. The boy dried himself with white cornmeal and the girl with yellow cornmeal. After this they told their story.

"While we were hiding from each other two persons were standing there. They were *xactc'elti* and *xactc'eoyan*. 'Come' our grandmother *yołgaiesdzan* said to us. Something white came to be spread near us. We felt nothing, but it alighted with us on the summit of *tc'ocgai* and then the top of the mountain called *tsịbɛl'qi*. There they washed us the way you have just done. Next we were taken to the summit of the jet mountain and then were conveyed to our grandmother's doorway. When we went in, our grandmother lay curled up, nearly killed by old age. She got up and walked with a cane of white shell to a room to the east. She came out again somewhat stronger. She then went into the south room, walking with a cane of turquoise. She came back walking by herself unaided.

"She went next without a cane into the room at the west. She came out a young woman. She went into the north room and came out a girl, so handsome, we were abashed. 'You came here within my view, my grandchildren,' she said to us. 'You went away without songs.' She began to sing and taught us the songs." When they had learned the songs they sang them. (I do not know those songs. I know the horse songs.) They found they had been there four days.

"'Some of the songs I will not teach you. My grandchildren who live over there will teach you those. Do not forget those I have taught you. The day you forget them will be the last, there will be no other days.' This is what our grandmother told us. Then two of the twelve people who live there came and began to sing the horse songs. We learned them. We were brought back to the summit of the mountain of jet, to the top of *tsịbɛl'qi*, to the summit of *tc'ocgai*, and then to the garden. We did not sleep last night. This grass on which we washed will be good. It will cause the people to increase, our grandmother told us."

Fall came and the Navajo camped across from *kiya'a* and lived there. During that time someone came up to the camp and reported the people on Red Mountain were being constantly defeated by their enemies. He said he was sent as a messenger to ask the loan of the bear which the people who came from their grandmother had for a pet. They wanted to have the bear to fight with. *ba'ni'* who was the caretaker of the bear, said, "All right, in five days we will come." When the fifth day came they started to war. When it was dark the party stopped. *ba'ni'* addressing his bear spoke as follows: "My pet, the people who live at Red Mountain are being beaten all the time by their enemies. We are going there to war." The bear went toward the south, pulled up some young spruce trees, and put them across each other. He sat on these and when it was very dark they heard songs:—

Consider me.
I am *naiye'nezɣani.*
Consider me, my moccasins being of black obsidian.
Consider me, my leggings being of black obsidian.
Consider me, black obsidian hangs down from my sides at four places.
Lightning strokes shoot out from me four times.
Where they go very bad talk kills you.
Over there the heads are bound in death.
Long life, I am the one they are afraid of.
Consider me.

When it was light, the war party attacked. The scouts helped them to go across the prairie. Song:—

I have become the heat mirage.
Toward the east I have become the black mirage with points projecting upward.
(Eight songs similar to the above.)

They crossed the prairie without being seen, due to the darkness caused by heat mirage   They camped at sundown and when it was good and dark the bear sat as before. He put young spruces across each other and songs were heard again. The bear was singing:—

Big black bear.
My moccasins are black obsidian.
My leggings are black obsidian.
My shirt is black obsidian.
I am girded with a gray arrowsnake.
Black snakes project from my head.
With zigzag lightning projecting from the ends of my feet I step.
With zigzag lightning streaming out from my knees I step.
With zigzag lightning streaming out from the tips of my fingers I work my hands.
With zigzag lightning streaming out from the tip of my tongue I speak.
Now a disc of pollen rests on the crown of my head.
Gray arrow snakes and rattlesnakes eat it.
Black obsidian and zigzag lightning streams out from me in four ways.
Where they strike the earth, bad things bad talk does not like it.
It causes the missiles to spread out.
Long life, something frightful I am.
Now I am.

It was light and they got up. So far the bear had walked and then he began to sing:—

Now we are getting ready to fight,
I, where I walk is danger.
I am *naiye'nezɣani.*
Where I walk is dangerous.
Where I walk with moccasins of black obsidian it is dangerous.
Where I walk with leggings of black obsidian it is dangerous.
Where I walk with a headdress of black obsidian it is dangerous.

Black obsidian with zigzag lightning spreads out from me in four directions.
Where it strikes the earth bad things and bad talk.
Long life being one that causes fear I walk.
Where I walk is dangerous.

Then there were two songs, not long ones, and he ran up the mountain and ran around them four times and took their hearts out of them. All bloody, they lay side by side. They took the scalps. The bear himself had killed them all. They started back home and passed a hill that stands there.

The bear stood up like a man, in his right hand he held a piece of *dzitdilgesi* and *tc'eji* with a red male arrowhead. In his left hand he held *l'onastasi, toikał,* and a red female arrowhead. Then he moved his hands across each other in four places. He made a curve four times. Speaking as if he were *naiye'nezɣani,* he made four curves. Speaking like *tobadjictcini,* he made four straight lines.

Speaking as if he were *naiye'nezɣani,* he made four curved lines. Speaking like *tobadjictcini* he made four straight lines. Then he moved his hands across each other in four places. He then stuck into the ground the branches of plants and the arrowhead he had in his hand. He did the same way with what he had in his left hand. He then moved over these things and began to sing.

I make a mark they won't cross it.
*naye'nezɣani* I am, they won't cross it
Black obsidian my moccasins they won't cross it.
Black obsidian my leggings they won't cross it
Black obsidian my shirt they won't cross it
Black obsidian four times my sides hang down
Black obsidian my headdress.
Black obsidian zigzag lightning darts four times from me stream out
Where it goes dangerous missiles will be scattered
I make a mark they won't cross
I come back with lightning streaming out from me in four places.
I come back, dangerous things and missiles being scattered.

There were six songs here. Then they came to a hill that stood there where he did exactly the same way. He made the lines again, sang six songs, and the party passed over the line again. When they had nearly returned he sang as follows:—

(?)          they stand
*naiye'nezɣani*
With moccasins of black obsidian.
With leggings of black obsidian.
With shirt of black obsidian.
With staffs of black obsidian hanging in four places.

> With headdress of black obsidian.
> Black obsidian and lightning.
> Shooting out from me in four directions.
> Bad talk.
> Missiles fly away from me.
> Long life and one to be feared.
> Now I am.

He sang six songs and the party all passed ahead of him. Again they heard songs.

> There is danger where I move my feet.
> I am whirlwind. There is danger when I move my feet.
> I am a gray bear.
> When I walk, where I step lightning flies from me.
> Where I walk, one to be feared.
> Where I walk long life.
> One to be feared I am.
> There is danger where I walk.

He did that because the wind told him to. There were eight songs. (There will be one more. I am tired.) When they came to the hogan from which they had seen (?) he began to sing.

> It moved with me, the male rainbow
> It moved with me, old age.
> It moved with me, I am the one inspiring fear.

There were two songs with the refrain, "With me we two start back?" Then there were two alike with the words, "With me they two get home," then two, "With me they two sit." The party then were home again. Hereafter when there is cough and fever ? ? That is why he sang that. When they returned with the bear he got angry and started to run off. *ba'ni'* caught him with a rope saying, "My pet, you were going to do something bad." He spread an unwounded buckskin and told his pet to sit on it. He put a string with five perforated white shell beads around his right wrist, and the same on his left wrist. He put similar strings of beads on each ankle and a string across his breast. Then between his ears he dusted specular iron ore, powdered turquoise, pollen from trees, and pollen from cat-tail rushes. He took turquoise from the bear's (?) mouth with his spit on it and pulled out his hair where it was twisted. The bear shook himself and the pollen fell off. "This will be called what was put in a bear's mouth. Hereafter when I live there will be danger from me. They will wish bad things to stay away." "My pet, I found you where it is the way of darkness. On this side is a mountain called black. Your relatives will be there. You will walk there."

He put some of the pollen which had been in his mouth on his head and sprinkled some of it before and behind him. He began to sing.

> Now big bear black mountain  ?  he walks.
> Black spruce being his door posts he walks.
> Pollen on his tail he walks.
> Pollen on the images of his foot he walks.
> Pollen on the image of where he sat he walks.
> Good fortune before him he walks.
> Good fortune behind him he walks.
> Good fortune below him he walks.
> Good fortune above him he walks.
> Good fortune all around him he walks.
> Good fortune his speech he walks.

It ends here. The bear went away to the mountain called, Black Mountain. It is because of that bears are mean there. My maternal grandfather, *baitnikǫsє* told me so. They decorated panther in the same way. "I found you at the place called yellow mountain, my pet. You will walk where it is called yellow stone. Because of that panthers are numerous there."

Made in the USA
Middletown, DE
25 October 2023

41388231R00106